Advance Praise for Survive a Shooting

"Alain Burrese has written the definitive guide to mass shootings—and how to maximize your chances of surviving one. And the common-sense steps he recommends aren't just relevant for shootings—they're well calibrated to help you keep yourself and your family safe generally."

- Barry Eisler
New York Times bestselling author and creator of John Rain, Ben Treven, and Livia Lone
www.barryeisler.com

"I have been studying the problem of active killer response for more than two decades. I've read every book available on the subject and have both attended and taught countless classes on the topic. Without question, Alain's book is the absolute best reference for active killer response available on the market today. His advice is both thorough and driven by industry best practices. If you want to learn how to prevail in an active killer attack, you need this book in your library."

- Greg Ellifritz
Veteran Police Officer and founder of Active Response Training
www.activeresponsetraining.net

"Way back in the 1990's, Alain Burrese established himself as a leading thinker in self-defense circles when he published *Hard-Won Wisdom from the School of Hard Knocks*. In the intervening years, Alain has continued to learn, grow, research, publish, and teach. I had the privilege to read a draft of his latest book, *Survive a Shooting*, which you now hold in your hands. Succinct, clear, and accurate are just what I expect from Alain. *Survive A Shooting* offers something else. Instead of jacking up the fear to create a market, Alain took a potentially terrifying subject and created a calming, empowering book. Yes, it's bad Alain points out. But there are things you can do. You are not helpless. That's the defining message of this very useful book. I hate touchy feely jargon, but *Survive a Shooting* is empowering. The kind of book that leaves you a little stronger, a little more ready."

- Rory Miller
Veteran corrections officer and author of multiple instructional books and videos including *Meditations on Violence*
http://chirontraining.com

"*Survive a Shooting* is a must read for anyone that may have to engage an active shooter or mass murderer. Alain did a great job detailing the history of mass shooting situations and what we must be prepared for in the future; as well as what we can do to mitigate this ominous threat."

- Dr. Dale Comstock
Former Delta Force, Author, and President of Strategic Outcomes Asia
http://strategicoutcomesasia.com

"*Survive a Shooting* is probably the best and most detailed resource available right now when it comes to active shooters. Alain provides not only the necessary background information to understand the problem, but he also points to specific cases of shootings to draw lessons from. Throughout the chapters, you learn the relevant statistical information and recommendations from law enforcement agencies and how to implement them. The knowledge you learn in this book is not just theoretical; Alain shows how to use it for your own safety or for those you have a responsibility for. From planning and prevention, to strategies to take action should the worst happen, followed by how to react when the police arrive and much more. Highly recommended."

- Wim Demeere
Martial Arts and self-defense expert, author of multiple instructional books and videos including the *Combat Sanshou* series
www.wimdemeere.com
www.wimsblog.com

"The CIA trains operatives to survive in hostile environments. *Survive A Shooting* trains people to survive active threats. Putting the knowledge in this book to use could literally save your life."

- Jason Hanson
Former CIA Officer and author of *Spy Secrets That Can Save Your Life*
https://spyescapeandevasion.com

"Alain Burrese has written what many will soon consider the definitive text on 'Slaughter in Progress.' From past incidents to current techniques on what to do in an active killer situation, Alain covers what you need to know to be ready for this increasing threat."

- Dave Spaulding
Founder of Handgun Combatives LLC and 2010 Law Enforcement Trainer of the Year
www.handguncombatives.com

"It's been twenty years since the last time I had bullets flying past me. I've never gone this long in my life without having been shot at. I wasn't a cop. Nor were these incidents on some foreign battlefield. They were in the streets and buildings in the U.S. - exactly the same environment you're going to be in. Alain's book is not regurgitated police and military tactics, it addresses the options and resources available to civilians and businesses when confronted with these terrible circumstances. The information herein works. But more importantly, it works with who you are and what you have. That's what makes this book unique."

- Marc MacYoung
Self-defense and personal safety expert, author of multiple instructional books and videos including *In The Name Of Self-Defense*
www.nononsenseselfdefense.com

"No one wants to be a victim, yet learning how to successfully defend against an armed threat can be a significant challenge. Nevertheless, with the right training it's a surmountable one. If I was going to put my life (or a member of my family's) in someone else's hands during an active shooting, I can think of no better person to safeguard it than Alain Burrese. His knowledge, experience, and pragmatic approach create powerful, trustworthy advice that everyone must know."

- Lawrence Kane
Bestselling author of *The Big Bloody Book of Violence* and 16 other titles
www.stickmanpublications.com

"As a highly accomplished martial artist, a former U.S. Army Sniper instructor, and an Active Shooter Response instructor, Alain brings a unique perspective to one of the most perplexing problems in modern society – the active killer. His book, *Survive a Shooting*, is an interesting and thought provoking read, but more importantly, it's a pragmatic guide that reveals simple steps anyone can take to increase their odds of surviving this nightmarish scenario. Read this book or bury your head in the sand and hope 'it' doesn't happen to 'you.' The choice is yours..."

- Richard Nance
Police Officer, Author, Active Shooter Instructor
www.wartac.com

Survive a Shooting

Strategies to Survive Active Shooters and Terrorist Attacks

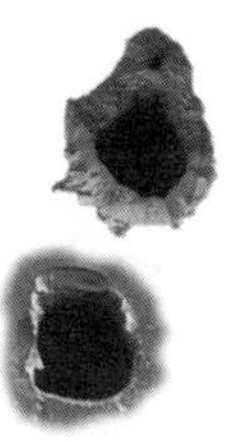

Alain Burrese

TGW BOOKS
Missoula, Montana

Survive A Shooting: Strategies to Survive Active Shooters and Terrorist Attacks by Alain Burrese

Print ISBN: 978-1-937872-12-0
eBook ISBN: 978-1-937872-13-7

Published by TGW Books, a division of
Burrese Enterprises, Inc.
Missoula, MT 59801, USA

Cover design and layout by Kevin Brett
V14

For more information, please contact Alain Burrese at
www.surviveashooting.com alain@surviveashooting.com 406-544-7410

Dedication

This book is dedicated to all those who run toward the gunfire to protect others and keep people safe.

And to all those who refuse to be a victim.

Also by Alain Burrese...

Books:

Hard-Won Wisdom From The School Of Hard Knocks
How To Protect Yourself By Developing A Fighter's Mindset
Lost Conscience: A Ben Baker Sniper Novel
Tough Guy Wisdom
Tough Guy Wisdom II: Return of the Tough Guy
Tough Guy Wisdom III: Revenge of the Tough Guy

eBooks:

101 Safety and Self-Defense Tips
101 More Safety and Self-Defense Tips

DVDs

Hapkido Hoshinsul
Streetfighting Essentials
Hapkido Cane
Lock On: Joint Locking Essentials vol. 1 Wrist Locks
Lock On: Joint Locking Essentials vol. 2 Arm Bars & Elbow Locks
Lock On: Joint Locking Essentials vol. 3 Shoulder Locks
Lock On: Joint Locking Essentials vol. 4 Finger Locks
Lock On: Joint Locking Essentials vol. 5 Combining Locks & Lock Flow Drills
Restraint, Control & Come-A-Long Techniques vol. 1
Restraint, Control & Come-A-Long Techniques vol. 2
Chokes and Sleeper Holds

Contents

Foreword

By Loren W. Christensen

As a Gang Enforcement Officer with the Portland, Oregon, Police Bureau, I once responded to one of the local high schools on an assault with a weapon by a gang member. This occurred less than 10 years before mass shooting events became what they are today. At that time, my only memory of a "school shooting" was when Charles Whitman climbed to the 28th floor of an observation tower on the University of Texas campus in Austin and gunned down 14 people. (He killed his wife and mother before going to the tower.) The press didn't call him a "school shooter," "active shooter," "mass shooter," or any other terms that sadly have become part of our modern-day vocabulary. Whitman was called the "Texas Tower Sniper."

The gangbanger I was investigating had used a machete to hack a wedge out of another kid's shoulder like a woodsman chops a big chunk out of tree trunk. The suspect admitted he had gone to an Asian market half a block away, bought the machete, returned to the school, chopped the kid who had "looked at him wrong," cleaned the blade, and returned it to the market for a full refund. The chopper was cold, calculated, and described his assault with an indifferent shrug.

I remember thinking that if more than one kid had "disrespected" the chopper with a wrong look, he might have just as easily, and without conscience, chopped others walking down the school hallway as well.

While this was just a passing thought at the time, eight years later in 1998, Kip Kinkel in Springfield, Oregon, and in 1999, Eric Harris and Dylan Klebold in Littleton, Colorado, would imbed the term "school shootings" and "mass killings," in our collective minds.

And more and more often knives and machetes are used.

Denial

While the number of mass shootings today has reached epidemic proportions (as I write this, mourners are still laying flowers at the scene of an active shooter event in Las Vegas that killed 59 and wounded hundreds), there are still people in denial.

"It won't happen to me."
"Why would anyone shoot people at our school carnival?"
"My kids go to a private school, and that wouldn't happen there."
"It's just an outdoor market where people go to enjoy a Saturday. Everyone is happy there."

Here is a classic example of denial. When I worked in the Gang Enforcement Team, I visited another high school to talk to the principal about something. In passing, I asked if there were any white supremacist students, especially skinheads, attending. Skins were my specialty in the gang unit.

"Oh, heavens no," the principal said as if offended by the question. "The staff and I keep a sharp lookout for gang symbols. We would never for a moment allow such ugliness on this campus."

I finished my business with him, and when I pushed open the office door to leave, it banged into a student passing by—a skinhead in full regalia: Doc Marten boots, green flight jacket, and shaved head.

When I was working on my small book *Surviving a School Shooting*, I contacted many schools to see what measures they had taken to secure their campuses to protect the children in their charge. To my disbelief, I learned that most hadn't done anything. Many school teachers and administrators refused to believe that it could happen on their campus.

One of my daughters is a school teacher, and she found the same problem. When she suggested preventative measures at her school, simple and inexpensive things, no one was interested, and she was dismissed with, "That would never happen here."

But it is happening, and it's getting worse, and the body count is going up. It's time for school campuses, movie theaters, shopping malls, stadiums, and every other place large groups gather to stop the denial and take measures to save lives.

As the bumper sticker says: "If you aren't completely appalled, then you haven't been paying attention."

Survive a Shooting

I am confident that you hold in your hand a book that will make a difference; a book that will save lives. *Survive a Shooting* gets right to the heart of the matter from the first page and continues to the very end. Alain Burrese doesn't waste time over-analyzing why someone would carry out such horror as a mass shooting, nor does he waste time talking about gun control and other issues that don't matter when red-hot steel is punching through innocent bodies.

Alain cuts to the heart of the matter and teaches you how to survive.

I have known Alain for many years, and I have always admired his drive to improve himself and his craft, specifically his earnest desire to help people protect themselves in all areas of their lives. In recent years, he has directed much of his work, study, and physical training on how to survive in the realm of mass shootings. So much so, that his expertise on the subject, especially his ability to communicate on all facets of it, has been called on by the media in the wake of such tragic events. I highly encourage you to read and absorb the critical information that Alain imparts in this book. Read it multiple times and contemplate the information.

Allow me to underscore just a few of the essential elements discussed in *Survive a Shooting*.

Chapter 4, "Your mind, adrenaline, and mindset" is critical to understanding what is happening to your mind and body when your frightened heart slams into your throat pounding at 200-plus beats a minute. Understand that when he discusses the loss of fine motor skills under stress that it just might be impossible to hold onto your cellphone—let alone poke 911. Knowledge is power; read this chapter carefully.

In Chapter 6, "Escape" is a topic you can practice in your mind anytime and anywhere. Maybe you're reading this in a classroom, on a bus, in a park, or in your easy chair at home. Right now, imagine the sudden thump of gunfire. Now, look around you. Where would you go? Where would you hide? Where is the exit? What if there isn't one? Factor this in: What if you can't determine from which direction the shots are coming? The sound of gunfire often gets distorted in an urban setting. But you still need to take cover or flee. But in what direction?

When you're in a shopping mall, movie theater, school, concert and other places where mass shootings have occurred, imagine a sudden explosion of gunfire and see yourself responding as Alain teaches in Chapter 11, "Develop your plan now."

Pre-thinking and mental rehearsal has been shown to be a powerful tool to help you respond more smoothly and tactically.

Think about the issues of planning and escaping every time you go out. If you're saying, "But I don't have time!" Yes, you do, because it only takes 5 to 10 seconds to look around, make a mental note where you could hide, take cover, or flee and then continue with your day. In less than a couple of weeks, you will find yourself automatically assessing your environment, sometimes without realizing you're doing it. As Alain discusses, if the worst happens, you will have already preplanned what to do and where to go.

Some readers might not see themselves fighting back as Alain discusses in Chapter 8, "Attack back." Well, your life might depend on it as well as other lives you hold dear. I have been teaching martial arts since 1965, and I know from having taught thousands of students that you possess the ability to bring forth your inner savage (a female martial arts friend calls it her "inner junkyard dog") and fight as if possessed. Study what Alain teaches and don't ever doubt for a second that you can do it.

Check Alain's website often to see if his group is offering classes in your area. He does an outstanding job instructing, and you will leave feeling confident that you're better able to handle yourself should the worst happen.

And it will happen again.

Loren W. Christensen is a retired police officer with 29 years of experience in military and civilian law enforcement. During his career, he specialized in street gangs, defensive tactics, street patrol, and dignitary protection. As an author, Loren has written over 60 books, fiction, and nonfiction. In nonfiction, he has written on such topics as martial arts, law enforcement, mental rehearsal, and self-defense. The latter includes two books: *Surviving a School Shooting* and *Surviving Workplace Violence.*

Introduction

www.SurviveaShooting.com

America is a rampage nation, where mass shootings now pose the greatest single threat to public safety, surpassing even terrorism.

Louis Klarevas
Rampage Nation: Securing America from Mass Shootings

You are holding the most important book I hope you'll never need. I hope you never have to escape a massacre, rampage, or spree shooting. I wish we didn't have the terms "active shooter" and "active threat" in our vocabulary. A world without terrorism would be ideal. But sadly, these events are becoming more common, and it only takes experiencing one such event to shatter your world and change your life forever, if you survive. These killings have occurred at elementary schools, middle schools, high schools, colleges, offices, factories, courthouses, hospitals, churches, nursing homes, malls, and military bases. Police don't ask "if" there will be another incident, they ask "when?" It can happen any time and any place.

This book will provide you with knowledge of life-saving skills and strategies for surviving active threats. I truly hope you never need any of the information this book covers, but if the unthinkable does happen, I want you to be a survivor. This book will help you be just that. But before I tell you what this book covers, I want to share the journey of how this book came to be.

On July 22, 2012, I stood in front of the local movie theater with *The Dark Knight Rises* posters behind me, talking about the terrible mass shooting that occurred inside the movie theater in Aurora, Colorado, during a midnight screening of that film on July 20, 2012. During that seven-minute video I provided some tips on staying safe during an active shooter event, but also made a commitment to do more, and to do everything I can to help people stay safe during these unthinkable acts.

On September 16, 2017, I stood in front of Freeman High School, just south of Spokane Valley, WA, filming another video. This time I was filming a tribute video to the two heroes of the shooting just three days earlier. Sam Strahan, the student who was killed trying to stop the shooter, and Joe Bowen, the custodian who did stop the shooter, were the two I honored in that video. They both deserve recognition.

A lot happened between the filming of those two videos. Much of it culminating with this book, *Survive a Shooting*, and the *Survive a Shooting* course I am teaching around the country, and hopefully internationally very soon. I'd like to briefly share some of that journey.

When I filmed that first video, I had considerable experience teaching people. I'd been teaching conflict resolution, safety, and self-defense classes and courses, as well as the martial art of Hapkido, for a long time. But I realized that these Active Shooter and Active Threat situations needed something a bit different. I started studying Active Shooter incidents and how to respond to them.

This study included books, DVD programs, on-line courses, and articles (both on-line and magazines) on all aspects of the topic. It included networking and discussing the topic with other experts. It also included attending an 8-hour *Emergency Response to an Armed Intruder* course taught by Safariland Training Group certified instructors. I then went through the instructor training and became certified myself. Over the last three and a half years, I have been part of a team that has taught this 8-hour course to around 4,000 community members on what to do when the unthinkable happens.

I then started appearing on radio shows around the country to share information to help people when these events happen. I've been on the radio over 70 times in the last sixteen months, including appearances on shows in Florida, New York, California, Montana, Nevada, Michigan, and Texas. I continue to appear on shows as time permits and when incidents happen.

Literally thousands of evaluations of the course we've been teaching here in Missoula commented on how empowering the training was. Unfortunately, because that course takes a team to teach, logistically it is difficult to take it beyond our community. The 8-hour time commitment was also a difficulty for many businesses and organizations that contacted me about training.

I wanted to empower people and show them that people don't have to be helpless victims, and that there are things that can be done before, during, and after these horrific events to increase the odds of surviving. My goal was, and is, to empower people and teach them to be survivors. I determined the best way to do this was to write this book and develop the 4-hour course I now teach.

Yes, there were other books on the topic. I've read most of them. Some of these books are not much more than pamphlets regurgitating the U.S. Department of Homeland Security message of Run – Hide - Fight. Others are more specialized for professionals in the industries of law enforcement and security, and while excellent resources, priced so most people will never read them. Some are very good books on the topic for the layperson, but they don't contain everything I want people to know, with the terms I chose for a reason, and the triangle example that I feel is so important for the survival concepts I teach. So, you now have this book, *Survive a Shooting*, with the most practical and applicable advice on surviving active threats for the layperson available.

What This Book Will Do for You

This book, above everything else, will show you how to be a survivor. You can't afford to turn your safety and security over to somebody else. As you'll learn, when seconds count, the police are only minutes away. You must take personal responsibility for your own safety and survival. Your response as a civilian is different than the response of law enforcement. This book focuses on what you can do to survive during that gap before law enforcement arrives. How you respond to an active shooter incident can mean the difference between life and death. Besides explaining why your response is important, this book will show you how to respond with the best strategies, tactics, and techniques to increase the likelihood of survival during these terrifying incidents.

Note what I just said, *this is the best information to increase the likelihood of survival*. Many people want the perfect answer, and there isn't one. The perfect answer is for no human being to ever hurt or kill another human being again. Now you see why there is no perfect answer. And along with that, there is no perfect response to an active threat situation. There are, however, responses that will increase your chances of survival and that will reduce the number of innocent casualties. These are the responses you will find within the pages of this book.

The **first chapter** looks at the history of active threats and why this history is important. From there, **chapter two** defines what an active shooter is, and provides information on motives, characteristics, and statistics of past studied events.

Chapter three addresses the topic of prevention. Hardening targets, threat assessment, reporting mechanisms, and indicators to be aware of are some of the items covered here.

Chapter four is extremely important when it comes to understanding how you will react when the unthinkable happens. The focus of this chapter is on your mind, adrenaline, and mindset. Areas covered include the OODA Loop, Denial, Accepting it Can Happen To You, Understanding Stress and the Adrenal Response, Combat Breathing, Situational Awareness, and how to Develop a Survivor's Mindset.

Chapter five looks at various active shooter response models; and **chapters six, seven, and eight** provide detailed instruction on my Active Shooter Response Triangle: Escape – Deny – Attack Back.

Chapter nine, "Stop the Bleeding," addresses the importance of trauma aid when it comes to saving lives. The instruction in this chapter will carry over to more than active threat situations.

Chapter ten will show you what to expect from the law enforcement response and how to avoid being mistaken as a threat. This chapter also covers how to report emergencies to a 911 operator, and includes details many people are unaware of.

The final chapter explains the importance of having a plan beforehand, and provides instruction on how to develop, visualize, and practice your own plans.

I've also included sections on lawsuits against businesses and organizations in response to active shooter events, considerations for business plans, additional training, and an extensive resource list.

I'm not kidding when I say you are holding the most important book I hope you'll never need. The information contained within these pages can mean the difference between life and death. I don't know how to stop the increasing trend of active shooter events, but I do know how you can increase your odds of surviving an attack. I've provided that information in this book. Read it, develop a plan, and be a survivor.

History of Mass Killings

www.SurviveaShooting.com

There are numerous instances, throughout history, where deranged suspects have sought out and killed as many innocent victims as possible. These mass murderers, also referred to as 'active shooters' since the Columbine High School tragedy in April 1999, have presented a unique tactical challenge to law enforcement officers.

J. Pete Blair, Terry Nichols,
David Burns, John R. Curnutt
Active Shooter: Events and Response

TOPICS

- ✓ School Killings Are Not New
- ✓ A Brief Look at Some Major Incidents
- ✓ Why the History of Shootings and Mass Killings is Important
- ✓ Killers Study Others

Reading newspapers or watching the news on television (or perusing your favorite on-line news sources) paints a picture of an increasingly violent world filled with mass murderers. And while it has never been in our face as prominently as it is now, the unfortunate fact is that there are numerous instances throughout history where sick deranged individuals have sought out and killed as many innocent victims as possible. I will share a few of these to illustrate that this isn't as new a problem as some seem to think. Not that this lessens the situation today, but it does help put things into a little better perspective. Besides teaching strategies and tactics to survive these incidents, I hope this book can also alleviate some of the fear people have due to the constant bombardment from our media that schools and other places are no longer safe.

Security Camera View of the Columbine High School Shooting

Since the Columbine High School tragedy in April 1999, many of these mass murderers have been referred to as "active shooters" due to their use of firearms to kill, wound, and create havoc among the innocent victims unfortunate enough to be in the location where these sickos decided to murder innocents. And while this book is titled *Survive A Shooting*, we must acknowledge that firearms are not the only way these murderers have killed people. I will share a few of the alternative ways killings have taken place because I want you to realize that it isn't just guns and shootings that you must be aware of, and that the principles, strategies, and tactics in this book to help you survive a shooting can also help you survive different types of attacks.

When was the first mass school killing in the United States? Think about this for a minute and come up with an answer before you read further.

When I ask people when the first mass school killing happened in the United States during live classes, "Columbine" is one of the most common answers. Was that the answer you came up with? Maybe you tried to come up with something earlier because of the title of this section. As I mentioned above, the Columbine tragedy happened in April 1999.

The first mass casualty attack at an American school happened on July 26, 1764. See why I state that school killings are not new? The first mass school killing happened even before our nation was even founded. It happened in a one-room schoolhouse in Western Pennsylvania. The schoolmaster, Mr. Brown, and ten students were killed and had the tops of their heads cut off. Only one boy, Archie McCullough, survived. They were massacred by a group of Native Americans who were retaliating for an earlier attack where members of their tribe were victims of similar brutality. The school was selected most likely for the same reason other schools are selected for these kinds of atrocious attacks. The victims were innocent and lacked the ability to protect themselves. The school was an easy target, just like many schools today.

Pennsylvania Memorial to the Victims of the 1764 school

Ninety-two percent of the occupants of the school were killed. Statistically, this can be considered the most lethal school attack based on mortality rates of building occupants. No attack on an educational institution in America has ended with such a high percentage of building occupants dead. In contrast, the horrendous attack at Sandy Hook Elementary school that unfolded on all of our television screens in 2010 had more than twice the number of deaths, but 96 percent of the building occupants survived.

If we want to skip percentages and statistics, and just look at total numbers killed, one of the deadliest mass murders at a school in the United States happened on May 18, 1927, in Bath Township, Michigan. The violent attacks of the Bath School disaster perpetrated by Andrew Kehoe included him killing his wife and firebombing his farm, detonating a bomb in the Bath Consolidated School, and killing himself by detonating a final explosion in his truck. 38 elementary school children and six adults were killed and at least 58 other people were injured.

Bath Township, Michigan, 1927

On Monday, December 1, 1958, a fire broke out at Our Lady of the Angel School in Chicago, Illinois. A total of 92 pupils and 3 nuns ultimately died. Many more were injured. While some sources share that the fire was started when a child struck a match in the basement of the school, a child who later confessed that he set the deadly fire because of his teachers, the cause of the fire was never officially determined. A family court judge concluded the evidence was insufficient to substantiate the confession. If we disagree with the judge and believe the confession was true, this incident becomes a deadlier mass murder than Bath, Michigan.

Major Mass Shootings

- Las Vegas, NV, Oct. 1, 2017 – 58 people killed at the Route 91 Harvest music festival on the Las Vegas Strip
- Orlando, Fla., June 12, 2016 - 50 people killed at the Pulse nightclub
- Blacksburg, VA, April 16, 2007 - 32 people killed at Virginia Tech
- Newtown, Conn., Dec. 14, 2012 - 27 people killed at Sandy Hook Elementary School
- Sutherland Springs, TX, Nov. 5, 2017 – 26 people killed at the First Baptist Church
- San Ysidro, Calif., July 18, 1984 – 21 people killed at a McDonald's restaurant
- Killeen, Texas, Oct. 16, 1991 - 23 people killed at Luby's Cafeteria
- Austin, Texas, Aug. 1, 1966 - 18 people killed at the University of Texas
- Parkland, Fla., Feb. 14, 2018 – 17 people killed at Marjory Stoneman Douglas High School
- San Bernardino, Calif., Dec. 2, 2015 - 14 people killed at the Inland Regional Center
- Edmond, Okla., Aug. 20, 1986 - 14 people killed at a local post office
- Binghamton, NY, April 3, 2009 - 13 people killed at the American Civic Association, an immigration center
- Littleton, CO, April 20, 1999 - 13 people killed at Columbine High School

Percentages and numbers don't really matter when bullets are flying. When it comes to numbers, one student killed is too many. And while it's not a contest to see which disaster can outdo the others, some of these sick individuals do set out to raise the body count and achieve higher numbers. But I think it is important to understand this historical perspective that school killings are not new. Too many people think this is a new phenomenon and have unrealistic and increased fears. I'm a parent and I understand the fear that arises when news stories focus on school shootings. Parents are afraid that their child may be shot and killed at school. And while I wrote this book to help you in case of a shooting, and I continue to teach at schools, universities, and businesses to arm people with the knowledge of what they can do in these extreme situations, I want you to remember if you're a parent that a young person's chances of being killed by gunfire on school property are lower than their chances of being killed by a medical emergency like a bee sting, or a simple but fatal accident. I am glad that the teachers at my daughter's school have gone through the course we teach here in Missoula, and I'm glad you are reading this book to better prepare yourself and your loved ones. But please keep the threat and your fears in their proper perspectives. Be aware and be prepared. But don't be afraid and paranoid.

A Brief Look at Some Major Incidents

Looking at previous mass killings allows us to recognize and identify components that can help us prevent and survive future events. Unfortunately, there is much history to study. Here are a few incidents that you may or may not be aware of.

July 26, 1764: Four Delaware (Lenape) American Indians entered a settlers' log schoolhouse in the Province of Pennsylvania in what is now Franklin County, near the present-day city of Greencastle. The schoolmaster, Enoch Brown, and nine children were shot and killed. Things to note: One of the earliest school shootings in what is now the U.S. An elder Delaware chief rebuked those that made the attack as cowards for attacking children.

September 28, 1850: George Pharoah, a 19-year-old student at Rocky Hill Schoolhouse West Chester, Pennsylvania, shot and killed Rachel Sharpless, an 18-year-old school teacher. Pharoah braced a rifle against a tree and shot the teacher as she unlocked the school door. Things to note: He used a Saturday Evening Post to muffle the sound of the rifle.

May 18, 1927: Andrew Kehoe killed his wife and firebombed his farm and then detonated an explosion in the Bath Consolidated School in Bath Township, Michigan. He then committed suicide by detonating a final device in his truck. The combined explosions killed 38 elementary schoolchildren and 6 adults. At least 58 others people were injured. Things to note: This is the deadliest mass murder to take place at a school in the United States. Kehoe was angry over increased taxes and his defeat in the 1926 election for township clerk.

May 6, 1940: Vieling Spencer, a disgruntled 38-year-old principal of South Pasadena Junior High School, in South Pasadena, California, shot and killed five school officials at the school. He used a .22 caliber semi-automatic pistol. Spencer's 30-minute shooting rampage left five of his colleagues dead and another terribly wounded. Three police officers cornered Spencer in the cafeteria, where he shot himself in the stomach in a failed suicide attempt. Spencer pleaded guilty and was sent to San Quentin with a life sentence. Things to note: Although he pleaded guilty and was given a life sentence, Spencer always maintained that he remembered nothing of the slayings. A possible explanation emerged three years into the 30-year prison term he ultimately served. It was only then that the former school principal learned that a blood sample taken shortly after his arrest showed that his system contained enough bromide to render him legally insane.

March 12, 1951: Charles Hugh Justice and Billy Ray Powell used a .22 caliber rifle to kill their school superintendent, W.E. Sweatt, and a fellow student, Wade Johnson, at Alexander School in Union Mills, North Carolina. The two boys believed they were unfairly reprimanded by Sweatt for walking with girls, and they thought Johnson, Powell's roommate, was telling on them. Things to note: This may possibly be the first active shooting with two shooters involved if you don't consider the American Indian raid of 1764 listed above.

August 1, 1966: Charles Whitman brought a number of guns, including rifles, a shotgun, and handguns, to the campus of the University of Texas at Austin. He killed three people inside the university's tower and eleven others firing from the 28th floor observation deck of the main building. Besides killing 14 people, he also wounded 32 others in and around the tower. Whitman was shot and killed by two Austin police officers. Things to note: Whitman is infamous as the "Texas Tower Sniper." Before going to the school, Whitman murdered his wife and his mother in their homes. The incident lasted approximately 90-95 minutes.

July 18, 1984: James Huberty went to the San Ysidro McDonalds with a 9mm Browning HP semi-automatic pistol, a 9mm Uzi carbine, a Winchester 12-gauge pump-action shotgun, and a bag filled with hundreds of rounds of ammunition for each weapon. He killed 21 people and injured 19 others. Huberty was fatally shot by a SWAT sniper. Things to note: When Huberty first tried to shoot his first victim, the gun did not fire. When the shooting began, most of the customers tried to hide beneath tables and booths. The incident lasted for 78 minutes. Huberty fired a minimum of 245 rounds killing 20 and wounding 20. The 21st person died the following day.

August 20, 1986: Patrick Sherrill, a part-time letter carrier, went to his workplace in Edmond, Oklahoma, and killed 14 and injured six others. He then committed suicide. Things to note: He had been reprimanded the afternoon before the rampage. One of the people killed was a supervisor who had spoken to him, the other was not at the location during the shooting. Sherrill locked doors behind him so that postal employees couldn't escape. Some wounded played dead and survived. The event lasted about 15 minutes.

August 19, 1987: Michael Ryan killed 16 people in the small market town of Hungerford, England, with a Kalashnikov rifle. He killed himself after being cornered by police. Things to note: Ryan was reported to be fascinated with firearms. The British government responded to the massacre with a ban on semi-automatic rifles.

September 14, 1989: Joseph Wesbecker went to his former workplace, Standard Gravure in Louisville, Kentucky, with a number of weapons, including a Chinese-made Ak-47 derivative, a 9mm pistol, two MAC-11s, a .38 revolver, a bayonet, and hundreds of rounds of ammunition. He killed eight people and injured twelve more. He then committed suicide. Things to note: The incident lasted about 30 minutes and he fired approximately 40 rounds. The murders resulted in a lawsuit against Eli Lilly and Company, manufacturers of the antidepressant drug Prozac, which Wesbecker had begun using during the month prior to the shooting.

June 18, 1990: James Edward "Pop" Pough went to the General Motors Acceptance Corporation office in Jacksonville, Florida, armed with an M1 carbine and a .38 revolver. He killed nine people and wounded four others. He committed suicide. Things to note: The day before he killed a prostitute and her pimp and wounded two teenagers. Pough systematically moved from desk to desk and shot at the GMAC workers, deliberately aiming at those hiding under their desks.

October 16, 1991: George Hennard drove his truck through the front window of Luby's Cafeteria in Killeen, Texas, and then started shooting with a Glock 17 pistol. He killed 22 people and wounded 20 others. The shooting stopped when a police officer shot Hennard as he was attempting to shoot another victim. Hennard then fatally shot himself. Things to note: Some diners initially went to help the driver after the crash, only to be shot. People were shot as they ran, hid behind tables, and crouched on the floor. The shooting lasted 12 minutes. Some speculated that he was influenced by a documentary he had seen on James Huberty, the gunman who killed 22 people and injured 19 at McDonalds in San Ysidro, California, in 1984.

December 7, 1993. Colin Ferguson boarded a Long Island commuter train in New York, New York, with a 9mm Ruger pistol and 160 rounds of ammunition. He killed six and wounded 19. He was stopped by three passengers who tackled him to the ground. Things to note: Stopped by unarmed passengers. Son of one of the wealthiest and most prominent businessmen in Jamaica.

June 20, 1994: Dean Mellberg, a former airman, entered the Fairchild AFB, Washington, hospital and shot and killed four people and wounded 22 others. Airman Mellberg was discharged from the Air Force as being unfit for military service. Mellberg used a Chinese-made MAK-90, an AK-47 clone, and was stopped by a security policeman, Senior Airman Andy Brown. Things to note: Brown was awarded the Airman's Medal by President Bill Clinton and has written a book detailing the events before, during, and after that tragedy titled *Warnings Unheeded*.

March 20, 1995: Domestic Japanese terrorists used Sarin gas to attack the Tokyo subway. 12 people were killed and more than 5,000 were injured. Things to note: Four suspects were found guilty. (I was living in Japan at the time, and I had been in the exact spot where the Sarin gas was released the day before the incident.)

April 28, 1996: Martin Bryant killed an elderly couple at the Seascape guesthouse in Tasmania, Australia. He then went to the Broad Arrow Café at the Port Arthur Prison Colony Historic Site and ate lunch. He then removed an AR-15 and a FN-FAL .308 from his bag and killed 12 people in the café and another 10 people in the adjacent gift shop. Bryant killed even more people before an 18-hour standoff with the police ended with him being captured. Bryant murdered 35 people. Things to note: The shooting in the café and gift shop areas took about a minute. The Port Arthur massacre remains Australia's single deadliest shooting spree. Twelve days after this incident, Australia enacted strict gun-control laws.

March 24, 1998: Andrew Golden and Mitchell Johnson went to their school, Westside Middle School, a consolidated school outside Jonesboro, Arkansas, with a van loaded with survival gear, camping supplies, and 10 weapons, including two semi-automatic rifles, one bolt-action rifle, and seven handguns. Johnson took the weapons to a field adjacent to the school while Golden pulled the fire alarm and then ran to join Johnson. They waited and watched the exits the teachers and students would come out of due to the fire alarm. The two shot and killed four female students and a teacher, and wounded nine other students and one teacher. The boys tried to escape back to the van, which was parked a half mile away, but were captured by the police. Things to note: Golden was 11 years old and Johnson was 13. They may have patterned their attack after an incident in Stamps, Arkansas, that occurred three months earlier. December 15, 1997: Joseph "Colt" Todd, who was only 14, hid in the woods by his high school and shot and wounded two students because he was tired of being teased and bullied.

April 20, 1999: Eric Harris and Dylan Klebold went to their school, Columbine High School, in Littleton, Colorado. Together, they killed 12 students and one teacher and injured 23 other students. Both shooters committed suicide. Things to note: Both wore long coats to hide the weapons they carried. When the shooting started, students thought it was a prank. Ten students were killed in the cafeteria in the first 7 ½ minutes. The incident lasted 46 minutes before they killed themselves. If the propane bombs had detonated as planned, and the pipe bombs had been used, many more could have been killed or injured.

July 29, 1999: Mark Barton went to his office, an Atlanta, Georgia, day-trading brokerage firm, and started shooting. He then crossed the street to another office and continued. He killed nine and injured twelve. He left and then committed suicide when confronted by police. Things to note: Hours after the event, his wife and two children were found dead in their home. He killed them before going on his shooting spree. In total, Barton killed 12 people.

September 15, 1999: Larry Gene Ashbroke went to the Wedgewood Baptist Church in Fort Worth, Texas. He had a 9mm handgun and a .380 handgun. He opened fire on the 150 teens who were gathered for prayer service. He killed seven and injured seven. He then killed himself. Things to note: Ashbroke threw a pipe bomb at the front of the church before the attack, but it did little damage. Materials for making more bombs were found at his house. He had no connection with the church, and no one knows why he targeted its congregation.

December 6, 1999: Seth Trickey took his father's 9mm semi-automatic handgun to his school, Fort Gibson Middle School, in Fort Gibson, Oklahoma. Outside the school, he fired at least 15 shots, wounding five people. He was subdued by a teacher. No one died in this incident. Things to note: Trickey was only 13 years old. He was greatly influenced by the Columbine incident that occurred eight months prior to this.

December 26, 2000: Michael McDermott, armed with an AK-47 variant, a 12-gauge shotgun, and a .32-caliber pistol, went to his place of employment, Edgewater Technology in Wakefield, Massachusetts. He killed seven coworkers and then waited calmly for police to arrest him. Things to note: Prosecutors claimed that McDermott was angry about the company's compliance with an order from the Internal Revenue Service to withhold part of his salary for back taxes. McDermott claimed that he was mentally ill and that he believed he had been "sent back in time to kill Nazis." He was convicted of seven counts of first-degree murder and sentenced to life in prison without possibility of parole.

February 5, 2001: William Baker was fired for stealing from the Navistar International engine plant in Melrose Park, Illinois. He went to the plant and shot and killed four people before shooting himself. He survived the suicide attempt. Things to note: Baker had worked at the plant for 39 years and had pleaded guilty to theft. He was scheduled to report to jail the next day to begin serving his five-month sentence.

July 8, 2003: Doug Williams took a 12-gauge shotgun, a rifle, and bandoliers of ammunition to the Lockheed Martin assembly plant in Meridian, Mississippi, where he worked. He shot 14 coworkers with the shotgun, killing six of them. When his girlfriend and a coworker began pleading for him to stop shooting, Williams committed suicide. Things to note: The spree lasted about 10 minutes. Williams was known to hold racist views, and eight of his victims were black.

August 27, 2003: Salvador Tapia went to the Chicago, Illinois, warehouse company from which he had been fired six months before. He had a semi-automatic handgun and used it to kill six former coworkers. He was killed during a shootout with police. Things to note: Tapia had a criminal record and was said to be angry about his termination.

March 4, 2004: al-Qaeda assisted terrorists bombed the train station in Madrid, Spain. 191 people were killed. Things to note: The bombing occurred just before elections in Spain. Spain then withdrew its troops from Iraq. Do you think terrorists learned from this?

July 2, 2004: Elijah Brown entered the meatpacking plant where he worked in Kansas City, Kansas. He shot seven co-workers, killing five, and then killed himself. Things to note: Three of the victims were from the same family, and it is believed Brown had had an argument with one of them. While described as strange, Brown had no previous criminal record.

September 1-3, 2004: The Beslan school siege (also referred to as the Beslan school hostage crisis or Beslan massacre) in the town of Beslan, North Ossetia (an autonomous republic in the North Caucasus region of the Russian Federation), started on September 1, 2004 and lasted three days. A group of armed Islamic

Militants held over 1,100 people hostage (including 777 children). On the third day of the standoff, Russian security forces stormed the building with the use of tanks, incendiary rockets, and other heavy weapons. At least 330 hostages were killed, including 186 children, with a significant number of people injured and reported missing. Things to note: *Terror at Beslan: A Russian Tragedy with Lessons for America's Schools* by John Giduck provides a detailed account of this incident along with lessons for American schools.

December 9, 2004: Nathan Gale rushed the stage during the heavy-metal band Damageplan's concert in Columbus, Ohio. He shot and killed the band's guitarist, Darrell "Dimebag" Abbott. He then began shooting at the audience, killing three more and injuring seven. Police shot and killed Gale while he was holding a man hostage. Things to note: The shooter reloaded at least once. He had 35 rounds remaining.

February 13, 2005: Robert Bonelli Jr. reportedly fired 60 rounds with a rifle into a crowd estimated at around 3,000 people inside a store in the Hudson Valley Mall in Upstate New York, near Glasco. Three people were injured. Things to note: He was a terrible shot or never intended on killing anyone. When he ran out of ammunition, a couple of shoppers restrained him until police arrived. Police found an altar to the Columbine shooters in his home.

March 13, 2005: Terry Ratzmann went into the Sheraton Hotel in Milwaukee, Wisconsin, where an evangelical group associated with The Living Church of God was meeting. Ratzmann killed seven and wounded four, including the pastor and his son. He then killed himself. Things to note: Ratzmann was about to lose his job and was upset over a sermon the minister had delivered two weeks before.

March 21, 2005: Jeff Weise went to Red Lake Senior High School, Minnesota, where he had been expelled. He grinned and waved to students as he shot them. He killed seven including a teacher and a security guard and wounded seven others. He briefly exchanged fire with police before killing himself. Things to note: Before he went to the school, Weise killed his grandfather and his grandfather's girlfriend.

July 7, 2005: Islamic extremists attacked a number of transportation lines of the London Underground with explosives. Four suicide bombers killed 52 people and injured more than 700. Things to note: The bombs of the second attack two weeks later failed to detonate, and there were no casualties during the July 21, 2005, incident.

January 30, 2006: Jennifer Sanmarco went to the Goleta, California, mail-processing plant where she had worked three years earlier. She killed six people. After the shootings, she killed herself. Things to note: Sanmarco had been removed from the postal facility in 2003 because she was "acting strangely." She was put on disability because supervisors thought she would be a danger to herself. She gained entry to the heavily secured facility by driving in behind an employee and stealing a badge. Before going to the postal facility, she killed a former neighbor whom she had argued with when they lived in the same complex.

October 2, 2006: Charles Carl Roberts went to the West Nickel Mines Amish School in the Old Order Amish community of Nickel Mines in Lancaster County, Pennsylvania. What started as a hostage situation turned into what is called the Amish massacre. By the time police were able to get inside, Roberts killed five young girls and wounded five others (plus the teacher's aide) before killing himself. Things to note: Roberts took with him a change of clothes, toilet paper, candles, sexual lubricant, and flexible plastic ties. He allowed a pregnant woman, three parents with infants, and all of the boys to leave. He kept 10 female students and the teacher's aide. The victims ranged in age from 6 to 16. Roberts' wife found four suicide notes he left behind to her and their three children.

February 12, 2007: Salamin Talbit (also spelled Sulejman Talovic) carried a 12-gauge shotgun and a pistol into the Trolley Square Mall in Salt Lake City, Utah, and started shooting people. He killed four before he was shot and killed by a police officer. Things to note: Many shoppers thought the shots were balloons popping and didn't do anything.

April 16, 2007: Seung-Hui Cho killed 32 people and wounded 17 others at Virginia Polytechnic Institute and State University (Virginia Tech) in Blacksburg, Virginia. He first killed two students at Johnston hall, went to his own dorm and cleaned up, went and mailed a package, and then went to Norris Hall where he resumed his killing about two hours after the initial killings. About 10 or 12 minutes after entering Norris Hall, Cho shot and killed himself. Things to note: Cho chained the doors of Norris Hall shut. Cho was armed with two handguns and fired over 100 rounds. At Norris Hall, he killed 25 students and five instructors in four different rooms. He had researched previous school shootings, including Columbine. This attack is the third deadliest shooting incident by a single gunman in the United States (surpassed by the 2016 Orlando nightclub shooting and the 2017 Las Vegas concert shooting).

The Impact of the Virginia Tech Mass Shooting

The mass shooting at Virginia Tech University (April 16, 2007), which claimed the lives of 32 people and left the country in shock, opened many people's eyes to the importance of emergency preparedness and marked the beginning of an overhaul of campus emergency operations that has transformed the way many college police and public safety departments function. It was one of the most scrutinized security incidents in higher education history.

After the attack, recommendations issued by the governor's review panel relating to university emergency planning and alerts included:

Virginia Governor's Panel Recommendations for Virginia Tech

- Universities should conduct threat assessments before deciding on the appropriate level of security for their campus.
- University threat assessment teams should include law enforcement, human resources, student and academic affairs, legal counsel and mental health services.
- Students, faculty, and staff members should undergo annual emergency response and notification training.
- Emergency communications systems must have multiple means of sharing information.
- Campus police and administration officials should have the ability to send emergency messages.

(Source: Zack Winn, 10 Years Later, Colleges Still Feel the Impact of the Virginia Tech Mass Shooting)

April 30, 2007: David Logdon shot and killed two people in the parking lot outside a Target store in Center Mall in Kansas City, Missouri. Logdon was killed by a police officer when he went into the mall. Things to note: Before the shooting, Logdon was stopped by police because he was driving a stolen car (the car's owner, Logdon's neighbor, had been found dead in her home). Logdon shot the officer in the arm and fled. The police tracked the stolen car to the mall and arrived much more quickly than if they had been called after the parking lot shootings.

December 4, 2007: Robert A. Hawkins shot and killed nine people in a busy mall department store in Omaha, Nebraska. He then committed suicide. Things to note: Police arrived six minutes after the initial 911 call. An hour before the shootings, Hawkins' mother found a suicide note that indicated he intended an act that would make him "famous." The note didn't give specifics. She contacted the sheriff's department.

December 8, 2007: Matthew Murray shot and killed two people at a Youth With A Mission training center outside Denver, Colorado, and then 12 hours later killed two more at New Life Church in Colorado Springs (70 miles south), which is affiliated with the Youth With A Mission program. He had a rifle and two handguns. After being shot five times by a female security guard, who was an off-duty police officer, he killed himself. Things to note: Murray detonated a smoke grenade to distract security and caused a panic among the parishioners. Murray had been a student at the school before being dismissed in 2002 for unspecified "health reasons."

February 9, 2008: Charles Thornton went to a city council meeting in Kirkwood, Missouri. He killed six people, including two police officers, two city council members, a city worker, and a news reporter. He also shot the mayor twice in the head, critically injuring him. He was killed in a shootout with police. Things to note: A suicide note was later found on his bed. Thornton had a long-standing feud with the city. He had received 150 tickets against his business (his trucks were parked overnight in residential areas where commercial parking was illegal) that he claimed were because he was black.

February 14, 2008: Steven Kazmierczak went to a lecture hall at Northern Illinois University in DeKalb, Illinois, armed with three handguns hidden under his coat, and a shotgun concealed in a guitar case. He killed five and injured 18 others. Kazmierczak then committed suicide. Things to note: Kazmierczak had a history of mental illness and had stopped taking his medications. He was described by faculty and students as an outstanding student and he had a girlfriend. It is reported that he researched previous school shootings, including Columbine and Virginia Tech.

June 8, 2008: A 25-year-old man plowed into a crowd with his truck and then got out and began stabbing people in a popular electronics and video game district of Akihabara, in central Tokyo, Japan. He stabbed 17 people, including a police officer. Seven people died. He dropped the knife when police threatened to shoot him and was arrested. Things to note: He used both a vehicle and a knife. The event occurred on the seventh anniversary of a mass stabbing at a Japanese elementary school.

February 25, 2009: Two men fired shots in a crowd during a Mardi Gras parade in New Orleans, Louisiana. No one was killed, but seven people hit by bullets, including a toddler. Things to note: Police apprehended both shooters. The shots were apparently random.

March 8, 2009: Terry J. Sadlacek went to the First Baptist Church in Maryville, Illinois. He shot and killed the pastor. Sadlacek walked down the aisle, and his handgun jammed. Two congregants struggled to restrain him as Sadlacek stabbed them and himself multiple times. Things to note: During the initial shots that killed the pastor, worshipers thought it was part of the program and didn't react right away. Sadlacek had three magazines with 10 rounds each for his gun. If it hadn't jammed, the body count would probably have been more than the one person he killed. The police found a note in a planner that described Sunday as "Death Day."

April 3, 2009: Jiverly Voong carried a high-powered rifle, two handguns and ammunition into the American Civic Center in Binghamton, New York. He killed 13 and seriously wounded five. He committed suicide. Things to note: He blocked the back door of the building with his car to prevent people from escaping. He wore a bullet proof vest. Two dozen people barricaded themselves in the boiler room and survived. The receptionist was shot as Voong came in the front door, but she survived by playing dead and hiding for 40 minutes until police arrived.

April 30, 2009: Karst Tates drove his car through police barricades in an attempt to ram the bus carrying members of the Dutch royal family during the Dutch Queen's Day Parade in Apeldoorn, Netherlands. Eight people were killed. Tates died from injuries received during the attack. Things to note: The people killed by being run over by Tates' car were not his intended targets.

November 6, 2009: Maj. Nidal Hasan killed 13 and wounded 31 at the Soldier Readiness Center at Ford Hood, Texas. Things to note: The soldiers inside were unarmed and tried to stop him by throwing chairs and charging him. A female civilian police officer, who was shot several times, was able to take Hasan down. It is believed that Hasan, a Muslim, was influenced by his religious feelings.

August 3, 2010: Omar Sheriff Thornton was at his place of employment, a warehouse owned by Hartford Distributors in Manchester, Connecticut, for disciplinary purposes for being recorded stealing beer. He was given the option to resign or be fired. He signed the resignation papers and was being escorted out of the building when he took two semi-automatic pistols from his lunchbox and opened fire. There were around 40 employees in the building. Thornton killed eight and seriously injured two others. He killed himself, after hiding in an office when police arrived, and after calling his mother and 911. Things to note: He told the 911 operator that he wished he had killed more people. Police arrived on the scene three minutes after the first 911 call.

January 8, 2011: Jared Lee Loughner shot U.S. Representative Gabrielle Giffords and eighteen others with a semi-automatic pistol during a meeting held in a supermarket parking lot in Casas Adobes, Arizona, in the Tucson metropolitan area. Six people died. Giffords, shot in the head, survived. Things to note: Loughner was stopped by unarmed individuals in the crowd.

October 12, 2011: Scott Evans Dekraai went to the Salon Meritage hair salon in Seal Beach, California, armed with three handguns. He shot eight people inside the salon and one person in the parking lot. Only one victim survived. Dekraai was arrested without incident after being stopped while driving a white pickup truck about one half-mile from the scene of the crime. Things to note: Dekraai was wearing body armor at the time of his arrest. Dekraai's former wife, who worked at the salon, was one of the victims. He reloaded at least once during the attack, which lasted two minutes.

July 20, 2012: James Eagan Holmes went to the Century 16 movie theater in Aurora, Colorado, during a midnight screening of the film *The Dark Knight Rises*. During the movie, he left the building through an emergency exit door, which he propped open. He returned with a shotgun, a semi-automatic rifle, and a semi-automatic handgun. He killed 12 people and wounded 70 more. Holmes did not resist when he was apprehended by a police officer behind the cinema, next to his car. Things to note: Holmes fired 76 shots in the theater: six from the shotgun, 65 from the rifle, and five from the handgun. Initially, audience members believed it was a prank or a film publicity stunt. Holmes was wearing a gas mask and he threw two canisters that emitted gas or smoke when he entered the theater and began shooting. The 82 casualties were the most victims of any mass shooting in the

United States until the 2016 Orlando nightclub shooting with 107 casualties. This was then surpassed by the 2017 Las Vegas shooting with over 900 killed and injured.

December 14, 2012: Adam Lanza went to the Sandy Hook Elementary School in Newtown, Connecticut, armed with a rifle and handguns. He shot and killed 20 children aged between 6 and 7 years old, as well as six adult staff members. Two others were injured. When police arrived, Lanza killed himself. Things to note: Lanza killed his mother at their Newtown home before going to the school. He shot his way through a glass panel next to the locked front entrance doors of the school. Authorities determined the Lanza reloaded frequently during the shootings, sometimes firing only fifteen rounds from a thirty-round magazine. The shooting occurred in the space of less than five minutes with 156 shots fired. 154 shots from the rifle and two shots from the pistol.

September 16, 2013: Aaron Alexis shot and killed twelve people and injured three others at the headquarters of the Naval Sea Systems Command inside the Washington Navy Yard in Southeast Washington, D.C. Alexis was killed by police. Things to note: Second deadliest mass murder on a U.S. military base behind the Fort Hood shooting in November 2009. Alexis entered with a valid pass carrying a disassembled shotgun that had had the barrel and stock sawed off in a bag over his shoulder.

September 21, 2013: Unidentified gunmen attacked the Westgate shopping mall in Nairobi, Kenya. The attack resulted in at least 67 deaths and more than 175 people were reported wounded. The extremist Islamic group al-Shabaab claimed responsibility for the incident. Things to note: a concealed-carry foreign national who was a resident in the country is reported to have helped over 100 people to safety providing covering fire for their escape. He is only one of the concealed-carry responders, and this incident is used as an example of how concealed-carry interventions can turn the tide and save lives.

October 1, 2015: Chris Harper-Mercer went to the UCC campus near Roseburg, Oregon, where he was enrolled. He shot and killed an assistant professor and eight students. Seven to nine others were injured. Police responded, and Harper-Mercer was wounded in a shootout. He then killed himself by shooting himself in the head. Things to note: Harper-Mercer fired a warning shot when he entered the classroom. He spared one student so that student could deliver a package to the police. He used two handguns. He allegedly asked students for their religion before shooting them.

December 2, 2015: Syed Rizwan Farook and Tashfeen Malik, a married couple, targeted a San Bernardino County Department of Public Health training event and Christmas party, of about 80 employees, in San Bernardino, California, for their deadly attack. They killed 14 people and seriously injured 22 more. After the shooting, the two fled in an SUV. Four hours later police killed them both in a shootout. Things to note: On December 6, 2015, President Obama defined the shooting as an act of terrorism. The couple has a large stockpile of weapons, ammunition, and bomb-making equipment in their home.

June 12, 2016: Omar Mateen went to Pulse, a gay nightclub in Orlando, Florida, armed with a semi-automatic rifle and a semi-automatic pistol. He killed 49 people and wounded 58 others. He was shot and killed by Orlando Police Officers after a three-hour standoff. Things to note: There were about 320 people in the club. Some people thought the initial gunshots were firecrackers or part of the music. The situation was a little different for police response because it went from an active shooter to a barricaded gunman with hostages. This attack was the deadliest mass shooting by a single shooter in United States history at the time. It was surpassed by the October 1, 2017 shooting in Las Vegas, NV.

July 7, 2016: Micah Xavier Johnson went to a peaceful protest held in Dallas, Texas, against police killings of Alton Sterling in Baton Rouge, Louisiana, and Philando Castile in Falcon Heights, Minnesota. He was armed with a semi-automatic rifle and at least one handgun. Johnson ambushed and fired upon a group of police officers. Five officers were killed and nine others and two civilians were injured. Things to note: Johnson fled and hid inside a building where a standoff ensued. The police killed Johnson with a bomb attached to a remote-control bomb disposal robot. It was the first-time U.S. law enforcement used a robot to kill a suspect. The shooting was the deadliest incident for U.S. law enforcement since the September 11 attacks, surpassing two related March 2009 shootings in Oakland, CA, and a November 2009 ambush shooting in Lakewood, WA, both of which four officers were killed.

July 14, 2016: Mohamed Lahouaiej-Bouhlel, a Tunisian resident of France, deliberately drove a 19-ton cargo truck into crowds of people celebrating Bastille Day on the Promenade des Anglais in Nice, France, resulting in the deaths of 86 people and injuring 458 others. The attack ended when Lahouaiej-Bouhlel was shot and killed by police. Things to note: Firearms, knives, and explosives are not the only means terrorists and evil people will use to kill and injure others.

June 5, 2017: John Robert Neumann, Jr., a 45-year-old former employee of Fiamma, killed five former colleagues and himself in Orlando, Florida. Neumann was armed with a handgun and a large hunting knife. He let himself into the building through a rear entrance and singled out his five victims and shot them in the head. He fatally shot himself as deputies responded to the scene. Things to note: Neumann was fired sometime in April 2017, for unknown reasons.

June 14, 2017: James Hodgkinson, in Alexandria, Virginia, shot Republican member of Congress and House Majority Whip Steven Scalise of Louisiana while he was practicing for the annual Congressional Baseball Game for Charity, scheduled for the following day. Also shot were Crystal Griner, a Capital Police officer assigned to protect Scalise; Zack Barth, a Congressional aide; and Matt Mika, a Tyson Foods lobbyist. Hodgkinson was shot and killed during a shootout with Capitol and Alexandria Police. Things to note: It is reported that Hodgkinson had been living out of a white cargo van in Alexandria on a block that borders the baseball field during the recent months before the shooting.

June 14, 2017: At 8:55 a.m., during a morning meeting, Jimmy Lam fatally shot 3 co-workers at a United Parcel Service (UPS) facility in the Potrero Hill neighborhood of San Francisco, California. Lam then shot and killed himself as police arrived at the facility. Two others were wounded by gunfire, and three people were injured while escaping. Things to note: Lam singled out specific employees to shoot.

October 1, 2017: Between 10:05 and 10:15 p.m., Stephen Paddock fired hundreds of rifle rounds from his suite on the 32nd floor of the Mandalay Bay hotel into a crowd of concertgoers at the Route 91 Harvest music festival on the Las Vegas Strip, Las Vegas, Nevada. 58 innocent people were killed and 851 injured (422 with gunshot wounds). Paddock was found dead in his room from a self-inflicted gunshot wound. His motive is unknown. Things to note: The incident is the deadliest mass shooting committed by an individual in the United States to date. It is atypical for many reasons, including the way the massacre was committed and the many questions still unanswered.

November 5, 2017: David Patrick Kelley killed 26 people and injured 20 more at the First Baptist Church in Sutherland Springs, Texas. Kelley was shot twice by a civilian as he exited the church and was found dead in his vehicle after a high-speed chase, with a self-inflicted gunshot wound to the head. Things to note: Deadliest shooting in an America place of worship in modern history. Kelley should not have been allowed to purchase firearms and ammunition due to a domestic violence conviction in a court-martial while in the U.S. Air Force, but the conviction was not entered into the FBI National Crime Information Center database that is used by the National Instant Check System to flag prohibited purchases. It was not entered because the Air Force never submitted this information – perhaps a change in how things are done will come about...

February 14, 2018: 19-year-old Nikolas Jacob Cruz killed seventeen people and wounded seventeen more at Marjory Stoneman Douglas High School in Parkland, Florida. Cruz was identified by witnesses and arrested shortly afterward. He confessed and was charged with 17 counts of premeditated murder and 17 attempted murders. Things to note: Cruz was armed with an AR-15 style semi-automatic rifle and pulled the fire alarms to cause confusion. For some reason, law enforcement did not immediately enter the building to confront the threat.

Sadly, this list is far from complete. It does illustrate that shootings and mass killings have been going on for a long time, and besides the senseless and tragic deaths of innocent people, the other factors vary.

Why the History of Shootings and Mass Killings is Important

The importance of studying previous shootings and mass killing incidents is to better understand what we can do to prevent future incidents and to be better prepared to respond when they do happen. Law enforcement has changed policies and tactics after learning from incidents, and we are now teaching civilians better responses to these attacks from what we have learned by studying the shooter events that have occurred.

For example, law enforcement started to develop SWAT teams after the August, 1966, incident with Charles Whitman in Austin, Texas; and police procedures in response to an active shooter were dramatically changed after the April, 1999, Columbine High School shooting.

In the civilian arena, different courses have been developed based on information gained by studying previous incidents. One such course developed by Safariland Training Group is the *Emergency Response To An Armed Intruder* class. I am certified by Safariland Training Group to teach this course, and along with my team members, we have taught close to 4,000 people in our community what they can do if they find themselves in an active shooter situation. This course is discussed more later, but I wanted to point out that the developer of the course, Sandy Wall, went to Sandy Hook Elementary School in Newtown, Connecticut, after that tragic shooting and it is believed by many that this course could have saved lives. As we study previous events, we continue to evolve and make our prevention methods and response options better with the single goal of saving lives.

The study and analysis of these events also provides the statistics of events found in the next chapter. These statistics are also used to help us teach and better our prevention methods and response options.

Killers Study Others

In *Shooter Down! The Dramatic, Untold Story of the Police Response to the Virginia Tech Massacre,* the author speculates that Seung-Hui Cho watched the news about Charles Roberts and the Amish massacre. Seeing how the barricades slowed the police response, a plan started to formulate in his mind. It is also reported that Cho had been obsessed with the Columbine massacre and had studied it relentlessly. Most likely he studied other shootings before going on his own rampage on April 16, 2007.

This is just one example, but there are many others, where the killers have been inspired by and studied other shooters before embarking on their own mass killings. Just days after the Fairchild AFB active shooter incident, a convicted felon in Spokane, WA, threatened to kill his mental health care workers, indicating he would "do it Fairchild style." Police were alerted and the man was arrested. Despite being a convicted felon, he was in possession of more than thirty firearms and a large quantity of ammunition. This is an example of why the good guys must study the history of these events and analyze them to try and stay ahead of the bad guys. Because the bad guys are studying them to learn more effective ways to thwart the police and up the body counts of innocent people to attempt to claim their 15 minutes of fame. Therefore, we are going to study everything we can to stay ahead and do everything possible to save lives.

2 The Problem Defined

www.SurviveaShooting.com

Laws concerning firearms, trespassing, theft, robbery, murder, and other crimes are of no concern to a prospective criminal or killer... someone who is capable of committing such a horrible act is past caring that it's wrong, and they will find a way to do it. They will find a gun or some other weapon, they will find dangerous chemicals, they will find gasoline and a book of matches. One way or another they will commit these murders. They are motivated and determined to do it, and there are too many logistics for us to cover for them to be stopped 100%. ”

Chris Sutton & John Graden
The Cobra-Defense Active Shooter Response Plan

TOPICS

- ✓ Definition of Active Shooter
- ✓ Active Shooter vs. Shooting Incident
- ✓ Active Threat
- ✓ Who are the Shooters?
- ✓ Some Characteristics of Active Shooters
- ✓ Active Shooter Statistics

Survive a Shooting focuses on a specific kind of violence; the active shooter or active threat.

Definition of Active Shooter

It is important to define problems before looking at options and solutions. Because there are several definitions of "active shooter" being used, it is important to discuss what an "active shooter" is and equally important, what an "active shooter" isn't. Also, spree killings and mass killings are not always committed with a firearm. Therefore, the term "active threat" is often better and more accurate than "active shooter." This chapter will address what an "active shooter" is, the use of the term "active threat," and provide some statistics and information to better understand the problem.

Active Shooter

"Active Shooter is a term used by law enforcement to describe a situation in which a shooting is in progress and an aspect of the crime may affect the protocols used in responding to and reacting at the scene of the incident." (FBI, 2015)

The U.S. Department of Homeland Security defines an Active Shooter as, "an individual actively engaged in killing, or attempting to kill people in a confined and populated area." (DHS, 2013)

Active Shooter vs. Shooting Incident

It is important both for what you need to do to survive, and how law enforcement will respond, to know the difference between an active shooter event and a shooting incident.

> **Mass Shooting**
>
> Gun Violence Archive defines **Mass Shooting** as "FOUR or more shot and/or killed in a single event (incident), at the same general time and location, not including the shooter."
>
> http://www.gunviolencearchive.org

Regarding what an "active shooter" is, Safariland Training Group uses this definition from the National Tactical Officers Association in the *Emergency Response to an Armed Intruder* course, "One or more subjects who participate in a random or systematic shooting spree, demonstrating their intent to continuously harm others. Their overriding objective appears to be that of mass murder, rather than any other criminal activity such as robbery, kidnapping, etc. Includes use of any deadly weapon."

Additionally, active shooter events are usually pre-planned, and the shooter has prepared to injure and kill as many people as possible before being stopped. Statistics show active shooter incidents average 12 minutes in duration and during this time, on average, a person is shot every 15 seconds. 69% of these incidents are over in 5 minutes or less, and 60% end prior to arrival of Law Enforcement personnel.

Contrast this with a shooting incident, which is typically spontaneous and emotionally driven, rather than predatory (not pre-planned.) Shooting incidents are often opportunistic or angry reactions, and sometimes accidental. These are common shooting incidents:

- A shot fired in a home, on campus, etc.
- An accidental discharge of a weapon
- A gun fight between two or more individuals (this includes many gang shootings)
- A gun fired to scare or kill during another crime such as robbery, kidnapping, etc.

Active Threat

There are other terms you may hear or come across. **Spree Killing** refers to two or more victims, but at more than one location. Although the murders occur in separate locations, the spree is considered a single event because there is no "cooling off" period between the murders. **Mass Murders** are when four or more people are killed at one location during one continuous period of time, whether it is a few minutes or over a period of days. Killers who murder several members of their family usually fall into the mass murder category. These are both different from **Serial Killers** who murder three or more victims, but each is killed on separate occasions. Unlike mass murderers and spree killers, serial killers usually select their victims, have cooling off periods between murders, and plan their crimes carefully.

Active Shooter is the term favored by law enforcement and the media when describing ongoing shootings. However, as we have seen, shooting is only one of the options used to kill innocent victims by these killers. Vehicles, knives, machetes, and explosives have also been used. This is why we use the term **Active Threat** in the classes we have been teaching, and why **Active Threat** may be the most accurate term when dealing with these types of incidents.

I use the terms Active Shooter and Active Threat somewhat interchangeably throughout this book, and titled the book *Survive a Shooting* because that is what is focused on more in the media. The strategies and information in this book are aimed at ensuring more people are prepared to survive any **Active Threat**, and not just **Active Shooter** incidents.

Who Are the Shooters?

It would save many lives if we could predict who will become a shooter. Unfortunately, while it is often easy to identify reasons why a person did what he did, it is not so easy to predict. Many of the red flags, or danger signs, associated with active shooters are not always obvious before the shooting. And even if they were, we are not allowed to arrest people for what they might do.

We do know that active shooters are not all alike. The previous chapter should have illustrated that pretty clearly. Ages have ranged from kids to the elderly, killers have been different races (although in the U.S. most have been white), and while most have been male, there have been female shooters as well.

Some shooters have specific targets and others select targets at random indiscriminately. Some are angry at specific people or institutions, while others are angry a society at large. Some act alone and others plot their acts and carry out their killing with like-minded individuals.

Some Characteristics of Active Shooters

Motives of Active Shooters

- Desire for attention or recognition (Herostratus Syndrome)
- Suicide or desperation
- Attempt to solve a problem
- Revenge
- Anger
- Felt bullied/persecuted or threatened by others
- Perceived grievance, either real or imaginary
- Ideology
- Multiple Motives

No consistent, clearly identifiable, profile currently exists. But, even though it is difficult to pinpoint who will become an active shooter, it is wise to look at some of the common characteristics of those who commit these heinous crimes to be more aware of the potential for violence to occur. It is important to note that not all people who exhibit these characteristics, even many of them, will become cold blooded murderers. And there are killers who won't exhibit characteristics on this list. But I find it lacking if I tell you to be more aware and don't at least provide some generalities of what to be looking for.

Characteristics During an Event

- Focus on assaulting persons with whom they come into contact.
- Intention to cause bodily harm, an expression of hatred or rage, rather than the commission of a crime.
- Likely to engage more than one target.
- Intent on killing as many people as they can as quickly as possible.
- Little or no warning. Often first indication of the presence of an active shooter is when they begin their assault.
- Often go to locations where potential victims are numerous and easily accessible such as cafeterias, classrooms, and libraries.
- Often go to locations that are "gun free" zones with less likelihood of someone being armed that could fight back.
- Often have some degree of familiarity with the location they choose for the assault.
- Usually don't attempt to hide their identity or conceal the commission of their attacks.

Characteristics Before an Event

- Someone with an "ax to grind."
- Go to great lengths to plan their attack.
- Argumentative.
- Uncooperative with supervisors; non-compliant with policy.
- Rage reactions; overreacts; impulsive.
- Always the victim; blames others.
- Manipulative; exploits others.
- Bullying; threatening or committing violence.
- Withdrawn; depressed; avoids coworkers.
- Increase in drug or alcohol abuse.
- Increased absenteeism; vague physical complaints.
- Noticeable decrease in grooming and personal hygiene.
- Increased severe mood swings.
- Noticeably unstable, emotional responses.
- Suicidal: talks about "putting things in order."
- Paranoia: "everybody is against me."
- Increasingly talks of problems at home.
- Brings domestic problems into the workplace; talk of serious financial problems.
- Talks of previous incidents of violence.
- Expresses empathy for individuals committing violence.
- Increased unsolicited comments about firearms, other deadly weapons, and violent crimes.

Active Shooter Statistics

In 2014, the Federal Bureau of Investigation initiated a study of active shooter incidents to provide federal, state, local, campus and tribal law enforcement with accurate data to better understand how to prevent, prepare for, respond to, and recover from these incidents. Since then, there have been some supplemental updates, and some major active shooter incidents such as the Orlando Nightclub incident of June 12, 2016. I still want to provide some statistics found in the FBI Quick Reference Guide, based on their larger report, because the information provides background and legitimacy to the courses of action this book recommends and that I teach in my classes.

According to the FBI, an active shooter is an individual actively engaged in killing or attempting to kill people in a populated area. The FBI identified 160 active shooter incidents between 2000 and 2013. Among the study results:

FBI Study Results

- An average of 11.4 incidents occurred annually with an increasing trend from 2000 to 2013.
- An average of 6.4 occurred in the first 7 years studied and an average of 16.4 occurred in the last 7 years.
- Incidents occurred in 40 of 50 states and the District of Columbia.
- 70% of the incidents occurred in a commerce (73, 46%), or education (39, 24%) environment.
- 60% of the incidents ended before police arrived.
- In 63 incidents where the duration of incident could be ascertained, 44 (69%) ended in 5 minutes or less, with 23 ending in 2 minutes or less.
- 64 (40%) incidents fell within the parameters of the federal definition of "mass killing" (3 or more killed). (Author's note: this is different than the definition above with 4 or more.)

Shooters

All but 2 incidents involved a single shooter.

In at least 9 incidents, the shooter first shot and killed a family member(s) in a residence before moving to a more public location to continue shooting.

The shooter committed suicide in 64 (40%) incidents. 37 before police arrived, 17 after police arrived, and 10 at another location.

6 shooters were female, the rest male.

At least 5 shooters from 4 incidents remained at large as of September 2014.

In businesses closed to pedestrian traffic, 22 of the 23 shooters were current/former employees.

Casualties

486 people were killed in the 160 incidents and 557 were wounded.

In at least 15 (9.4%) incidents, family members were targeted resulting in 20 killed and 1 wounded.

In 16 (10%) incidents, current, former, or estranged wives as well as current or former girlfriends were targeted resulting in 12 killed, 3 wounded and 1 unharmed. In addition, 42 others were killed and 28 wounded.

Resolutions

90 (56%) incidents ended on the shooter's initiative, by the shooter committing suicide, fleeing, or stopping shooting.

21 (13.1%) incidents ended after unarmed citizens successfully restrained the shooter (Off-duty officers assisted in 2). In 5 of those incidents, the shooting ended after armed, non-law enforcement officers exchanged fire with the shooter.

In 45 (28.1%) incidents, law enforcement engaged in gunfire to end the threat. In 21 of those 45 incidents (46.7%), 9 officers were killed and 28 were wounded.

Locations

The FBI study divided incidents into 11 distinct location categories with most incidents occurring in commercial and educational areas. Below are the summary categories of this study.

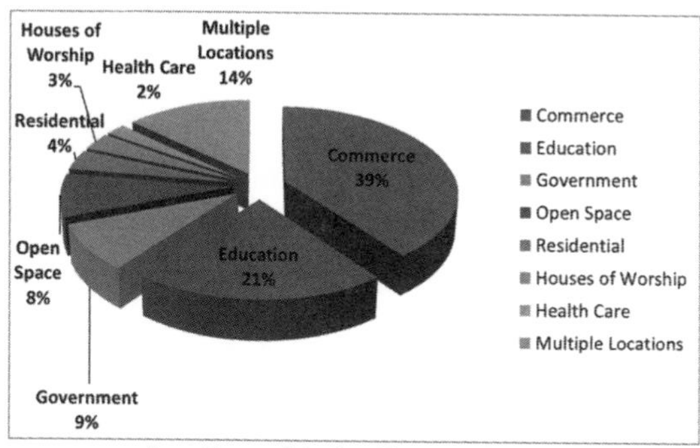

Locations of Active Shooter Events

Education Environment

Institutions of Higher Education:

- 2 of 12 shooters were female; 5 were former students, 4 current students, 2 employees, and 1 patient at a medical center.
- 5 of 12 incidents occurred on a Friday.

Pre-Kindergarten to 12th Grade

- 17 of 20 high school and middle school shooters were students at the affected school.
- The majority of school shooters were students (12 of 14 high school and 5 of 6 middle school/junior high).
- 9 of the 27 school incidents occurred on a Monday.
- 11 incidents ended when unarmed school employees and students successfully confronted shooters to end the threat.
- At least 14 school employees were killed and 16 wounded.

Conclusion

I think one of the most important things we can get out of these statistics is that the number of incidents is increasing. I think most people inherently know this because of the frequency we hear about these incidents on the news. It is for this reason that this book and the courses I teach are more important now than ever before, and why you, just reading this book, will be better prepared for such an incident than those who don't have a plan of what to do.

It is also important to note that both armed and unarmed citizens have stopped active shooters. This confirms my assertion that you don't have to be a victim. You can, and must, act to save yours and your loved one's lives. And when you have no option to escape or deny the shooter access to you, you can attack back, armed or unarmed, and prevail. Others have, and so can you.

Active Shooter/ Killer Prevention

www.SurviveaShooting.com

There is no silver bullet nor single psychological or personality trait that clearly and undeniably pinpoints who will or who will not become an active shooter.

Kevin T. Doss and C. David Shepherd
Active Shooter: Preparing for and Responding to a Growing Threat

TOPICS

- ✓ Hardening Targets
- ✓ Threat Assessment
- ✓ Reporting Mechanisms
- ✓ Indicators

While there is no specific identifiable profile of an active shooter, many of these killers exhibit signs of their intentions before they commit their atrocious acts. These signs range from certain behaviors, telling a certain friend or peer, and even publicly posting plans on social media websites. I read one source that stated that the Safe School Initiative Report claimed that in around 80 percent of school attacks at least one person had information that the attacker was thinking about or planning the school attack. (Remy, page 27)

A week before I taught a couple of *Survive A Shooting* courses in Virginia, a Maryland teen was thwarted in her attempt to commit a mass shooting at Catoctin High School in Thurmont, Maryland. Talk about a recent and relevant situation to discuss in the classes. Nicole Cevario's father alerted law enforcement of his daughter's plans, which were outlined in detail in her diary. Frederick County Sheriff Charles Jenkins stated, "There is no doubt in our minds that we averted a disaster out there," when comparing the possible destruction to the deadly attacks on Columbine High and Sandy Hook Elementary. This is only one example of many possible mass killings that have been prevented by aware citizens and responsive law enforcement. Pre-attack detection happens more than many realize and more often than reported by the media.

This chapter will look at a few of the measures to help detect potential attacks and prevent them from occurring. Preventing attacks in the first place is the surest way for people to survive.

Safe Hiring Practices

> *Every good security program begins with the human resources department. The ability to screen out potential threats during the hiring process, or the identification of risky behaviors in existing employees, is vital to protecting the organization.* ”
>
> *Kevin T. Doss and C. David Shepherd*
>
> *Active Shooter: Preparing For and Responding to a Growing Threat*

One aspect of prevention, and of creating a safe work environment, is the ability to screen out potential threats during the hiring process. Another is the identification of risky behaviors in existing employees. These are often done by the human resources department and may include conducting background screenings, drug testing, and interviews. Human resources are also involved with disciplinary actions and employee separations. For these reasons, human resources departments should be involved with security programs for the business.

In the book *The Safe Hiring Manual*, author Lester S. Rosen provides a S.A.F.E. hiring system that consists of these practices:

The S.A.F.E. Hiring System

Set up programs using written policies, procedures, and practices to achieve a safe workplace.

Acclimate and train all staff with hiring responsibilities to use safe hiring practices.

Facilitate and implement the safe hiring program throughout the organization.

Evaluate and audit the program to ensure compliance and understanding.

Hardening Targets

Developing a plan and emergency preparedness efforts are important for active shooter incidents. However, it is equally important, or maybe even more important, to spend time, energy, and money on trying to prevent such catastrophes in the first place.

There are strategies that can help prevent planned attacks, and a comprehensive approach using multiple strategies will be more reliable in stopping an attack than a single or minimal number of concepts. One of the things we can do is harden our location as a target. This doesn't necessarily prevent a criminal from committing a crime, or stop a massacre from happening, but it stops them from occurring at the harder target. Sometimes, when we can't stop bad things from happening, the best we can do is prevent them from happening here. That is what hardening targets is about.

Many active shooters are set on destruction and achieving a high body count, and their own mortality is not a concern. Many intend to not live through the incident. This limits some measures of deterrence, and is a big difference between active killers and other criminals. There are things that can be done to make a location a harder target and increase the survivability rate of an active shooter incident. This section will look at a few of these.

Hardening Targets through Environmental Design

Crime prevention through environmental design (CPTED) concepts are being used more these days, but there is still a battle between designs that enhance security and those that are aesthetically pleasing. We have gone into schools that were beautifully designed with glass walls that from an active shooter threat point of view were terrible for security. In an article for *Campus Safety*, Executive Director of Safe Havens International, Michael Dorn states, "the proper utilization of CPTED can help improve the connectivity between people, the ability for building occupants to see a potential threat in time to react to it, can improve access control and can help to make more overt physical security measures less intimidating."

20 Active Shooter and Active Killer Prevention Strategies

The following list is from an article by Michael Dorn for *Campus Safety* magazine. The article describes each strategy more in depth. This list is to stimulate thought and what kinds of things can be explored and implemented to increase the chances that a planned attack will be averted.

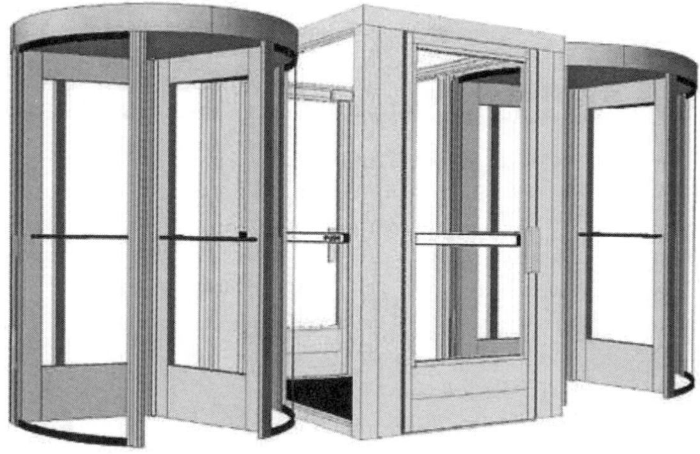

Access control vestibules can be used as an active killer prevention strategy

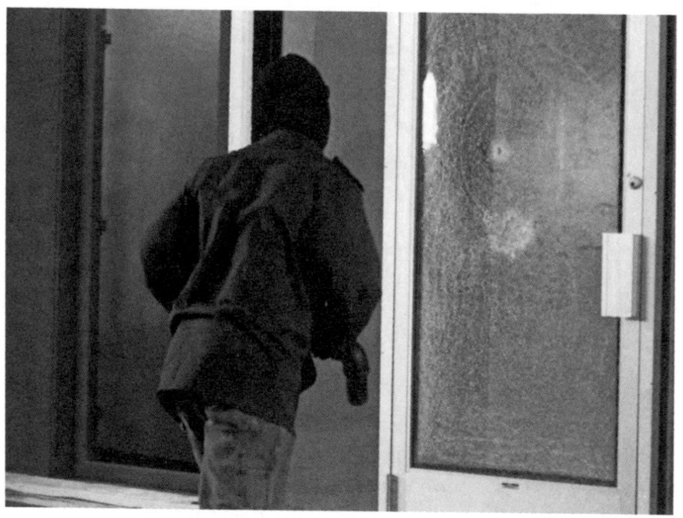

Window Safety and Security Film

20 Active Shooter and Active Killer Prevention Strategies

1. Multi-Disciplinary Threat Evaluation and Management
2. Visual Weapons Screening
3. Pattern Matching and Recognition
4. Anonymous Reporting Systems
5. Banning Potential Violators from Campus
6. Effective Use of Crime Prevention Through Environmental Design (CPTED) Concepts
7. Good Physical Perimeter Security
8. Robust Visitor Screening and Management
9. Security and Ballistic Windows in Key Areas
10. Properly Screened, Trained and Equipped Security and Law Enforcement Officers
11. Monitoring of Social Media
12. Intelligence Databases
13. Internal and Interagency Information Sharing
14. Traffic Enforcement
15. Proper Background Checks of Employees and Volunteers
16. Gun Detection Canines
17. Security Cameras with Facial Recognition Software
18. License Plate Recognition Cameras
19. Entry Point Metal Detection
20. Robust Intrusion Detection Systems

Better Door Locks and Windows

Superior doors and locking mechanisms along with security and ballistic windows may prevent a potential killer from entering a building, as well as help facilitate better lock downs. If cost is a factor, and it almost always is, use these in key areas first. Installing protective laminate film on windows is less expensive than bullet proof glass.

Lt. Col. Dave Grossman (U.S. Army, Ret) is an internationally recognized scholar, author, soldier, and speaker who is one of the world's foremost experts in the field of human aggression and the roots of violence and violent crime. In a presentation Grossman gave to law enforcement officers, he discussed a lawsuit that families of two of the 20 first-graders killed in the Sandy Hook Elementary School shooting brought against the town of Newton, Conn., and its board of education, alleging security measures at the school weren't adequate.

Grossman makes a case for having clear laminate on windows. The Sandy Hook doors were locked, but the killer shot out the glass next to the door to gain entry into the school. Grossman recommends Tru Armor, a division of Clear Armor as a quality laminate. (www.truarmor.com)

No windows would be preferred from a security standpoint, but that may not be practical for various reasons. This makes it important to use laminated glass that provides some resistance to ballistics attack and forced entry. If a gunman can shoot through glass and reach in to unlock the door, secondary devices (see below) may stop the killer from entering. Researching active shooter events has shown that shooters will not spend significant time trying to get through a particular door if it is locked or blocked. This is why the "deny strategy" using lock-downs is effective. They move to their next target knowing law enforcement is on the way and time is limited.

There are other laminates available, and it is prudent for businesses, schools, and organizations to look at these and include them as one of the layers in making locations a harder target. I recommend getting the highest quality and highest rated laminate your budget will allow.

Grossman also makes a great argument against how the teachers had to lock their doors. It's not enough to have a solid door with a good lock. At Sandy Hook, in order to lock the classroom door, the teachers had to step into the hallway, expose themselves to the killer, and then have the fine motor control to put the key into the lock. Grossman states that there isn't anything much more negligent than that the only way to lock the door is to step into the hallway and expose yourself to the killer.

I have seen this when teaching. We had teachers that wore their key around their neck so they could quickly lock the door. However, in adrenaline producing stress scenarios, teacher after teacher failed to lock the door quickly. We must remember that under extreme stress, we lose the ability to perform fine and complex motor skills. Putting a key into the key hole when terrified and under stress becomes extremely difficult.

There must be a quick and easy way to lock doors and deny killers access to your location. This lock down procedure must be tried and practiced. One simple procedure that can be used without a financial expenditure, is to keep the doors locked but cracked open. In an emergency, the door just needs to be quickly shut and it is locked. No fumbling with keys, and no going into a hallway exposing yourself to a killer.

Secondary Locking Devices

Besides reinforced doors lockable from the interior, secondary door blocking devices such as simple triangular door stops can provide additional stopping resistance for open-in type doors. For those that open-out, there are commercial and improvised ways to increase the difficulty in opening the door besides the installed locking mechanism. One measure would be to install a dead-bolt type lock where you only had to slide a handle (gross motor movement) to push the sturdy dead bolt into a reinforced door frame. This could secure either an open-in or an open-out type door. Pre-installing, or having devices readily available, is one more way to make a location a harder target.

There is no guarantee that an active threat won't occur in a particular location. However, hardening a target with appropriate strategies to reduce the risk of an attack can increase the probability of active threats being averted. Many planned attacks have been successfully thwarted by institutions implementing target hardening strategies. The strategies don't all have to be implemented immediately. Security measures can be increased as resources are available. An initial assessment can assist with this prioritizing. Each institution and location will have to determine which strategies to implement depending on their specific risk, location, and available resources.

Master Lock Security Bar

Sandy Hook Elementary School Shooting Lawsuit

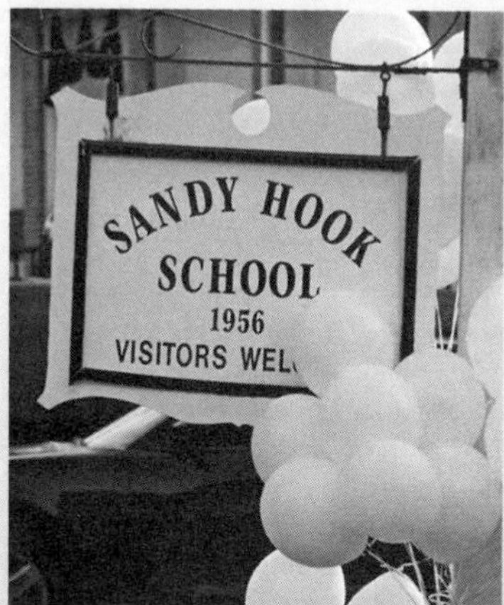

As reported in the Chicago Tribune, January 13, 2015.

Families of two of the 20 first-graders killed in the Sandy Hook Elementary School shooting are suing the town of Newton, Conn., and its board of education, alleging security measures at the school weren't adequate.

The wrongful-death lawsuit served on the town Friday is being filed by the parents of Jesse Lewis and Noah Pozner, who were among the children fatally shot Dec. 14, 2012. The families are seeking unspecified damages in the lawsuit, which is expected to be filed in state Superior Court in Danbury in the coming weeks.

Among the allegations is that Sandy Hook Elementary School had security policies and procedures in place that teachers weren't able to follow on the day of the killings. Classroom doors could only be locked from the outside with keys, leaving teachers vulnerable to intruders, and the front of the school didn't have security glass to protect against gunshots, according to the lawsuit. The lawsuit alleges a teacher in one of the two classrooms where students were killed was a substitute, didn't have a key, and didn't receive training on the security protocols.

Cameras Don't Stop Active Killers

Cameras have a place in security measures, but they don't stop active shooters and killers. When we are dealing with these mass murderers, cameras are not a deterrent. The Columbine killers actually posed for the security cameras, and a still from that footage appeared on the Dec. 20, 1999 cover of TIME magazine. Many of these sick individuals want to be famous and seen. Security cameras are filming their video for them.

For other situations, security cameras and the footage they provide is very valuable. And they can be a deterrent for some types of crime. But never think that a security camera is going to stop a massacre. All they provide in these incidents is a documentation of the killing and a means to help make the murderer famous. You could even make an argument that some of these killers may seek out locations where the security cameras are located so more people will see their atrocities.

Install security cameras as part of your overall security measures, but do not include them as a deterrent to active killers, or as a measure in active shooter prevention.

Threat Assessment

All of us are continually assessing potential dangers and threats as we go through life. Some, like crossing the street, are so routine that we do this without really thinking about it. When crossing the street, you assess the threat of being run over by determining the speed in which the oncoming vehicle is approaching and if you can cross safely. You then decide to cross the street or wait until the oncoming vehicle has passed. By the time we are adults, we are pretty good at judging the speed of oncoming vehicles and knowing how long it will take us to cross. When it comes to assessing the threat of an active shooter, most people have nothing to base their assessment on. And because of the complexities involved, it is often best to form a threat assessment team within your organization.

Businesses, organizations, hospitals, schools, and universities can establish threat assessment teams, or committees, to investigate reported instances of threatening behavior. These teams will determine the seriousness of the potential threat and advise administrators with appropriate responses. Threat assessment teams can consist of administrators, mental health workers, security staff, local police officers, and pertinent social service agencies. Teams will vary depending on the organization, but these are often the kinds of people involved.

Establishing a threat assessment team provides a specific place where people can report their concerns. (See Reporting Mechanisms below.) The threat assessment team can also work with potential offenders by working to prevent a violent outburst. This can be done by getting the person counseling to alleviate their sense of hopelessness, depression, or rage. It is important that the threat assessment team have access to social services and resources that can help individuals, and to do so confidentially.

> “*Many people who make threats never carry them out.*”

Establishing a threat assessment team, or committee, is the first step. It then must be communicated to the organization, whether that be a business, church, school, university, hospital, or any other institution. People need to know the program exists in order to be able to report concern and abnormal behavior to the team. In his book, *Surviving a School Shooting*, Loren W. Christensen recommends schools that form a threat assessment program inform students via school newsletter, homeroom presentations, and posters of the following details:

- The team exists, and it's user-friendly
- Students are doing the right thing by reporting their concerns.
- The team consists of dedicated people who listen and take students' concerns seriously.
- Their concerns and information will be handled discreetly.
- Their information protects both the victim(s) and the potential shooter.

Christensen continues by saying, "Let students know that the members of the threat assessment team are trained to help them, and that they will use all their resources to accomplish the following goals:

- Treat every contact with respect, discretion, and seriousness.
- Document the threats.
- Evaluate the motivation of the complainant.
- Determine the intervention needed.
- Interview the alleged offender.
- Present the complaint to all members of the team.
- Bring in more experts as necessary, including mental health professionals and police.
- Take appropriate disciplinary action and/or law enforcement action.
- Implement security measures against the threat.
- Respond to media queries.
- Conduct a follow-up investigation."

Christensen's lists are aimed at schools, but it doesn't take much to adapt them to different organizations. The formation of a threat assessment team and the communication of the team's existence and what its goals are can be as simple as three or four people, or as complex as a team of multiple individuals from a variety of community programs. The size of the team isn't as important as the team's existence and the collaborative effort exerted with the goal of making the organization, and actually the entire community, safe through prevention and help to those who need it.

Reporting Mechanisms

Mr. Cevario was hailed a hero by law enforcement for turning in his daughter, Nicole. I'm sure it was a difficult thing for him to do, but I'm sure he saved many lives by doing so. Unfortunately, many people are not comfortable and won't readily report information to law enforcement, administrators, or authority figures. Some may feel embarrassed and feel they would be viewed as being paranoid. Others may not like authority figures or law enforcement. Some people don't want to get involved for various reasons, including the fear of retaliation. Uncertainty of who to tell and the fear of relaying inaccurate information may prevent some people from stepping up. Others may just refuse to believe the warning signs they witness are legitimate. This is the same kind of denial that people have to overcome in an actual killing spree.

Anonymous tip lines can be an excellent way for those not wanting to be identified as going to the authorities to report threats and other suspicious activities and behaviors. These can be used by students, teachers, employees, parents, and any concerned citizens. These can be manned by live operators or voice mail services. Additionally, they can be set up to incorporate e-mail or text message reporting. Providing more options and making it easy and comfortable for people to give tips will be most effective.

It's not enough to just establish reporting mechanisms such as tip lines, anonymous or direct. Information about the reporting mechanisms must be disseminated to everyone so it is commonly known how to report threats or suspicions. It is especially important for students and employees to know that their concerns will be listened to without fear of judgment or retaliation.

Additionally, there must be a timely assessment of all tips with appropriate actions taken. This may be done by an organization's threat assessment team, a school's School Resource Officer, or a designated law enforcement officer of the department reported to. The most important factor is that all tips are taken seriously unless proven otherwise, and an assessment is performed in a timely and thorough manner.

Attacks and killings have been averted due to tips and information sharing. While not as "sexy" as models teaching what to do when bullets are flying, prevention really is the best way to save the most lives and have everyone survive. The Cevario incident was a success story, just as the May, 1999, Holland Woods Middle School incident in Port Huron, Michigan, was a success story. Four pupils were charged with conspiring to massacre students and teachers. The boys' intent was to do something worse than the youths at Columbine High School in Littleton, Colorado. The Assistant Principle, Nancy Schoenebeck, was told by two students that four boys were talking about getting guns "to shoot up the school." Fortunately, those students told the Assistant Principal, and she took them seriously and contacted appropriate law enforcement. The four boys, age 14, 14, 13, and 12, were all arrested, and a tragedy was prevented because the two students had the courage to tell their Assistant Principal.

Indicators

> "An anomaly is any variation from the baseline – and what we are primarily searching for is anomalies. Anomalies are things that either do not happen but should, or that do happen but shouldn't."
>
> *Patrick Van Horne and Jason A. Riley*
>
> *Left of Bang: How the Marine Corps' Combat Hunter Program Can Save Your Life*

There is no specific demographic profile of an active shooter, but many active shooters have had a history of disturbing thoughts, actions, verbalizations, and other warning signs. Sadly, many of these warning signs have been overlooked or ignored. This is why Andy Brown's book, detailing the events that led up to the Fairchild AFB shooting in 1994, is titled *Warnings Unheeded*. Many researchers and professionals have analyzed the available data to attempt to identify the psychological traits or behaviors of active shooters. Unfortunately, none of the conclusions are definitive. Not all active shooters possess all indicators, and there are individuals who possess many indicators that never commit an attack. Nor is there a single common denominator trigger when it comes to active shooters, regardless of age, social status, or education.

Red Flags

Garret Machine, veteran of the Israel Defense Forces and bodyguard for the Israeli Ministry of Defense, provides this list of red flags, or most common warnings, that should set off your security antenna in his book *Israeli Security Warrior Training*:

Red Flags

The first sign is inappropriate clothing, such as a winter coat being worn in the heat of the summer or a man wearing a suit when everyone else is in casual attire. Bizarre or unsuitable clothing is often the most obvious tell that the person may be a security threat. The next sign consists of behavioral characteristics, including but not limited to the following:

Fidgeting. This could include nervous movement of the hands or feet. Keep your eyes on this person.
Sweating excessively for the situation. For example, you should keep your eye on anyone sweating profusely even though the temperature is not hot enough and his activity is not strenuous enough to produce that much perspiration. Nervous tension makes people sweat.
Refusing to make eye contact. This is a telltale behavioral sign in people who are ashamed of their actions or are afraid of attracting attention to themselves.
Pacing frenetically. This is common in people too amped up to calm down. This is a typical sign that something is about to happen.
Repeatedly looking at a watch or cell phone. This could indicate that the person is nervously waiting for a certain time or signal to act.
Communicating secretly with another person in the area. This could help you identify two terrorists planning an act of violence. In the case of suicide bombing, this might mean that one terrorist has the actual bomb on his person and the other is there to remotely detonate the bomb if the first person is reluctant to set it off or is caught by the authorities.
Appearing to be in a trance. Anyone who is walking around or sitting in an apparent daze could be so brainwashed to carry out his mission that he is no longer able to engage in normal dialogue or respond to any type of interaction. Keep your eyes on a person displaying this behavior.

The final indication of a suspicious person is the presence of inappropriate belongings, such as a suitcase at a park, a large electronic device in a movie theater, or a child's backpack on an adult who is unaccompanied by a child.

This does not mean there aren't certain behaviors, traits, and circumstances that we should be more aware of and pay closer attention to. There are. We just must remember that no list of indicators or triggers is definitive and one-hundred percent conclusive. The totality of available information must be assessed, and then hopefully the correct course of action will be taken by appropriate professionals.

> "*Combat Rule of Three*: When you observe three anomalies or indicators, you *must* make a decision. Do not wait for more information."
>
> *Patrick Van Horne and Jason A. Riley*
>
> *Left of Bang: How the Marine Corps' Combat Hunter Program Can Save Your Life*

The following list of indicators is from the U.S. Secret Service and Department of Education Safe School Initiative Report of 2002. It should be noted that not all active shooters possessed all indicators.

The FBI identified a four-pronged assessment model in the report "The School Shooter: A Threat Assessment Perspective." The model is to be used to assess someone who has made a threat and evaluate the likelihood that the threat will actually be carried out. The four prongs include:

- Personality of the student,
- Family dynamics,
- School dynamics and the student's role in those dynamics, and
- Social dynamics.

The following list of indicators is from the same FBI report "The School Shooter: A Threat Assessment Perspective."

U.S. Secret Service
Active Shooter Indicators

Anger	Lacks compassion and empathy
Anxiety	Laughed at
Bullied	Low self-esteem
Classroom or work disruptions	Mental illness, possibly undiagnosed
Conflict with peers	Mood swings
Conflict with management	Nonconformist
Conflict with religion	Obsessed with lucid dreaming
Conflict with social contacts	Paranoid
Conspiracy thinking	Prejudice
Demanding	Personality change
Depression	Pressure
Disturbing writings	Psychological reward
Empowered	Resentment
Fear	Retaliation
Frightened of world	Revenge
Frustration	Self-centered
Hallucinogen use	Severe anger reactions
Hanging out with outcast group	Severe social anxiety
Harassed	Suicidal
Hatred of almost anything	Trapped, feeling no way out
History of issues reported	Thrill
History of issues not reported, yet people were aware	Unsuccessful
Hostility	Vengeance
Ignored conversation attempts	Victimization
Isolated	Volatility

FBI Active Shooter Indicators	
Leakage (giving prior knowledge of impending event)	Externalizes blame
Low tolerance for frustration	Masks low self-esteem
Poor coping skills	Anger management problems
Lack of resiliency	Lack of trust
Failed love relationship	Intolerance
"Injustice collector"	Inappropriate humor
Signs of depression	Seeks to manipulate others
Narcissism	Closed social group
Alienation	Negative role models
Dehumanizes others	Rigid and opinionated
Lack of empathy	Change of behavior
Exaggerated sense of entitlement	Unusual interest in sensational violence
Attitude of superiority	Fascination with violence-filled entertainment
Exaggerated or pathological need for attention	Behavior appears relevant to carrying out a threat

The FBI continues, "It is important to note three important cautions highlighted in the report, which be considered whenever lists are provided:

1. No one or two traits or characteristics should be considered in isolation or given more weight than the others.
2. Behavior is an expression of personality, but one bad day may not reflect a student's real personality or an unusual behavior pattern.
3. The four-pronged threat assessment model cannot be a substitute for a clinical diagnosis of mental illness.

Stereotypes?

Loren W. Christensen summarized the findings of the United States Secret Service in his book *Surviving A School Shooting: A Plan of Action for Parents, Teachers, and*

Students. (If you are a parent or work in a school system, add this book to your library.) Loren writes:

"Some experts consider the following a list of stereotypes since it presents profiles that are true for some shooters, but not for all:

- Some are lonely and lack good relationships with friends and family
- Some feel rejected and bullied by others
- Some are fascinated with firearms and explosives
- Some are insecure
- Some have fantasies of grandeur
- Some suffer from mental problems, including depression
- Some try to boost their lack of social skills and influence by bragging that they are going to commit violence on someone or several people
- Some want a sense that they have ultimate control over people and they want others to recognize it.

Important: Notice the liberal sprinkling of "some" to describe the above characteristics. It's used for the simple and problematic fact that not all of these characteristics fit the known shooters while many, many other students share these traits but don't gun down their peers and teachers.

In 2002, The United States Secret Service and the United States Department of Education released a report titled 'The Final Report and Findings of the Safe School Initiative: Implications for the Prevention of School Attacks in the United States.' It runs for 63 pages; to sum it up: ***There is no useful profile of a school shooter.*** The report included the following descriptions of attackers:

US Secret Service and Department of Education Report Findings

- They were 11 to 21 years old.
- They were 75 percent white. The rest were Hispanic, African American, Native Alaskan, Native American, and Asian.
- They were from happy families, neglectful families, and foster homes. Nearly three-quarters came from two-parent homes. Only 5 percent came from foster homes or a legal guardian situation.
- They were doing well in school, with 41 percent getting A's and B's. Only 5 percent were failing.
- They revealed no pronounced change in their schoolwork, relationships with friends, interest in school, or disciplinary problems prior to their attacks. A few of them actually showed improvements in their studies prior to the event.

- More than half showed an interest in violence as shown in movies, video games, books, and other media. More than 25 percent were interested in violent movies, another 25 percent liked violent books, 12 percent were interested in violent video games, and 37 percent were interested in their own violent essays, poems, and journal writings.
- Contrary to the popular belief that shooters are loners, only one-third were loners or thought to be; 41 percent socialized with mainstream students; only 12 percent had no close friends. A quarter of the shooters socializes with students disliked by mainstream kids or considered part of a fringe group. Forty-four percent were active in school activities in or outside of school.
- Nearly two-thirds of the shooters had never been in trouble while 27 percent had been suspended from school in the past.
- Most attackers (78 percent) showed some history of suicide attempts, a history of thinking about it, or a history of depression.
- More than 50 percent had been documented in the past as feeling exceptionally depressed.
- Only 34 percent had ever received a mental health evaluation. Of those, 17 percent had been diagnosed with mental health or behavioral disorders prior to their attack.
- Nearly all of the attackers had experienced some type of loss prior to their event. Around 66 percent felt they had lost status in some way.
- Half had lost a loved one or lost an important relationship. About 15 percent had experienced an illness or someone close to them had been ill.
- Nearly all of the attackers (95 percent) planned their shootings – some just one or two days prior, while others thought about it for a year.
- Some 71 percent of the shooters felt bullied, persecute, threatened, attacked, or injured prior to their school attack. In a few cases, these incidents had occurred over a long period of time; some had been severe.

The one common denominator? In every case examined for the report, the attacker was male."

(**Author's note:** While this report was from 2002, current research and data provide no further conclusions; and although no female active shooters were included in the report, there have been female active shooters.)

The 5 Stages of an Active Shooter

The Washington County Sheriff's Office in Oregon put out information on the 5 stages of an active shooter. Here are the stages they present:

1. Fantasy Stage

During this stage the shooter has daydreams of the shooting. He fantasizes about the news coverage. He idolizes other shooters. He might draw pictures of the event and make Web postings.

Would-be Active Shooters in the Fantasy Stage will often discuss their desires with friends and foes alike. If news of these fantasies are shared with you, believe them and pass them on to law enforcement. If police can intervene prior to the suspect acting on their fantasy there may never be a headline.

2. Planning Stage

The suspect is deciding on the "who, what, when, where and how" of his day of infamy. He will put his plans down in writing. He will quite often discuss these plans with others and sometimes seek out an accomplice. He will plan the time and location to ensure the most victims, or in some cases to target specific victims.

He will determine the weapons he will need and where he will get them. He will decide how to travel to the target area and how to dress to conceal his weapons without arousing suspicion.

> **The Five W's**
>
> **What to Remember When Reporting Suspicious Activity**
>
> 1. **What** is happening?
> 2. **Who** is doing it?
> 3. **Where** is it taking place?
> 4. **When** did you observe it?
> 5. **Why** are you suspicious?
>
> *Source: U.S. Department of Homeland Security*

If the police are tipped during this stage, once again, intervention can be made prior to people dying and families crying.

3. Preparation Stage

The suspect may be obtaining gunpowder for his improvised explosive devices. He might break into grandfather's house to steal some weapons and ammunition for the event. He might stockpile or pre-position weapons and explosives for the assault. He might train with the weapons by shooting regularly and testing explosive devices. He might conduct surveillance of the target location. Active Shooters have been known to call friends and tell them not to go to school or work on the scheduled day of the attack in an effort to keep them out of the line of fire.

4. Approach Stage

This is a very dangerous stage. The suspect has made his plans and decided to act. He will be walking, driving, or riding toward his intended target, armed with his tools of death.

Contact with the soon-to-be active shooter could come in the form of a traffic stop, a citizen call, or a stop and frisk. A thorough investigation can still lead to an arrest of the suspect before he brings down a multitude of victims in a needless shooting or bombing.

5. Implementation Stage

Once the shooter opens fire, immediate action needs to be taken. The Active Shooter will continue to kill until he runs out of victims or ammunition, or is stopped. This suspect is unique, because he is fully dedicated to going for the "top score," which is measured in kills.

The sooner an on or off-duty officer or citizen intervenes with an effective, efficient act of courage, the fewer casualties there will be. In past incidents, active shooters have been thwarted by police officers, security guards, school teachers, and students. One principal recently died successfully stopping an active shooter in a Wisconsin school. There is a risk in doing something, *but the greatest risk lies in doing nothing.*

8 Signs of Terrorism

1. **Surveillance:** Individuals monitoring security operations or watching and logging emergency response times.
2. **Elicitation:** Gaining or attempting to gain information about operations, capabilities, or people. Attempts may be made by mail, email, telephone, in person, or even by gaining employment at the location.
3. **Tests of Security:** Attempts to measure reaction times of security and safety personnel, attempts to penetrate physical security barriers, or monitor procedures to assess strengths and weaknesses.
4. **Funding:** Attempts to raise money for operations that don't draw attention.
5. **Supplies:** To conduct an attack, terrorists might need supplies, such as weapons, uniforms, badges, and communication systems.
6. **Impersonation:** Terrorists might impersonate officials or company employees to gain information.
7. **Rehearsal:** Terrorists often rehearse an attack to make sure their operation runs smoothly. This could include measuring response time by emergency responders, mapping routes, and determining the timing of traffic lights.
8. **Deployment:** This is when terrorists are putting their plans into place, getting into position, and moving equipment and supplies.

Source: *U.S. Department of Homeland Security*

Conclusion

If nothing else, this chapter illustrates the difficulty in hardening targets and identifying potential active shooters. But I hope it also showed you that it is possible. Remember, the goals are to prevent an actual shooting and to minimize the amount of carnage a shooter can commit if he does go on a rampage.

Hardening targets, forming a threat assessment team, initiating effective reporting mechanisms, and becoming familiar with potential indicators of violence and potential shooters can all aid with these goals.

Working toward hardening targets and continued vigilance in hopes of recognizing and preventing an active shooter event are on-going procedures that shouldn't consume all of our thoughts, but it shouldn't be neglected either. Every active threat prevented equals lives saved.

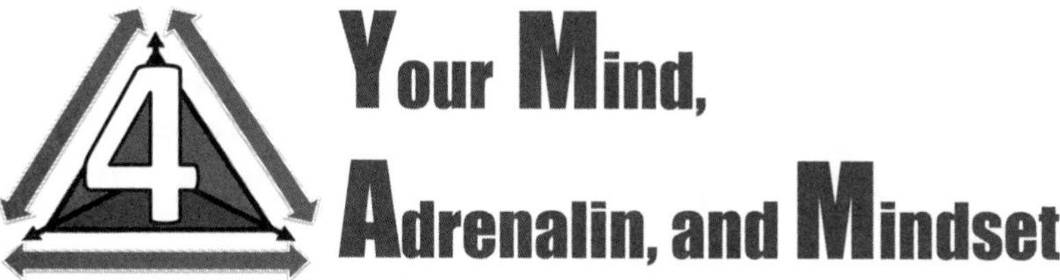

4 Your Mind, Adrenalin, and Mindset

www.SurviveaShooting.com

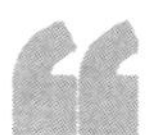

The single most important factor in effective self-defense is the ability to deal effectively with the adrenaline and fear that naturally arise in a stressful situation.

Bill Kipp

TOPICS

- ✓ The OODA Loop
- ✓ Denial
- ✓ Accept That It Can Happen to You
- ✓ Understanding Stress and the Adrenal Response
- ✓ Combat Breathing
- ✓ Situational Awareness
- ✓ Know Your Exits
- ✓ Develop a Survivor's Mindset

To better be able to escape, deny, or attack back during an active shooter event, it is important that we understand our mind, stress, adrenaline, and how we can better perform under such stress and adrenaline. We must also practice situational awareness and develop the proper survivor's mindset.

The OODA Loop

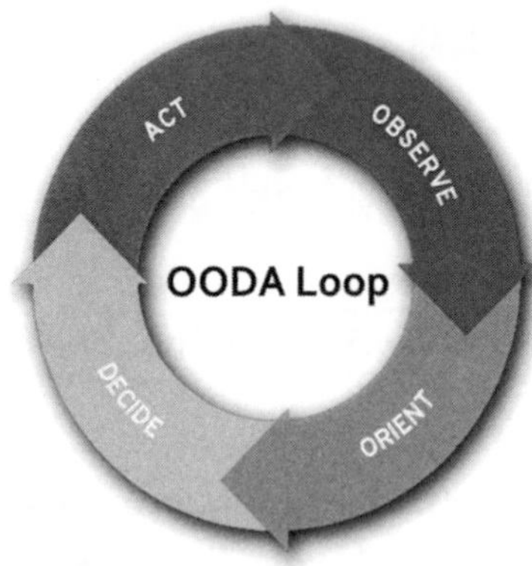

When we talk about mental aspects, or the survival mindset, it is important to look at the decision-making process. A concept that was applied to combat operations in the military, and is also applied to commercial operations and learning processes, is the OODA Loop. It's a concept that is important when reacting to an active threat.

The OODA Loop, also referred to as Boyd's Law, was developed by military strategist Colonel John R. Boyd (USAF). OODA stands for Observation, Orientation, Decision, and Action (Sometimes Observe, Orient, Decide, and Act). This was Boyd's way of quantifying reaction times in combat.

Much has been written about Colonel Boyd and the OODA Loop, but for our purposes here, a brief explanation will suffice. In a nutshell, here are the basics to understanding this model of decision making. Before we Act (the A in OODA), we must first go through the first three steps of Observation, Orientation, and Decision. Each of these three phases takes time, even if miniscule. Let's look at each:

1. **Observe**. We observe our physical surroundings, ourselves, and for purposes of this book, a threat. How long it takes us to observe will depend on various factors, one of the most important being how aware a person is.
2. **Orient**. Once a threat is observed, we must orient ourselves to the situation. We make a mental image of the tactical situation. This image will be based on our past experiences, knowledge, and training. We interpolate what we know with the current environment and situation before deciding how best to respond.
3. **Decide**. Once you take in the various factors present at the time of your orientation, you must decide what to do. This decision will also be based on previous experiences, training, and knowledge.

It takes a quantifiable amount of time to observe, and then there is also an orientation delay because we cannot process information as quickly as we perceive it. Once the decision is made, there is another delay between thought and action. We continue to cycle through this OODA Loop as we act and decide what to do next. As you can see, this "loop" takes time, and therefore the quicker we can process through the cycle, the better advantage we have of staying alive during a crisis.

How do you cycle through the loop more quickly? Training and experience. The more comprehensive your training, and the more experience you have, the faster you can move through the cycle. Preparing a plan of action ahead of time can significantly reduce your OODA loop cycle time. This can give you a significant advantage in being able to successfully escape, deny, or attack back in the event of an active threat. Being aware, as I discuss in that section, allows you to start the loop sooner than someone oblivious to their surroundings, also decreasing the time before you take action.

Inside the Killer's OODA Loop

The killer is also going through the same OODA Loop decision making cycle. Unfortunately, their loop will often be shorter because they have already made the decision to kill people, and are actively observing and orienting on targets. If you can do something to disrupt their cycle, you may be able to delay action, and thus save lives.

For example, if a shooter enters a cafeteria and is observing and orienting on targets to kill, and then all-of-a-sudden gets hit in the head by something, his cycle will be thrown off. He will then have to observe and orient on what hit him, before deciding to proceed with his original intent, and re-observe and orient on potential targets. The time it takes him to do this may be enough for people to escape, deny, or attack back with something else.

> “While you may know and even practice hundreds of techniques in your martial training, a limited subset is required in self-defense situations. During the OODA loop, the orientation and decision flow time will be adversely affected if you think too much, ultimately leading to disaster.”
>
> Lawrence A. Kane
>
> *Surviving Armed Assaults: A Martial Artist's Guide To Weapons, Street Violence, & Countervailing Force*

Essential Elements of Information (E.E.I.)

In his DVD, *Active Shooter Survival*, Alon Stivi points out these six essential elements of information you want to be aware of as you are processing through the OODA Loop and determining your course of action:

- Number of Threat/s
- Location of Threat/s (if stationary)
- Action of Threat/s (direction of movement)
- Description of Threat/s (appearance)
- Capability of Threat/s (weapon type)
- Number & Location of victims/hostages

Denial

Often, before you can even get to the decision-making cycle described above as the OODA Loop, we must get past the initial denial that something is happening. And before we take training and learn how to respond to threats which explode terrifyingly, violently, and seemingly out of the blue, we must get past the denial that such a terrifying event could take place in our place of work, place of recreation, or even place of sanctuary such as a house of worship. Denial is a powerful factor that must be overcome to increase your safety and survivability.

Denial Training is Needed

The simple, easy to learn, and effective responses to an active threat, taught in this book and in the classes I teach, can and will save lives. One of the main reasons people don't read books such as this and take the class is denial. Fear-induced denial is a well-documented phenomenon. The fear of being in an active threat situation, especially one with an active shooter, tends to make many deny that it may happen to them. This denial prevents them from taking the precautionary measures such as reading this book or attending a *Survive A Shooting* class.

To some of us, this seems illogical. Why wouldn't you want to better prepare yourself to survive an event that you are afraid of? Sometimes, those in denial will tell those who prepare and have a plan that they are paranoid. This is far from the truth. Those with training and a plan are often the most comfortable and confident because of having a plan. Those who don't know what to do and have never trained or planned tend to be the more scared and paranoid.

Because you are reading this book, I doubt you are in denial regarding the benefits of education, training, and planning. It will be up to you to break through the walls of denial put up by family members, friends, co-workers, and supervisors. I personally would like to know that those I am with, family, friends, and people I work with, are all on the same plan if an emergency occurs. During the chaos of an active threat is not the time to start thinking about what to do. You must already know what you will do beforehand to increase your chances of surviving the situation. Talk to your family members and discuss what you will do in different situations. Get your friends onboard to. And at your place of work, get your management to provide regular training that deals with workplace violence and active threats. If you are part of management, provide this for your employees. Don't be in denial, be prepared.

Denial During an Event

People will also experience a form of denial during the initial onslaught. It is easier, and less scary, to dismiss the loud sound as something other than gun shots. Others, because of the intense terror of the situation will tell themselves, "this isn't really happening." Both responses are a form of denial.

Another type of denial often experienced with a sudden terrifying attack is neurosensory distortion. Examples of this are when things seem to be in slow motion. People in car accidents or other scary events will share stories of how time slowed down. Others may say it sped up. Tunnel-vision and auditory exclusions are other distortions that frequently occur in life-threatening situations. These are also a type of denial to reality.

All of these "denials" can cause a person to freeze when action is required. You must get past the denial phase before the OODA Loop can begin. It is proven that training, even infrequent and simplistic, helps overcome the freeze reaction. Even after simplistic training, the body reflexively responds as it was trained when faced with overwhelming fear.

You do not need to be a high ranking martial artist or a military special forces operator to survive an attack by a gun or a knife. You need to get past denial and assess the situation and respond appropriately. That is what this book and my classes are all about. You need to be aware, you need to know how to escape, deny, or attack back. You mustn't let denial prevent you from doing what is necessary to survive.

Accept that it Can Happen to You

I just explained why it is crucial to get past denial so you can get to the decision-making cycle described as the OODA Loop. An important consideration when getting past the denial stage is accepting that things can happen to you. They can!

You cannot count the number of times surviving victims say things like, "I never thought it would happen here." After horrific incidents you will often hear, "things like this don't happen in this town." Or, "this is such a quiet place, nothing happens here." No one thinks these tragedies will happen when and where they do.

In the *History of Mass Killings* chapter, I illustrated that there is no particular place, or type of place, that these events occur. Just like we can't profile the exact type of person who will become a potential killer because of the wide variance in people that have become active shooters, we can't tell you what

> **Pay Attention and Listen to Your Gut**
>
> 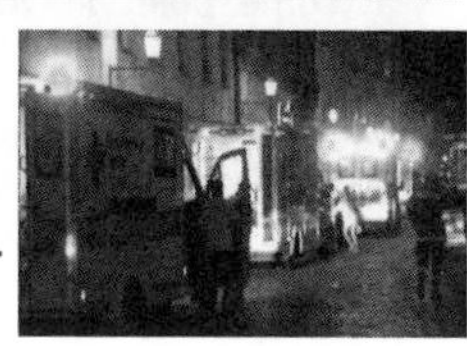
>
> In all of my safety programs, *Survive a Shooting* programs included, I instruct people to pay attention to their intuition. *Listen to your gut!*
>
> Pascal Bohm listened to his instincts and saved many lives at the summer Ansbach Music Festival, Nuremburg, Germany, July 24, 2016. He noticed a suspicious character, Mohammad Daleel, and paid attention. Paying attention to Daleel, and not allowing him into the event, caused Daleel to move away from the entrance where his backpack exploded outside a nearby café. 15 people were injured, but Daleel was the only person killed. If he would have gained entry to the target-rich event, the incident would have been far worse. Bohm's intuition and awareness saved lives.

locations these events will take place in the future. They can, and do, happen anywhere to anyone.

I don't say this to make you paranoid. I'm into planning and preparation, not paranoia. But you must absolutely accept that fact that you could find yourself right in the middle of an active threat situation and the only way you'll survive is by escaping, denying, or attacking back. The odds of this happening are slim. Even with the increase of active shooter events, the odds are still minimal. But isn't it prudent to have a plan just in case? I'm guessing you agree with me because you've read this far in the book. Make sure those you care about - friends, family, and co-workers - think so too.

Accept that an active threat event can happen to you and you will be that much quicker in getting past denial and making the decisions that will allow you to act and stay alive.

Understanding Stress and the Adrenal Response

You have probably experienced a serious adrenal stress response at some point in your life. This is also known as fear. You have probably experienced it more than once. We all feel fear, and fall prey to its effects when under stressful situations.

There are situations that are stressful, and then there are high stress situations that have these four characteristics as described by Driskell, Salas & Johnston and cited by Asken, Grossman, and Christensen in *Warrior Mindset: Mental Toughness Skills for a Nation's Peacekeepers*: 1. Sudden and unexpected demands that disrupt normal procedures. 2. Consequences of poor performance are immediate and severe. 3. Task environment is complex and unpredictable. 4. Personnel must perform multiple tasks under adverse conditions.

If you find yourself in an active shooter situation, it will most likely be the highest stress situation you will ever encounter. Events will unfold quickly and require immediate response. This obviously disrupts your normal routine and procedures.

Understanding stress will allow you to better manage it if you ever face a high stress situation.

It is important to realize that stress isn't all negative. The effects of adrenaline and the other chemicals released when we are in demanding situations can increase our strength and energy. We have all heard the stories of people who performed extraordinary acts during an emergency; from the mother who lifts a vehicle off her child, to the soldier who performs a superhuman heroic act in the chaos of battle. We don't want to eliminate the adrenal stress response, we just want to better control and use it to respond quickly and appropriately.

Research has been done on the potentially debilitating effects of adrenaline and fear in high stress situations. Understanding what the body is going through will enable you to train more realistically and learn to better control and use the adrenal stress response to prevail in active threat or self-defense situations.

Adrenal Stress Response

When the human body perceives stress, the body increases the production of adrenal hormones. This adrenal rush causes blood to rush from the major organs to the muscles. This increases a person's strength in order to flee or fight (the flight or fight response that you may be familiar with). Gross motor skills can be performed under stress because the extra strength assists in these movements. However, the increase in adrenal hormones interferes with fine motor skills and accuracy during high stress events. This is an important distinction when determining responses to an active threat. Techniques and procedures that involve fine motor skills may not only be difficult, they may even be next to impossible for some people under high stress. A couple of the most important physiological and psychological effects of adrenaline as related to surviving a shooting are:

- ***Heart rate:*** Your heart rate will increase with the adrenal dump. There is a direct correlation between adrenal stress and increased heart rate.

- ***Motor performance:*** At 115 beats per minute (bpm), gross motor skills can be enhanced. However, as noted above, most people lose fine motor skills. Things such as finger dexterity, eye-hand coordination, and multitasking become difficult. Note: It doesn't take a lot of stress to elicit a 115-bpm heart rate. At 145 bpm, complex motor skills break down entirely for most people. This means things like putting a key in a key hole, or performing a fancy complicated martial art technique, become extremely difficult, and should not be part of your active shooter response plan.
- ***Vision:*** At about 175 bpm, pupils dilate and flatten, causing what is commonly referred to as "tunnel vision." When you get to this state, visual tracking becomes difficult (this can be very important when dealing with multiple threats or attackers), and the ability to focus on close objects becomes impaired. (This is significant when weapons are involved. Many victims fail to see the weapon that could kill them.) It is strange how the body works. Sometimes people won't see the firearm, and other times that is all they see. Our eyes will also play tricks on us under stress. During scenario training, instructors never point the gun we are shooting blanks from at students. It will always be pointed in a safe direction. I remember one training when a student swore the instructor was pointing the gun at them when shooting. The instructor was actually holding the revolver in his left hand behind his body pointed at the floor when firing the blanks. But he had his right hand up and was pointing at them with his hand in the configuration of a gun like kids playing will do. The student, who saw the instructor after the sound of gun-fire got her adrenaline dumping, was sure it was the gun pointed at her and not his finger. This effect must also be taken into account when interviewing witnesses to a stress inducing event.
- ***Mental Function:*** At approximately 175 bpm, memory is impaired. The term they use to describe this loss of memory is "Critical Stress Amnesia." Tests show that after a traumatic event, many people recall approximately 30 percent of what happened in the first 24 hours, 50 percent within 48 hours, and 75 percent or more after 72 to 100 hours. This is another effect that must be considered when interviewing witnesses to a stress inducing event. This also happens to trained professionals – Law Enforcement Officers included – which is why departments typically want officers off the clock for 72 hours before making any statements involving incidents involving use of deadly force.

I mentioned flight or fight above, but there is another "F" when it comes to the adrenal response. The third "F" is freeze. This is also called temporary paralysis. Around 185 to 220 bpm the freeze response begins. This is the "deer caught in headlights" response. When this happens to people, they often won't be able to do anything. They won't scream, yell, or move. It can be very difficult to break this "freeze." According to Bill Kipp, a leader in adrenal stress training and self-defense, the best way to break this freeze is to breathe. When discussing this with Bill, he explained from his years of teaching adrenal stress self-defense classes, that he's watched when the Adrenaline Rush hits, and the first thing that happens to people is their breathing gets very constricted, causing their brain and body to go into adrenal activation. He says that those that can breathe well in this state will be able to continue to control the adrenaline and can actually bring the neocortex back online. Those that do not will experience the amygdala hijack and lose control, which at the far of the spectrum is "freeze." He states that the problem is lack of proper breathing and in his opinion, the solution is proper breathing. He continued by saying he feels breathing is absolutely core to everything we do in combatives at the most basic level. It's also how we transform the adrenal rush into Optimal Performance or that zen-like no-mind state. He added that there is some great research with extreme athletes that really hits this concept home.

Freezing

While a little blunt and not Politically Correct, Eugene Sockut makes a good point about freezing in his book *Secrets of Street Survival – Israeli Style: Staying Alive in a Civilian War Zone*. This is what Sockut says about freezing:

"This phenomenon occurs when an individual faced with danger finds he or she cannot even run. It is a severe form of fright and is not uncommon. Of the three choices (Fight, Flight, Freeze), freezing is the most dangerous. In human beings it may be brought about by an utter lack of the ability to face even the idea of danger. These are usually the individuals who live by the mottos, 'I couldn't live that way,' 'I don't want to hurt anyone,' or 'I would rather die than kill.'

These poor souls have never made any scenario plans in their minds, deeming them too painful and horrible to even consider. Many of these individuals are against firearms of any kind and fear them along with anything else even remotely related to self-defense. They are usually more capable of feeling sorry for the vicious murderers they read about in newspapers or see on TV than for their helpless victims.

They believe in a most cowardly manner that appeasement of evil can stop evil. They are like dogs who roll over in a subservient position when faced with the presence of a more dominant dog. Incidentally, in nature, the dominant dog usually accepts their submission. This is not true in the human context, the nature of criminals being that anyone in the freezing position excites and enrages them, stimulating them to mayhem and murder. Avoid the 'freezers' like the plague. They are born victims."

Like I said, Sockut is pretty blunt with his opinions. But the fact is, you can't afford to freeze in an active shooter event or other emergency. Not if you want to survive. You must act! Having a plan, having visualized the plan, and trained to execute it will ensure you don't freeze and won't be one of the victims Sockut mentions. Reading this book and following its advice is a great way to learn what to do and start working on your plans.

I think Bill hit the nail right on the head with his answer. Breathing is one of the most important things we can do to minimize the effects of stress. I teach the four-count Combat Breathing technique in all of my Survive A Shooter, safety, and self-defense classes. I was also the instructor that introduced teaching this technique during the Safarialand Training Group certified active shooter classes here in Missoula, MT. I got some kidding by other instructors calling it "Alain's Combat Lamaze," but everyone agrees with its vitality and importance. I'll provide the details on this breathing technique in the next section.

I also like Rory Miller's three-steps to breaking the freeze:

Breaking the Freeze

Step 1. Recognize you are frozen.

Step 2. Make yourself do something.

Step 3. Repeat Step 2.

In his excellent book, *Facing Violence*, Miller explains it like this: "In order to break the freeze, you must recognize that you are frozen. If you believe or know you should be doing something and you aren't, you are frozen. If you are taking damage or seeing someone else take damage and you have a warm, comfortable feeling and hear a rushing noise in your ears like the ocean, you are frozen.

Recognize it. Acknowledge it. Say, 'I'm frozen.' Out-loud is better because it reminds you that you can affect the world. It is easy to say stuff in your head and not do it. Then tell yourself to do something – scream, hit back, run – and do it. Then, again, tell yourself to do something, maybe even repeat the same action and do it."

Remember to breathe and tell yourself to do something. And then, as Rory stated, Do it! These techniques have helped others break the freeze and they can help you too.

Besides the physical effects and the mental function mentioned above, research also shows that our brains work on two levels. The higher level is what separates us from the lower animals lacking the complex brain capacities of humans. It helps us with cognitive processes of deliberation, analysis, creative thinking, and the myriad other elaborate brain functions that occur daily. The lower level is our reptilian brain and is responsible for survival. It is this lower level that takes over when a dangerous threat is perceived. This isn't bad, it's been crucial for the survival of every species on Earth. However, when the body and brain shift into this survival mode, many simple tasks and thought processes become not only difficult, but nearly impossible.

In this section, I've tried to give you a quick introduction to understanding the stress and adrenal response that will occur during an active threat. When shots ring out, your mind and body will do things unexpected if you have never learned how people respond to stress and the adrenaline dump. I encourage you to study this subject further. It's quite fascinating to learn how our bodies and minds react to different stress and stimulus, and what we can do to change those reactions. The two most influential ways to change reactions are breathing, which was previously mentioned, and scenario-based adrenal stress response conditioning, which will be discussed near the end of this book.

Gross Motor Skills vs. Fine Motor Skills

Bruce K. Siddle describes gross and fine motor skills this way:
Gross motor skills are skills which generally involve the action of large or major muscle groups. Examples of a gross motor skill would be simple actions such as walking, jumping, swimming, or squatting or pressing movement. Since gross motor skills utilize large muscle groups, they could also be referred to as strength events. For the purpose of studying survival skills, consider a gross motor skill as a pushing or pulling event, or any event which has double-appendage symmetry. As a strength event, a high level of arousal (motivation, excitement, or psyching-up) will increase the optimal performance level due to increased adrenal secretions.

Fine motor skills are skills which are performed by small muscle mass or groups, such as hands and fingers; and frequently involve hand-eye coordination. Actions such as typing, handwriting, or playing the piano would be considered fine motor skills. In the survival skill category, a fine motor skill would include any action that requires precision hand-eye coordination, such as shooting a firearm accurately.

Countless studies have found that to maintain optimal performance conditions for fine motor skills, the conditions should maintain at low or nonexistent stress levels. This seems especially true of skills that require a high degree of accuracy and cognition.

(From *Sharpening The Warrior's Edge: The Psychology & Science of Training*)

Acute Signs of Stress

Most of us know at least some of the physical signs of stress. These include reactions such as:

- Stomach upset
  - Butterflies
  - Nausea
- Increased heart rate
- Increased blood pressure
- Increased perspiration
- Increased respiration
- Sweaty palms
- Bowel/Bladder urgency
- Muscle tightness
- Dizziness
- Visual Changes
- Dry mouth/throat
- Fatigue

- Restlessness
- Concentration problems
- Word-finding problems
- Chest pain
- Tremors/shakes
- Decreased emotional control

(From: *Warrior Mindset: Mental Toughness Skills for a Nation's Peacekeepers*)

Common Physical Disruptions with Stress

Stress will impact performance, and some of the common physical disruptions of stress include:

- **Choking**
- **Freezing**
- **Death Grip**
- **Muscle Tension and Fatigue**
- **Disrupted Coordination**
- **Blurred Vision**

(From: *Warrior Mindset: Mental Toughness Skills for a Nation's Peacekeepers*)

Perceptual Distortions with Sudden Stress

Typical perceptual changes in high-stress situations include:

Auditory Exclusion; Diminished Sounds
- Muffled Gun Shots
- Failure to Hear Shouts, Directions

Intensified Sounds
- Cylinder of a Weapon Turn and Lock

Tunnel Vision
- Tunnel on the Gun Not Center Mass

Heightened Visual Clarity
- Objects in Tunnel are Highlighted

Automatic Pilot

Time Distortion
- Slow-Motion Time
- Fast-Motion Time

Memory Related Distortion
- Forgetting Events

Inserting Events that Did Not Occur
Disassociation
Intrusive Distracting Thoughts
Friends and Family
Temporary Paralysis

(From: *Warrior Mindset: Mental Toughness Skills for a Nation's Peacekeepers*)

Performance Effects of Stress

Performance Effects of Stress can include:

Decreased awareness of environmental cues
Decreased ability to manage anxiety
Decreased tolerance for pain and frustration
Decreased ability to deal with errors
Decreased efficiency in mental processing
Increased mistakes and injury

(From: *Warrior Mindset: Mental Toughness Skills for a Nation's Peacekeepers*)

Combat Breathing

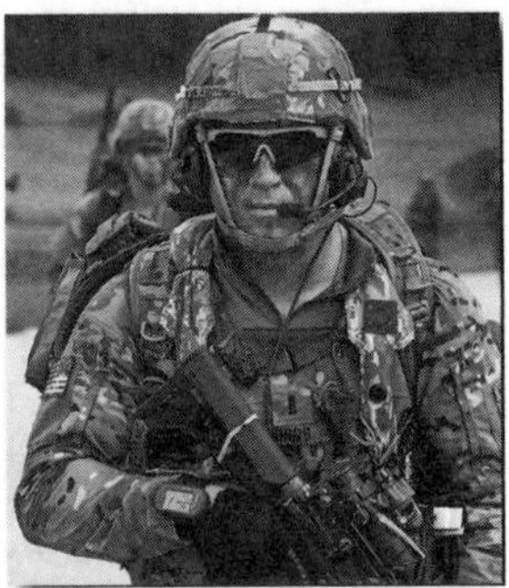

One of the greatest challenges we face when scared and confronting fear is the ability to control physiological reactions and keep "cool." There is a technique that will help us slow or stop its crippling effects. It's often referred to as autogenic or combat breathing. I've also heard it called tactical breathing by some. It is a simple four-count breathing pattern that is highly effective in slowing your racing heartbeat, reducing the trembling in your hands, and clearing your mind so you are able to perform tasks rather than be frozen in fright.

Combat breathing is not new. It's been used in the martial arts, yoga, and medical fields for many years, if not decades and centuries. Lawrence Kane compares it to ibuki breathing in Japanese martial arts, and a fellow *Safariland Response to an Armed Intruder* instructor liked to joke and call it "Alain's Combat Lamaze" when I'd teach the breathing exercise in our classes. In recent years, it has become more popularized in military and law enforcement communities by authors such as Loren Christensen, Lt. Col. Dave Grossman, and others. And that is because it is effective and works.

> **Lamaze and Controlled Breathing**
>
> The **Lamaze** method, developed by the French obstetrician Ferdinand **Lamaze**, has been used in the United States since the late '50s and remains one of the most commonly taught types of childbirth classes. In the early days, the focus was on using controlled breathing techniques to cope with labor.

How to Do It

Breathe in through your nose to a slow count of four. Breathe deep and feel your lower belly expand rather than your chest. Hold your breath for a slow count of four, and then slowly exhale through your mouth for a count of four. Your stomach should deflate. Hold empty for a slow count of four before repeating. In classes I will lead the class through a cycle like this:

- Breathe in, two, three, four. Hold, two, three, four.
- Out, two, three, four. Hold, two, three, four.
- In, two, three, four. Hold, two, three, four.
- Out, two, three, four. Hold, two, three, four.
- In, two, three, four. Hold, two, three, four.
- Out, two, three, four. Hold, two, three, four.

It really is that simple. Some people teach to use a count of three. I prefer four, but if three is more comfortable for you, do what works. If you meditate a lot and prefer slower cycles of 5 seconds each, that is fine too. Customize the technique to what works best for you.

It may take more than three cycles to calm you down and gain control. This can depend on a couple of factors. The first is what has you stressed. Obviously, an active threat killing people and wanting to kill you may take more breathing to calm you down than having to give a presentation to a group of colleagues. (Unless you are extremely terrified of public speaking.) The second factor is how much you have practiced this combat breathing technique beforehand. The more you practice it, the easier you will be able to control the effects of fear when you encounter a dangerous situation. So don't wait for a dangerous situation to try this. Practice beforehand so it will be there for you when you need it.

This breathing technique can be used in any situation which can cause stress: before meetings, public speaking engagements, presentations, or any event that would cause an elevated heart rate. I had a woman come up to me one day who remembered me from a safety presentation she had attended a year before. She told me, "You know that breathing you taught? I do it before every presentation I have to give at work and it really helps." Practice it, use it, and it will help you too.

Breathe Like the Navy SEALs

Mark Divine served in the U.S. Navy SEALs for 20 years. He now trains civilians on how they can succeed using principles learned from the military. In his book, *The Way of the Seal: Think Like an Elite Warrior to Lead and Succeed,* he calls this four-count breathing "box breathing." This is what he says about practicing box breathing, "Repeat this process for a minimum of five minutes and practice it until you can do it for up to twenty minutes at a time. Over time, you can also increase the duration of the inhale, exhale, and hold period. Seek to settle your thoughts and any fidgeting. If a thought arises, just let it go and bring your attention back to the breathing. Use Box Breathing as part of your morning ritual and during the day as 'spot training' whenever you have the opportunity – such as when reading e-mail – or when you feel excess stress building up."

I included this segment by Divine to illustrate that many of the strategies and tactics I teach such as awareness and breathing have many benefits other than during an active threat. Even if you never experience an armed intruder or life-threatening emergency, this breathing technique can benefit you in other ways.

Situational Awareness

> *Situational awareness is a cumulative alertness to threat and your environment. It enables you to notice pre-incident indicators, which are odd movements or anomalies given the situation. Cumulatively, pre-incident indicators create a visual unlikely circumstance consistent with either a contrived situation or predatorial behavior.*
>
> *Kelly McCann*

Situational awareness is probably the most important topic I cover in any of my active shooter response, safety, or self-defense classes. It is the cornerstone to staying safe, including surviving a shooting or active threat incident. People need to get their heads out of their apps and pay more attention! This alone will increase a person's safety, and it will allow you to more readily see and recognize the different threat indicators discussed earlier. Part of the survival mindset, of a survivor's mindset, is being aware of one's surroundings and being aware of how you interact and affect those surroundings. This chapter will provide you with additional information and encouragement on how to be situationally aware.

This is so important, I'm going to repeat it. Situational awareness, or simply being aware of your environment and how you interact with that environment, is not only the foundation to surviving a shooting, but the core of staying safe in general. Being aware is the most important thing I teach people, and it is absolutely the most important thing you can do for your safety and to increase your survivability when disaster strikes.

I have always paid attention to the flight attendants at the beginning of each flight. I still do. Part of it is that I just believe it is common courtesy and good manners to pay attention to people who are talking to you. When I look around at people reading, talking, or now more common texting on their phones, I can't help but think to myself, "how rude." I've usually already read the safety card in the back pocket before the flight attendants provide the safety briefing, or the safety video plays. I read it because I like to know. But after the safety briefing, I always look at the two nearest exits and count how many seats away I am. Often, when not flying with my daughter, I try to sit in the exit rows. That makes it much easier to count. When I'm figuring out how far I am from the nearest exit, another thought that goes through my mind besides, "how rude," is, "odds are, in an emergency, I'll live and you won't, and that's a high cost for being rude and not paying attention."

I'm not being flippant with that thought, but realistic when it comes to who survives. Amanda Ripley, in her excellent book, *The Unthinkable: Who Survives When Disaster Strikes – And Why*, describes the terrible collision at the Tenerife airport in the Canary Islands on March 27, 1977. A Pan Am 747 awaiting takeoff was sliced open without warning by a Dutch KLM jet that had come hurtling out of the fog at 160 mph. Everyone on the KLM jet was killed instantly. But many of the Pan Am passengers survived.

When the collision occurred, many of the Pan Am passengers sat in a stupor, including seventy-year-old Floy Heck. But her sixty-five-year-old husband, Paul Heck, reacted immediately. He told his wife, "Follow me!" as he unbuckled his seat belt and headed toward the exit. Floy snapped out of her daze and followed him. She later said she followed through the smoke "like a zombie." Before Paul and Floy Heck jumped out of a hole in the left side of the aircraft, Floy looked back and saw her friend Lorrain Larson sitting in her seat looking straight ahead, mouth slightly open, and hands folded on her lap. Larson died, like dozens of other passengers, not from the collision but from the fire that came afterward.

Airplanes are meant to be emptied fast and they are designed that way. All passengers are supposed to be able to exit within ninety seconds. The people on that Pan Am 747 had at least sixty seconds to escape to safety before fire engulfed the plane. But 326 of the 396 people onboard were killed.

A few months after the accident, Floy and Paul Heck were interviewed by psychologist Danial Johnson, who was working on safety research for McDonnell Douglas and was fascinated with the paralysis behavior observed in plane crashes. Johnson made this discovery. Before the crash, Paul Heck studied the 747's safety diagram. He even walked around the aircraft with his wife to point out the nearest exits. It turns out, Paul had been in a theater fire as a boy and always checked the exits of unfamiliar environments. Ripley concluded, "Maybe this is a coincidence. But it is also possible that when the planes collided, Heck's brain had the data it needed to take action."

I believe the "file" in Heck's brain allowed him to escape when others were killed. Ripley also reports that "The National Transportation Safety Board has found that passengers who read the safety information card are less likely to get hurt in an emergency. In a plane crash at Pago Pago three years before the Tenerife accident, all but 5 of 101 passengers died. All the survivors reported that they had read the safety information card and listened to the briefing. They exited over the wing, while other passengers went toward other, more dangerous but traditional exits and died."

That's good enough for me. I'm going to continue to be polite and listen to the safety briefings on every flight I'm on, and I will continue to read the safety information card and determine where the exits are in relation to where I'm sitting. Besides being polite, I'll be better prepared in the event of a disaster.

> "*Dealing with a lethal encounter is a multi-step process. It is usually accomplished so quickly that you are not consciously aware of the process. In order to survive a threat, three primary elements need to work together. First and foremost, you need to become aware of the threat. Secondly, you need to assess the threat. And finally, you must decide upon and carry out the appropriate response.*"
>
> *Kelly McCann*

But this thinking goes much further than just paying attention when you board an aircraft. Just as reading the card and paying attention to the briefing only takes a few moments during your flight, paying attention and being aware, when a habit, takes minimal time from your daily activities. In fact, once you develop this habit, it's just a part of your being.

Benefits of Awareness

Situational awareness encompasses several main elements. A few keys for surviving a shooting include:

- Looking for potential threats/shooters
- Knowing and finding locations of cover and concealment
- Knowing and finding exits and means of egress
- Knowing and finding potential weapons

This can allow you to avoid or escape trouble before it begins, or be better prepared to escape, deny, or attack back if a situation occurs.

Pull Your Head Out of Your Apps!

This bears repeating. Pull your head out of your apps and pay attention. I've stated that situational awareness is probably the most important topic I cover in any of my active shooter response, safety, or self-defense classes, and that it is the cornerstone to staying safe, including surviving a shooting or active threat incident. In today's society, I believe smart phones are the number one distraction that keep people from being more situationally aware.

Rather than increasing situational awareness, people are choosing situational blindness. There are so many incidents captured on security cameras where people are victims because they had their heads in their apps and were unaware of obvious dangers. You can search for yourself on the Internet and find countless examples of people being blindsided because their eyes were glued to a screen.

An example directly related to surviving a shooting happened in San Francisco in 2013. Train riders were too consumed with phones to see the gun before the shooting. According to an article on CNN by Kyung Lah and Lateef Mungin, "The killing of 20-year-old Justin Valdez on that busy train was shocking enough. The shooter, apparently picking the victim at random, shot the San Francisco State University student in the back. Also shocking, the prosecutor says, was the initial actions of bystanders. Or inaction. 'Some are no more than two to three feet to him,' said San Francisco District Attorney George Gascon 'We're seeing people that are so disconnected to their surroundings. This is not unique. People are being robbed, people are being hurt, people are being run over by cars because they're so disconnected because of these phones.'" Before the shooting, the criminal pulled the gun out and no one noticed. He put it away, and then pulled it out again and shot Valdez. I agree wholeheartedly with another comment by Gascon, "Just for our own safety, wouldn't you want to know if somebody standing next to you is pulling a gun out? I think I would." I would too! Wouldn't you? Well, you won't if you are staring at a screen.

Don't think that you are different and that you are aware of your surroundings even when using a smart phone. Science of the brain's executive function proves different. Human beings simply do not multi-task well, and if your head is in an app, you will miss most if not all of what is going on around you. Walking into someone, falling into a fountain, or the guy who looks up to see a black bear in front of him (I show this video in my live presentations) might all be funny. Not seeing someone with a gun and getting killed is no laughing matter.

The draw and addiction to these technologically advanced devices is incredible. For your own safety, I challenge you to wean yourself if you are one of those that have eyes constantly glued to a screen. You can't be aware of your surroundings if your head is in your apps checking every ping, chime, and buzz. Smart phones and technology have tremendous uses for good, but as my friend Tom often says, "they can also be the most dangerous thing you own." Use your phone and technology when it is safe to do so. But when you are out and about and should be paying attention to your surroundings, keep your head out of your apps.

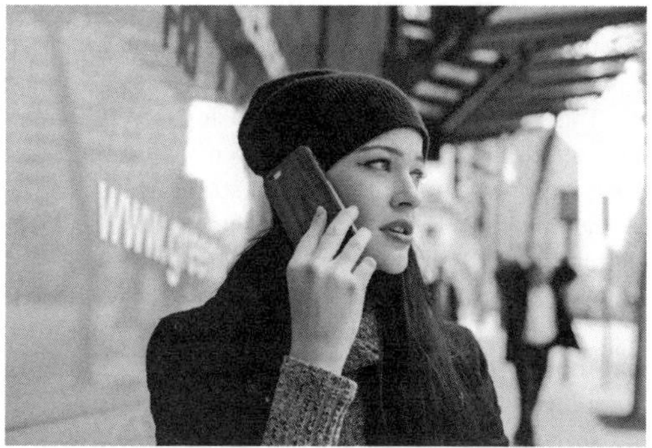

Colonel Jeff Cooper's Awareness Color Code

White	Unprepared and unready to take action.
Yellow	Prepared, alert & relaxed. Good situational awareness.
Orange	Alert to probable danger. Ready to take action.
Red	Action Mode. Focused on the emergency at hand.

Situational awareness really is the most important thing you can practice for your personal safety, and this is for all emergencies, including a shooting. Just as you must know how to exit an aircraft during a disaster such as the Pan Am crash described above, you should always know how to get out of anyplace you enter. Knowing where the exits are and how to get out can be critical toward you surviving a shooting. But situational awareness is much more than just knowing the exits. A famous model, and one I use a lot in my classes and courses, is Colonel Jeff Cooper's Color Code. This "code" has been taught in various ways by many people. Some use levels; others use stages, and many use colors, to include a model that added the color black to the existing white, yellow, orange, and red. For purposes here, I want to share my interpretation of the simple four-color code to get you thinking about how they relate to your own awareness levels. Once we have the color code framework, we can better understand how we can be more aware and what to look for.

Level 1: White. This is the first level, and unfortunately the level where most people exist. This is especially true with so many people walking around with their head in their apps. Devices have people so distracted that awareness levels are almost nonexistent at times. This is why you see people walking into fountains, falling into holes, and walking off cliffs (all real examples from the news). Some places have passed laws making it a misdemeanor to cross a street while using an electronic device due to people being hit by cars while texting or talking on cell phones as they walked out into traffic.

In white, you are oblivious to your surroundings and unaware of any potential threats. In this state, you are not prepared mentally or physically to escape or attack back if confronted with a violent or life-threatening encounter. The only times you should be in white are when you are secure in a locked safe place such as being in your home with the doors locked. You can let your guard down, relax and veg out if you want to. Otherwise, when you are out and about, I recommend you stay at level 2, or yellow, the majority of the time.

Level 2: Yellow. My friend Ray Terry, a martial arts and firearms instructor, likes to say, "Yellow is a great place to live." I agree with him. Condition yellow is having the mindset of paying attention and being aware of what is going on around you. Again, this is the cornerstone of the survivor's mindset and of staying safe. This does not mean you are paranoid. You are just aware. This allows you to be aware of the general threats that surround you, such as being in a bad part of town, as well as noticing things or people that don't seem right. Your awareness will enable you to detect the indicators before an active shooter event and hopefully prevent it, and your awareness will enable you to determine and choose your response to an active threat incident. Being aware better prepares you to escape, deny, or attack back.

Besides living a much safer life and being prepared for an active threat or other emergency by being in condition yellow and aware, you can live a fuller more enriched life by noticing the good things surrounding you, that otherwise go unnoticed as you blindly go along in condition white with your head in your apps, oblivious to your surroundings. You don't only notice potential or actual threats when you are aware, you also notice the new store that just opened across the street, the ten-dollar bill blowing across the sidewalk, or numerous other positive things you would miss if you were not paying attention to your surroundings. This is being aware. You notice everything: good, potentially bad, and bad. But it is NOT being paranoid, looking for danger around every corner. It's just being aware of your surroundings.

Level 3: Orange. The third level, orange, is for when you notice a specific or potential threat. You raise your perception of your surroundings to a higher, more acute, level because you have recognized some danger. Beware of getting trapped in tunnel vision and only focusing on the threat. With your heightened sense of awareness, you want to be more aware of everything around you, while paying attention to the threat that caused you to go to level three. You look for avenues of escape, potential weapons, and other people that may help you. You also look for other people or things associated with the potential threat.

This heightened awareness at level orange is where you could burn out if kept up too long. You don't want to stay at this level all the time. It's only when you are generally aware and paying attention in yellow, and you recognize something that needs extra attention, or action, that you raise your awareness level to orange. When the situation is over you drop back down to your general level of yellow and pay attention as usual.

Level 4: Red. Time to act! You must escape, deny or attack back. On the street, this is where the punks on the corner that were eyeing you start to advance drawing weapons, or when the drunk that has been talking trash grabs a bottle and swings at your head, or when the car door opens after the car had been slowly creeping up the street toward you walking on the sidewalk. In the office or classroom, this is when you see a person with a gun or other weapon, when you hear gun shots, or screams and commotion that indicate a threat.

You need to realize that you won't necessarily be walking around telling yourself, "stay in awareness level yellow. Oh, he looks scary, go to level orange. Oh no, he's attacking, I must go to level red and escape, deny, or attack back."

The colors let us conceptualize these mental states and make them easier to discuss and understand. I hope the colors also make them a bit easier to remember too. At first, you just might have to tell yourself, "I'm out-and-about, stay in level yellow." Training and drills will allow you to go up and down through the levels as situations dictate. Your surroundings will constantly change, and you must be able to change your awareness level appropriately with these changes as you go through your daily routines.

It's also important to recognize that sometimes you will go from yellow to red without the third level of orange. Sometimes you must react instantly upon the first hint of a threat. The sound of gun fire while sitting in a class room or office should send you immediately to level red, taking the best action to survive.

Pay Attention to Your Surroundings

Being able to protect yourself in an active shooter situation begins with having a good sense of what's going on around you.

- Limit your use of cell phones, headphones, or any other electronic device in public that pulls your attention away from your surroundings.
- Before entering any public place, make sure you get a good feel for your environment. Scan the area, looking for anyone who looks out of place.
- If anything looks out of place, or your gut tells you something isn't right, you need to trust your instincts.

(Source: The Ultimate Situational Survival Guide by Robert Richardson)

Unfortunately, some teach situational awareness at a level that becomes hard for many to maintain. It is difficult to remain at a high level of hyper-vigilant awareness always scanning for danger. You can burn out at this level, and it is more appropriate for members of the military in combat zones. (And they have to be careful not to burn out too.) For the normal civilian, you don't need to be a paranoid, hyper-vigilant, super-duper, ninja-commando, looking for deadly threats around every corner, under every rock, and behind every bush and tree. Just be aware of what is going on around you; and be sure to notice that beautiful sunset too (and take a moment to enjoy it).

The Counting Game

This is an exercise to build the habit of situational awareness from Cecil Burch. It's designed to keep people alert in the most vulnerable times. Burch calls it the Counting Game, and this is how he explains how it works: "every time you leave a building – any kind of building, from your place of work, to a grocery store, bank, restaurant, etc. – you need to count how many people you see. That's it. Just count them up. It takes only a few seconds, at most, and even then, that would only be on occasion, such as leaving the shopping mall during the Christmas season. Most of the time it is the work of one to two seconds at best. Easy to do, and easy to remember, and it does not take any special training. We are not asking you to see the potential bad guys, or judge actions. Just count."

Burch goes on to explain the multiple benefits of practicing this exercise. Here are a few of the top benefits:

1. We immediately know those around us.
2. By making sure we actually count, we have to pay attention to what is beyond our head and keeps us from burying our nose in a Smartphone or something similar that puts blinders on us. Or, in other words, it forces us to pull our heads out of our apps and look around.
3. It tells potential bad guys who are doing their own scan that we are paying attention and have seen them, even momentarily. This is a great way to be deselected as a victim. Bad guys prefer if they can get close without being noticed.
4. It starts to let our subconscious start to make thin-slicing judgments of what we have seen. This further allows us to be aware of the situation and general environment.

Burch's simple mental exercise only takes a couple of seconds, but the return on investment is increased situational awareness. And that could mean the difference between being a victim or a survivor.

The Kim's Game

A fun exercise to help with your awareness, observation, and retention skills is called the Kim's Game. The game is derived from Rudyard Kipling's 1901 novel *Kim*; and helps develop a person's capacity to observe and remember details. In Kipling's novel, the young hero, Kim, plays the game while training to become a spy.

While it is taught to Boy Scouts, Girl Scouts, and other youth groups, I didn't learn it until I attended the 2nd Infantry Scout Sniper School at Camp Casey, South Korea while stationed in Korea with the U.S. Army. This is how we learned it and played during sniper school:

We were first instructed to prepare a sheet of paper. We numbered it one to twelve down the side, and then made five columns. The headings for the columns were: Appears To Be; Shape, Size, Color, and Condition.

We then went outside where a blanket was on the ground. We were told to gather around the blanket and look at the items underneath when the blanket was removed. There were twelve items under the blanket, things such as a stapler, coin, cup, spent cartridge, paper clip, pen, etc. After two minutes, we were told to go back inside. We then had to fill each column per item to receive a point. Maximum points were twelve.

For example:

1. **Appears To Be:** stapler
2. **Shape:** draw an outline of the stapler
3. **Size:** approximately 6 inches long, 2 inches high, 1 inch wide
4. **Color:** black
5. **Condition:** good, no marks or damage

That was the first time we played the game. The cadre then made it more difficult as the class went on. The time we were allowed to observe was shortened, the time we were allowed to recall and record what we'd seen was shortened, and the length of time between observing and recording was lengthened. But it wasn't just lengthened, we had to do things to distract us and make us forget what we'd observed. Things from simply having each student telling a joke to the circle of students, to learning the *Brady Bunch* theme song.

Learning the *Brady Bunch* theme song? Yes, you heard that right. It's something I will always remember. After observing the items and having the blanket put back over them, the class was instructed to lay on our backs with our feet six inches off the ground. Those that have been in the military know the position. One of the instructors, Eric Allen, then proceeded to teach us the *Brady Bunch* theme song. You know the one, "Here's the story of a lovely lady…"

The Brady Bunch aired from 1969 to 1974 and I was a fan as a kid. I was familiar with the song, but I didn't know it by heart. I soon learned. Each time someone messed up on the lyrics or didn't sing along with the rest of the class, we were stopped, did flutter kicks (moving your feet up and down in the air, but still never letting them touch the ground), and started over. If an instructor caught someone's feet touching the ground, we were stopped, did flutter kicks, and started over. This went on until the entire class sang, together, the entire theme song without anyone's feet dropping. We were then allowed to get up and go back into the classroom to be instructed to recall what we had seen under the blanket in what seemed like eons ago.

That's the Kim's game, and I strongly recommend you try it out and play some. It's fun, and it will help your observation and recall skills. I'll leave it up to you if you want to incorporate flutter kicks and the *Brady Bunch* theme song. You don't have to do it with a pile of objects and a blanket. You could be at the mall, in the woods, stopped in traffic, or wherever. Have the players look around for 30 seconds and then close their eyes. Whoever remembers the most details about what is around them wins.

If you want to make this more challenging, try this: Go to the mall, a university, school, park, or even someone's house. Play at different locations. When the players are not expecting it, tell them to close their eyes and start identifying things they observed and where the items are located. Make this more real-world applicable by having them name things like: where are the escape routes and exits, cover, objects that can be used as weapons or barricading materials, and so on. This helps train us to notice things that could come in handy during an emergency or survival situation. With some creativity, you can devise ways to look for indicators, and train yourself to recognize them more readily. Keep it simple and have fun with it.

Visual Information Retention: "KIMS"

Maj. John L. Plaster, USAR (RET.) is the author of *The Ultimate Sniper: An Advanced Training Manual for Military and Police Snipers (Updated and Expanded).* This manual sets the standards for sniper training. I had the opportunity to meet Maj. Plaster and his knowledge and dedication to our military and law enforcement snipers is exemplary, and his books and DVDs are top notch resources. For a little extra information on the Kim's Game, this is how Maj. Plaster describes it in *The Ultimate Sniper*:

"The ability to retain brief visual images is a critical sniping skill. Not only must a sniper record and report detailed intelligence, but he must remember exactly where targets are located or where last observed.

During World War II, the American OSS intelligence agency trained its personnel to memorize an entire scene with a single glance so that with only one passing view of a railway yard, for instance, a spy still could report details about every Nazi train in the station.

This mental snapshot technique was made famous by Rudyard Kipling's novel Kim, in which his youthful hero plays it as a game. Called 'Kim's Game,' or just 'Kim's,' it has become so standardized in sniper training that it's equally known as the 'Keep in Memory System' (KIMS,) which also spells the Kipling character's name. Whatever it's called, playing it is simple in concept and execution.

Pay Attention to Your Gut

"Whether you call it 'a gut feeling,' 'a sixth sense.' or 'a mother's instinct,' it's important that you believe in it. Think of it as a compilation of your life's experiences raising a red flag, a warning that a situation or a person needs to be watched. Heed this feeling because it's telling you something."

\- Loren W. Christensen
Surviving Workplace Violence: What to Do Before a Violent Incident, What to Do When the Violence Explodes

Take an ordinary blanket and a half-dozen commonplace items, such as coin, a fired cartridge, a business card, eyeglasses, a piece of string, and a pencil. Lay them out randomly and cover them with the blanket.

Now, expose the items for two minutes and allow your fellow snipers to study them but not take any notes. Re-cover the items and then direct your audience to write notes in as much detail as possible, recording what they saw. They can even draw a sketch, depicting the relative sizes and spacing of the objects.

Now, ask them highly detailed questions. They probably all noted the coin's date, but how many wrote that it was facing the business card, which was about 5 inches away? And that string – which end was frayed and which end was cut?

To keep the mood competitive, it's excellent to allow a person who answers one question correctly to ask the group the next question – but in order to ask it, his own notes must record, say, that the business card had a phone number with an area code of 612. Or you can direct questions at people, with any wrong response eliminating a competitor and the final winner owed a brewski or relieved of policing brass from the range, etc.

To make KIMS even more challenging, increase the number of items displayed, reduce the amount of exposure time, or lengthen the time gap between observing and recording information. We've had our school cadre act out gunfight scenarios as a real-life kind of KIMS that was especially popular with students. It sometimes required observing through optical devices.

But just the blanket and trinkets technique works fine, too, and makes for an exercise that can be conducted anywhere with two minutes' preparation."

Situational Awareness isn't Perfect

It's easy to say, "Stay in condition yellow!" And as I mentioned above, some teach to be hyper-vigilant 24/7/365. But you can't be hyper-vigilant all the time. And even those that are more aware of their surroundings can't take in everything all the time. It's just not possible to take in everything at all times. When you are doing activities, they are going to take your focus, and therefore you won't be as focused on everything else. This is reality. And when you go to orange because you notice a potential threat, you will most likely see even less of everything else because that object or person has your focus and attention. That's why I reminded you not to become trapped in tunnel vision and force yourself to look around. And this is a key to being more aware.

To make the best decision possible, you need information that you can process and tools or knowledge to use that information. The information that is available is out of your control (pre-attack indicators, available cover and concealment, available exits and improvised weapons, manner of attack, weapons being used in the attack, number of threats, etc.). You can, however, optimize your potential to take in that information.

As I said above, pull your head out of your apps and walk around with your head up looking around and being aware of things around you. You'll notice good things and potentially bad. When working, take pauses once-in-a-while to be aware of your surroundings. Avoid other distractions that detract from your awareness such as wearing headphones in public. Don't inhibit your hearing. Auditory cues can be early warning signs. You can hear gun shots even when you can't see the gunman. Sit in places that offer the best visibility of exits and others. Watch people for cues and indicators that they may be up to no good. Trust your intuition. That "gut" feeling is there for a reason, and you need to pay attention to it. Study more about situational awareness from different sources and practice being aware. It is a skill, like others, that improves with practice.

Use opportunities from occurrences in your life to test yourself. Test your awareness and how quickly you can analyze situations. Work at being more aware. Developing these alertness and awareness skills is an important ingredient to your personal safety. You will be at a tremendous disadvantage in recognizing danger and ultimately escaping, denying, or attacking back if you are not first aware. Being aware is the foundation of your survival mindset. So, take care, be aware, and stay safe!

Be Aware of Yourself

The second part of awareness is being aware of yourself. Here is a section from one of my earlier books that explains this important concept:

"So far, everything regarding awareness has been targeted toward paying attention to what is going on around you, and what to look for to help ensure your safety. It's extremely important to pay attention and be aware of external things, but you must also be aware of yourself. You must be aware of your strengths, weaknesses, and limitations, as well as how you affect your environment.

First, take a good assessment of your strengths and weaknesses regarding self-defense and attacking back. Are you in great shape? Are you in terrible shape? Do you have physical limitations? Do you have martial art training? Have you trained with weapons before? What kind of lifestyle do you lead? Do you go out partying a lot, or do you stay home with the family?

Take a real close look at yourself: physically, mentally, emotionally, your habits, and your lifestyle. I'm not going to tell you what life to lead, just know yourself, and what you do, so that you can prepare accordingly. If you are in better shape with no physical limitations, you will have a better chance at being able to attack back. Additionally, you may not be a primary target for the criminal looking for an easy score.

If you look like someone who will fight back, the criminal may just go somewhere else. If you party a lot in places where violence occurs, know this, and take extra precautions. Go with friends, limit your alcohol consumption, and stay extra alert. There are no absolutes, but knowing yourself will help you make decisions and be better prepared.

Second, be aware of how your actions affect a situation. Your actions can antagonize or diffuse; they can escalate or de-escalate; they can assist you in going home safely, or result in you having to attack back for your life – and possibly losing. Acting like a jerk or being obnoxious and aggressive can lead to violence.

Being polite and taking an assertive but non-aggressive position with obnoxious people can help de-escalate potentially violent situations. Being aware of how your actions are affecting the situation, is as important as being aware of what's going on around you, and they go hand in hand.

A theoretical example I often use consists of the options available when going into a bar frequented by bikers. I can go in and get along just fine, or I can go in and start bad mouthing anyone who rides a Harley. Which is the most conducive to my health? Obviously, this is extreme, and one would need to be suicidal to go into a bar filled with bikers badmouthing Harleys. People do things just as obvious all the time that get themselves into trouble and hurt. These actions are obvious to everyone but them. They wake up in the hospital wondering what happened, and a friend says, "Man, you should have kept your mouth shut."

Another example that is fairly common involves the type of person who gets loud or vicious with words when angered but doesn't expect the confrontation to go physical. This type of person will yell, call people names, and swear profusely when angered. It can be directed at anyone anytime the person is riled. Some people will cower away or avoid such behavior, while others may take it to the next level and become physical.

Many people have been surprised when what they figured would be a loud argument got them punched in the mouth. Many men have been punched or worse for comments or looks directed at someone's girlfriend or wife. I could go on for several chapters about the stupidity I've seen, and the violence that erupted over such acts. Don't go there. You need to be aware of what you are doing and how it is affecting those around you. Do not provoke a situation that could have ended without violence. Paying attention to this, while paying attention to your surroundings, will keep you out of most trouble." (Burrese, Alain. *How To Protect Yourself By Developing A Fighter's Mindset*, p. 36-39.)

Know Your Exits

One of my favorite movie quotes when it comes to staying safe comes from the 1998 film *Ronin,* staring Robert De Niro. After De Niro's character, Sam, retrieves his gun from behind some crates as they leave the small shop, he tells Deirdre (played by Natascha McElhone), "Lady, I never walk into a place I don't know how to walk out of." I want you to live by this too. You should always be aware of the ways out of wherever you are. Know your exits.

Unfortunately, many people don't pay attention to the different ways in and out. Most often, people will only think of the way they came in, and that will be where they flee during an emergency. The way you came in may not be the closest or the wisest direction to escape.

I'm sure that I was one of the only people making a quick mental note of each emergency exit as I waited in lines with my wife and daughter at Universal Studios, Hollywood last summer. I didn't dwell on them, but as I was paying attention, I noticed each exit and always knew which direction I'd be rushing my family toward if something happened. We enjoyed The Wizarding World of Harry Potter™ and everything else the theme park had to offer, and my awareness didn't take away from any of that enjoyment. Remember, being aware allows you to notice the good things that sometimes go missed too. But if an emergency had occurred, I'd have ushered us out the nearest exit while most people would have been heading back toward the entrance they came in. This would have gotten us out quicker, and we would have avoided the larger hysterical crowd where trampling is more likely to happen.

Always Know Your Exit Points

Part of being aware of your environment means knowing how to get out when things go bad. One of the first things I do when entering a building, or any other public place, is to look for every possible escape route and exit. Not only can it help during a shooting, but it's also an important part of being prepared for natural disasters and building fires.

- When entering a building, immediately scan the area, looking for exit signs and doors.

- Continue to make mental notes on the building's layout, and think about how you will reach your exit points should it become necessary.
- Look for alternative exits like windows, emergency doors, and fire escapes.
- Be aware of corners and hallways that can be used as cover while you are trying to exit the building (turning a corner can help put you out of the shooter's line of fire).

(Source: *The Ultimate Situational Survival Guide* by Robert Richardson)

I often quiz people during classes about exits in a nearby mall or store. It is surprising how many people forget about the back or service doors. In malls, everyone thinks of the main doors or those in the anchor stores where people regularly enter and exit. They forget about all the back doors that are not used by customers. In an emergency, these back ways out may be the closest avenue of escaping the danger zone. The quickest and safest way out of a restaurant may be through the kitchen and out the back. Are there windows that would provide an avenue of escape?

In many plane crashes, more passengers have died from smoke inhalation in fires after the impact than have died from the impact of the crash itself. We learned earlier that the FAA requires that all of a plane's passengers must be able to be evacuated in ninety seconds. This is the approximate amount of time you have to get out before you are likely to succumb to smoke inhalation or fire and die. This is one of the reasons that before every flight, the attendants tell you to locate the nearest exits. I'm telling you the same thing. In order to escape, you must know the way out. So, wherever you are, know your exits.

The Station Nightclub Fire

On Thursday, February 20, 2003, the Station nightclub caught fire. The fire was caused by pyrotechnics set off by the tour manager of the headlining band Great White. The fire caught quickly and within five and a half minutes, black smoke engulfed the club. It was the fourth-deadliest nightclub fire in US history, killing 100 people. 230 people were injured and only 132 escaped uninjured. The important thing to note for our purposes are the four exits and how many people went out of each.

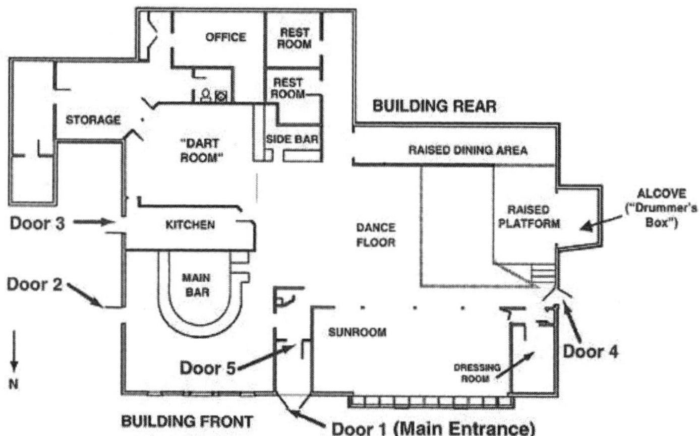

Floor plan of the Station Night Club

It is also important to note that within minutes, most of the club reached a point that firefighters call untenable: when the heat from the fire and the density and toxicity of the smoke make survival or escape no longer possible. Both an active shooter incident and a fire require immediate action. This reinforces the "Move!" in the center of the Active Shooter Triangle. (Explained in the next chapter.) The time to escape an active shooter and the time to escape a fire is immediately when able to do so.

Returning to the exits of the Station nightclub, it is estimated and reported that at least half of the 462 people in the building attempted to leave the same way they came in; through the club's main entrance. Without prior thought or planning of how you will exit a building in an emergency, you will often default under stress to where you came in. This default reaction in the Station nightclub led to over 200 people rushing the main entrance. Because of the congestion, people were injured and only 127 of them made it out the front door. According to Steven Casner, in his book *Careful: A User's Guide to Our Injury-Prone Minds*, "Sixty-two people managed to turn back from the frenzied rush at the front door and find another way out. And while rescuers were able to pull some people out of the pileup in the narrow hallway that led to the front door, 31 people perished there along with 58 others in the building who never found a way out." (Author's note:

Casner's numbers don't add up to the 100 fatalities reported elsewhere on this fire, but the differences don't negate the importance of knowing exits.)

Some patrons were in a different room that had its own exterior exit and they were able to escape to the outside through that door. Others, near the stage, escaped through an exit beside the stage. The fourth exit was an exterior door located at the back of the club's kitchen, and only a few people knew about it. Two people that were aware of this exit were the club's sound engineer and a bartender. Both of these employees had put some thought into where they would go in case of an emergency. Casner reports, "the sound man was later quoted as saying, 'This is the exit to use if someone pulls out a gun and starts shooting, or if there's a fire in this building. I know this is an exit that's going to be accessible because it's unknown.' Another survivor reported having been to the club between fifteen and twenty times. He'd seen the exit sign by the swinging doors of the kitchen, and when the fire broke out he immediately headed for it. Another man, who also knew about the kitchen exit after being at the club many times, grabbed his friend and led the way. He wrote in his witness statement, 'About halfway the smoke had overcome the room and I had to feel the wall to find (the) door.' He knew the building well enough to find the door in complete darkness. Through their interviews of survivors, investigators learned that 19 of the estimated 440 people inside the club exited through the kitchen door." (Author's note: Again, Casner's numbers differ from the 462 people reported in other sources, but the difference has no significance regarding knowing where your escape avenues and exits are located.)

Casner also writes, "In most situations we have an opportunity to stop and think about the possible outcomes for whatever it is that we're about to do. In this most tragic example, a failure to think ahead by a trusted few resulted in many lost lives. At the same time, thinking ahead by a few staff and patrons resulted in saved lives. Thinking ahead can be a powerful thing, but it's not something that we always stop to do." And that brings us to my number one goal for this book and the courses I teach on the topic. I want people to think ahead and have a general plan of what they would do when the unthinkable happens.

Many lessons were learned through the tragic loss of life at the Station nightclub fire. One important one is Know Your Exits.

Survive a Shooting | Alain Burrese

Develop A Survivor's Mindset

> *"You can be riddled with bullets or slashed into an unrecognizable shred of blood and tissue and survive."*
> Gabe Suarez

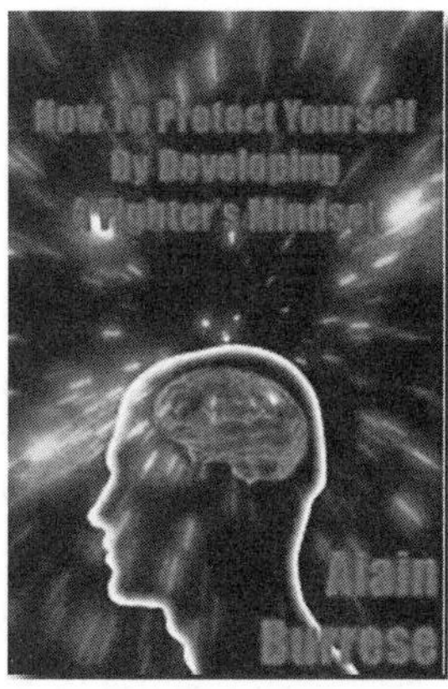

After teaching physical defensive tactics to students in the active shooter response classes I teach, I always tell them, I don't care if they are injured, they must fight until the threat is stopped. I don't care if they are stabbed, and I don't care if they are shot. They must continue escaping, denying, or attacking back until they are safe. If that means killing the shooter with their bare hands, so be it. If that means pressing on through pain, blood, and exhaustion, that's what must be done. Surviving is not an option. It's a given! They, and now you, must do everything possible to survive! It's your duty to yourself and everyone you care about and that cares about you. And to do that, it's necessary for you to develop a survivor's mindset. And it's critical that you start developing that mindset right now.

After telling people this, I will ask them how many times they can be shot and continue fighting. Sure, I get replies saying it depends, or asking where they are shot, or with what kind of gun. I deflect these and ask for numbers, "How many times can you get shot and keep fighting?" I will then start getting answers from the group, "three," "five," "ten..." I'll incredulously ask, "What? Can you really get shot ten times and keep fighting?" People will shake their heads negatively, and others will fall back on the, "it depends," answer. Some people will stick with their answer, and some will have doubts. I then provide my answer to the question. But before you read ahead to my answer, what is yours? How many times can you be shot and still keep fighting?

My answer, "I'm not sure just how many times you can be shot and continue fighting, but I do know you can be shot 27 times and keep going." I'm often looked at in disbelief. Twenty-seven times? I know for a fact you can be shot 27 times and keep fighting. I then tell them about a US Navy SEAL who was shot 27 times during one incident while on tour in Iraq and made it home to his family.

On April 6, 2007, Navy SEAL Sr. Chief Mike Day engaged in a brutal fire-fight with four al-Qaeda insurgents when he was the first of his team to enter a room in a town near Fallujah, Iraq. The insurgent enemy fighters opened fire, hitting Day with 27 separate bullets. 11 of the shots struck Day's body armor and were stopped, the other 16 bullets penetrated his body and left him perilously wounded. A grenade then exploded about 10 feet away from him, knocking him unconscious. According to Day, when he woke up roughly a minute later, he managed to kill two of the insurgents with his pistol. When the fighting stopped, he miraculously got up and walked himself to a medical helicopter.

Day has described his injuries as, "I was shot in both legs, both arms, my left thumb was almost amputated, I was shot in the abdomen and had a colostomy bag for a year, my right scapula was shattered, I was shot twice in the buttocks, once in the scrotum, and my body armor was hit multiple times which caused fractured ribs and contusions on my lungs." In an interview he stated, "Anywhere you can put a finger on me, I was shot, except for my head."

Day's thoughts at the time were, "God, get me home to my girls," extreme anger at being shot, and then he went to work doing what he was trained to do. In interviews, he discusses his faith and his family. While the body armor definitely saved Mike Day's life, I believe both of those, his faith and the love for his family, are critical components to Day's survival and especially to his survival mindset. Without that mindset, Day wouldn't have killed those who shot him and lived through being shot 27 times.

Most Gunshot Victims Survive

"Yes, on television and in the movies, 'shot' actors fall and don't get up. In real life, though, most gunshot wounds are survivable. Sometimes the victim continues to function at the scene. When I was shot in the shin, I continued to move about for an hour afterward. I know of two people, a man and a woman, who in separate incidents, survived five gunshots to their heads – five – and one of them was still running around when the police arrived."

(Source: *Surviving Workplace Violence* by Loren W. Christensen)

People like Day live through injuries that should kill them. Others die from injuries that shouldn't be life-threatening. The mind and the determination to survive versus quitting and giving up are deciding factors. It is amazing what we can do when we have the right mindset. This is why you must develop a survivor's mindset right now. Don't pass go, don't wait till later, start right now on developing and strengthening your survival mindset as quickly as possible and never stop believing it.

Don't dismiss this. It is imperative that you determine what it is that you will live for. Why will you survive? It can be a particular faith, it can be family, friends, or a cause that you believe in. I don't care what it is, just so it's something that means something to you. Something worth enduring the fires of hell to live for. It shouldn't matter to me or anyone else, it has to be personal and relevant to you. Why will you survive? You need to determine this, and you need to have this as part of your survival mindset.

Conclusion

This chapter covered some important concepts. Understanding the decision-making process and the OODA Loop, along with stress, denial, and the adrenal response, allows you to better prepare yourself and accept that extreme situations such as an active threat can happen to you. Practicing combat breathing, keeping your head out of your apps and staying aware, especially of your exits, and developing a survivor's mindset will all increase your odds of surviving life-threatening situations, which includes active threats. Don't just read the chapter, take action to prepare yourself to be a survivor.

"We can't always avoid high-threat areas – and sometimes the high-threat area doesn't avoid us. In the world today, conflict and danger can occur anytime and anywhere. So it is important to maintain situational awareness at all times. Pay attention to your surroundings. Look at suspicious people. Look at unsuspicious people. What are they doing? Where are they going? What are they looking at? Assess. While you assess, think of contingencies. Where is your closest escape route? Where is the closest cover and concealment – 'cover' being a place to shield you from bullets and 'concealment' being a place to hide. If you are maintaining situational awareness, you should be very hard to surprise. If you sense something is going wrong or you sense a threat, proactively move away from it. Walk to the other side of the street. Accelerate your car. Walk out the door. Don't wait for things to get worse."

Jocko Willink
Discipline Equals Freedom Field Manual

www.SurviveaShooting.com

You have to think a little smarter, be proactive, not reactive.

Frank Abagnale
American security consultant known for his history as a former confidence trickster, check forger, and imposter

TOPICS

- ✓ Active Shooter Response Models
- ✓ Why Another Model?
- ✓ Escape – Deny – Attack Back
- ✓ Active Shooter Triangle vs. Linear Models

There are a number of different models for responding to an active shooter or active threat. Most of these are very similar, but they use different terminology in their title and/or descriptions. It is worth looking at these and understanding the basic concepts, as well as looking at the different terms and why I chose the specific language for the model I teach and present both in this book and my live classes.

What the Shooter Needs to be Successful

The shooter's goal is to create as many casualties as he possibly can in whatever time he has before he is stopped. In order to effectively carry out his plan, the shooter needs the following:

- He needs easy access to the targets.
- He needs unchallenged access to freely roam from room to room.
- He needs untrained victims and targets.
- He needs to have selected a group with no active shooter plan.
- He needs to be able to reload at will.
- He needs to retain a functioning weapon.
- He needs a clear line of sight in order to be able to shoot effectively.
- He needs little or no physical contact with his intended victims.

(Source: *The Cobra-Defense Active Shooter Response* Plan by Chris Sutton & John Graden.)

Run – Hide – Fight

This is the most known model due to the "Run > Hide > Fight >> Surviving An Active Shooter Event" video. The video is a Department of Homeland Security Grant Funded Project of the Regional Catastrophic Planning Initiative. It was produced by the City of Houston Mayor's Office of Public Safety and the Department of Homeland Security. This is a good video and worth six minutes of your time to watch if you haven't already. We actually show this video in the Safariland Training Group created course, but we explain why we changed the terminology from the video. (See the section: Run – Lock – Fight.)

The video provides this information:

Run

When an active shooter is in your vicinity:

- If there is an escape path, attempt to evacuate.
- Evacuate whether others agree to or not.
- Leave your belongings behind.
- Help others escape if possible.
- Prevent others from entering the area.
- Call 911 when you are safe.

Hide

If evacuation is not possible, find a place to hide.

Your hiding place should:

- Be out of the shooter's view.
- Provide protection if shots are fired in your direction.
- Not trap or restrict your options for movement.

Fight

As a last resort, and only if your life is in danger:

- Attempt to incapacitate the shooter.
- Act with physical aggression.
- Improvise weapons.
- Commit to your actions.

911

When Law Enforcement Arrives:

- Remain calm and follow instructions.
- Keep your hands visible at all times.
- Avoid pointing or yelling.
- Know that help for the injured is on its way.

The "Run – Hide – Fight" model is also taught by the Texas State Office of Risk Management in their four-minute video *How to Survive an Active Shooter.* This is a good short video reiterating the basic model found in the previously described video.

Armed Intruder Training for Schools

The Wichita Public Schools and WPS-TV also produced a video based on the "Run – Hide – Fight" model. Their six-and-a-half minute video is titled *Run, Hide, Fight: Armed Intruder Training for Schools*. Key points from this video:

Run

When attacker is spotted:

- If there is an escape route, move quickly to a safe area.
- If staff is present, follow their instructions.
- Escape by exits or windows.
- Leave your belongings behind.
- Help others escape.
- Prevent and warn others along the way about the danger.

Hide

When attacker is spotted:

- Hide until help arrives.
- Lock and/or barricade your door.
- Silence all electronic devices.
- Hide behind large objects.
- Remain calm and quiet.
- Your hiding place should be out of attacker's view, provide protection, not trap or restrict your options.

Fight

- Fight as a last resort.
- Attempt to incapacitate the attacker.
- Improvise weapons, use any means.
- Commit to your actions.

When Law Enforcement Arrives

- Remain calm.
- Keep your hands visible.
- Avoid pointing or yelling.
- Know that help for injured is on the way.

Parents

- Do NOT come to the school!
- Do NOT call your child!

The *Surviving an Active Shooter* video is a six-minute video by the Ohio State University that also adopts and uses the "Run – Hide – Fight" model. This video also reiterates the basic responses of run, hide, and fight similar to the other videos teaching this model.

Surviving an Active Shooter in a Healthcare Environment

MESH Coalition, Indianapolis Coalition for Patient Safety and the Indy Public Safety Foundation, produced an eleven-minute video based on the "Run – Hide – Fight" model for hospitals and health care facilities: *Surviving an Active Shooter in a Healthcare Environment*. The key points this video emphasizes are:

Run

- Leave immediately.
- Leave belongings behind.
- Don't wait for others to follow.
- Discontinue all patient care.
- Secure patient room upon exiting.
- Do not stop for victims.
- Keep others from entering area.
- Keep hands raised and visible.
- Don't point, scream or yell.
- Follow law enforcement instructions.
- Don't make sudden movements toward officers.
- Move a safe distance from facility.
- Report the incident: call 911 or security.
- Do not re-enter the scene.

Hide

- Get out of the shooter's view.
- Look for protection from gunfire.
- If possible, choose a place that doesn't trap you.
- Hide behind large objects.
- Stay quiet, silence phones and pagers.
- Report the incident, if you can do so safely.
- Do what you can to help any injured who are with you.
- Stay in place until "all clear."
- Plan for "Fight."

Fight

- Last resort action.
- Act as a team.
- Use improvised weapons.
- Disrupt and incapacitate.
- Act aggressively.

Run – Lock – Fight

This is the model I've taught to thousands of people when teaching the Safariland Training Group *Emergency Response To An Armed Intruder* course. This 8-hour course teaches more than just the "Run – Lock – Fight" model, but for purposes here I will only include some of the key points related to these three topics.

Run

- Always Be Aware.
- Know Escape Routes.
    - Exits.
    - Windows.
- Decide to Leave at First Opportunity and Report.
- Go into Lockdown Mode.

Lock

- Lock Doors.
- Barricade access points.
    - Door stops.
    - Furniture.
    - Rope doors closed.
- Cover windows.
- Darken room.
- Go into Run mode again.
- Lockdown Considerations.
    - Barricading doors:
        - Outward opening.
            - Eye bolts.
            - Rope.
        - Inward opening.
            - Furniture.
            - Kick bars.
            - Door stops.

Fight

- Escaping Always First Option.
- Be mentally prepared to fight for your life and those around you.
    - Use any weapon.
    - Use pack mentality.
    - Attack weak spots.
- Get as close as you can to the access point before the shooter enters.
- Try to get ahold of the gun and get it pointed away from people.
- Have a survivor's (not a victim's) mindset.
- Decide right now that you are going to do whatever it takes to survive.
- Getting shot does not mean that you are dead.
    - You can and must keep going!

Get Out – Hide - Fight

The *Shooter on Campus: Know You Can Survive* video by Concordia University College of Alberta uses this model. This is a good eight-minute video that resembles the "Run – Hide – Fight" model.

When a Shooting Occurs:

- Scan and assess your situation.
- Consider your options.
- Act.

Get Out

- Get out *now*, if you can.
- Choose a safe exit.
- Don't attract the shooter's attention.
- Protect yourself first before helping others.

Hide

- Barricade your hiding place.
- Turn off lights.
- Lock and barricade doors.
- Stay out of the line of fire.
- Be quiet.

Fight

- Improvise weapons from nearby objects.
- Commit to an aggressive physical attack.
- Stop the threat.

Choose action over fear.

Get Out – Secure Your Location – Defend Yourself

The Los Angeles County Sheriff's Department produced a more graphic video than the one by the Department of Homeland Security and the City of Houston. It is titled *Surviving an Active Shooter*, and is close to 9.5 minutes long. It is also worth watching. Some key points taught in this video:

Get Out

- Use cover and concealment, and any available means to get out.
- Assist the injured if safe to do so.

Secure Your Location

- If you can't move safely to an exit, get to a room or a confined area you can lock down. Then secure the location.
- Lock or barricade the doors.
- Turn off the lights.
- Move away from any windows.
- Silence your cell phone.
- Do not alert the shooter to your presence.

Defend Yourself

- If you cannot escape the location, and you can't shelter in place, you may have to defend yourself as a last resort.
- Improvised weapons.

Law Enforcement

- Keep hands visible and follow any commands given.

Escape – Lockdown - Fight

The Indiana State Police produced a video titled *Unarmed Response to an In-School Shooter Event*. This eight-and-a-half minute video expands the paradigm of "Run – Hide – Fight." The main points include:

Escape

- Determine a safe path to a safe area.
- Escape via a safe path to a safe and secure site.

- Remember principles of cover and concealment.
- Have a safe path and destination with an alternate destination in mind.
- Do not attempt to evacuate if you do not know where the threat is located.
- Leave your possessions.
- Warn others, but do not let it slow you down.

Lockdown

- Lock and secure the door.
- Call 911 if you think you are safe.
- Stay out of the line of sight and line of fire.
- Barricade the door with any and all furniture and equipment.
- Put as much cover between you and the threat as possible.
- Turn out the lights.
- Turn off any source of noise and remain quiet.
- Do not make yourself an easy target.
- Stay on your feet ready to move.
- Remember that cover is your goal. Cabinets, desks, solid walls.

Fight

- Fight option is your last resort.
- Be loud and aggressive.
- Secure the door to prevent breach from additional shooters.
- Use age appropriate students to assist you.
- Prepare yourself mentally to incapacitate the shooter.

Evacuate – Take Shelter In Place – Fight Back

This is essentially the "Run – Hide – Fight" model but with different terms being used. This model is presented in a short video titled *Practical Responses to Active Shooter* by Rock Valley College in Rockford, IL.

Avoid – Deny – Defend

This is the ALERRT (Advanced Law Enforcement Rapid Response Training) model that can be found in the book *Active Shooter: Events and Response* by Blair, Nichols, Burns, and Curnutt as well as the eleven-and-a-half-minute video titled *Surviving an Active Shooter Event – Civilian Response to Active Shooter* produced by the ALERRT Center at Texas State University.

Avoid

- Avoid the attacker.
- Be Aware of your Surroundings.
- Do Not Hesitate.
- Go to the Closest, Safe Exit.
- Use cover and concealment

Deny

- Deny the attacker access to your area.
- Keep the Attacker Away from you.
- Lock doors, Lights off, Out of Sight.
- Have a Back-Up Plan

Defend

- Defend yourself. It is a personal decision, but you have a right to do so.
- You Have the Right.
- Do Not Fight Fair.
- Be Aggressive.

911

- Call 911 as soon as you are in a safe location.
- Provide only information you know, don't guess.

When Police Arrive

- Follow Commands.
- Show Your Hands
- Do Not Move.

(Note: Laura J. Kendall recommends the ALERT model in her books *Active Shooter Response and Tactical Trauma Training for Laypersons* and *Active Shooter Response Training Tactical Trauma Care for First Responders*.)

React – Escape – Survive

This model comes from the video titled *Active Shooter Prevention Training with OSHA Message* on YouTube. Watching the credits, the video is titled *How to Recognize and Survive the Active Shooter* presented by Countermeasure Consulting Group, LLC and Paroco Television. The free 27-minute training video features a team of Active Shooter Prevention Experts including Chris Grollnek,

Dave "Bo" Bolgiano, Dr. Morgan Banks, Jim Patterson, and Dave Rodriquez. Here are some of the key points from this video:

React

- React to the threat.
- You MUST Do Something.
- Train your mind to react.
- Observe, Orient, Decide, Act (OODA Loop)
- Don't think, KNOW. Be Prepared.
- Preplan YOUR options.

Escape

- Escape from the threat.
- Self-Preservation is Key.
- Evacuate yourself out of the danger area.
- "Wait and see" is not an option.
- Move to cover.
- If you hide, always be preparing to evacuate.
- If can't run or hide and have no options: Attack!
- Use anything you can find.
- Don't stop until you are safe.

Survive

- Survive the threat.
- When Police Arrive, stay calm, the police are there to help you.
- Stay still with hands visible to police.
- Cooperate with police.

Situationally Aware – Flight – Evade – Rush (SAFER)

This model is taught by Delta Situational Awareness Training, or DESAT. They have a short video that covers these concepts. This is what the video covers:

SITUATIONALLY AWARE

- The video only mentions this and then quickly goes into the next steps.

TAKE FLIGHT When an Active Shooter is in Your Area.

- Take flight if it is safe to do so.
- If possible, help others escape.
- Leave, even if others do not.

- Leave your belongings.
- Stop others from entering the dangerous area.
- Call 911 from a safe place.

EVADE If You Cannot Escape Safely.

- Lock and blockade door if possible.
- Silence cell phones.
- Hide behind large objects.
- Be as quiet as possible.
- Be out of the shooter's view.
- Try to protect yourself if shots are fired in your direction with cover of large objects.
- Do not trap or restrict your options for movement if possible.

RUSH as a Last Option, if Your Life is in Danger.

- Try to incapacitate the shooter.
- Act as aggressively as possible.
- Yell.
- Use any improvised weapons available, throw items.
- Commit to these actions.

Finally

- Be aware of your surrounding environment. Always have an exit plan. Understand that in these kinds of incidents, victims are often chosen randomly. These events are fluid and unpredictable, and can evolve rapidly. Your actions CAN make a difference for your safety and survival. Be prepared and be aware. SAFER:
- Be Situationally Aware.
- Take Flight if it is safe to do so.
- Evade your attacker.
- Rush your attacker if you are left with no choice.

Guard – Evacuation – Avoid – Resist (G.E.A.R.)

This model is from Personal Protection Training G.E.A.R. (PPT G.E.A.R.) offered by Go2FirearmTraining.

Guard: the things you do to guard against an Active Shooter event.

Evacuation: Creating a standard protocol of Active Shooter events including an evacuation plan including various routes, reunification points, and medical/safety procedures to ensure ultimate survival.

Avoid: If evacuation isn't possible, do anything you can to avoid an Active Shooter to include hiding, barricading, or evading. Knowing cover vs. concealment, safe rooms vs. unsafe rooms, and knowing how and when to help yourself or others who are injured.

Resist: When there is no way to avoid the Active Shooter, then resistance is your only option. Defend against and attack the shooter until law enforcement arrives on scene.

Alert – Lockdown – Inform – Counter – Evacuate (ALICE)

The ALICE Training Institute teaches this ALICE model. They provide live instruction as well as on-line courses. From their website, this is the breakdown of the ALICE model.

Alert

- Initial Alert may be a gunshot, PA announcement, etc... Avoid code words.

Lockdown

- If Evacuation is not a safe option, barricade entry points. Prepare to Evacuate or Counter if needed.

Inform

- Communicate real time information on shooter location. Use clear and direct language using an communication means possible.

Counter

- As a last resort, distract shooters ability to shoot accurately. Move toward exits while making noise, throwing objects, or adults swarm shooter.

Evacuate

- Run from danger when safe to do so using non-traditional exits if necessary. Rallying point should be predetermined.

Note that these five responses are not in any specific order. They are not sequential, but arranged simply to help people remember them. What you do will be determined by the situation. Refer to the ALICE Training Institute website (listed in the resources of this book) for additional information on this model and other resources related to Active Threats and training.

Many schools and organizations have adopted the ALICE model and training. The Oak Hills Schools District in Ohio combined with the Delhi and Green Township Police forces to train people and produce a training video based on the ALICE model titled *Active Shooter Response Training for High School and Middle Schools*. The video illustrates the five responses taught in this model.

Escape – Deny – Fight

This is the model Steven Remy presents in the chapter "Response to a School Attack" in his book *Indomitable Spirit: How to React and Survive in a School Shooting.*

Remy presents some sound advice regarding escaping the area through the most reasonable escape route given the circumstances and building layout; denying by barricading or hardening the immediate area and concealing yourselves from view of the attacker; and fighting back as a last resort with any means available.

Act Immediately - Take Cover – Escape – Engage – Communicate – Recovery

This model is presented by James C. Jones in his book *The Live Free Book Of Total Survival: Principles For Organizing Your Life, Home Vehicle, And Family For Natural Disasters, Civil Unrest, Financial Meltdowns, Medical Epidemics, And Political Upheaval*. In the section on Active Shooters, Jones describes the steps to his model under "What to Do When the First Shots Are Fired:"

Act Immediately

If you have accepted the possibility of an active-shooter situation and taken the steps above (be observant and alert, make an escape plan, and identify potential bulletproof cover), you can skip from denial to action while others freeze and get shot.

Take Cover

If you are already in the shooter's vision or if there is no covered escape route that will not expose you to the shooter, taking cover may be your only option. Immediately get behind the strongest, thickest object possible. Stay low or lie flat. If you are wounded or among wounded people, lie down and play dead. Shooters will instinctively shoot at anyone they see moving.

Escape

If the shooter has his back to you, you have a chance to escape or at least reach good cover before he turns around. But remember that there may be more than one shooter. If you go through a door, get to the right or left of the door and keep moving toward cover since the shooter may shoot through it or follow you out.

Engage

The Washington, D.C., chief of police and many others have now recognized that civilians may need to take action on their own before law enforcement arrives to save themselves and others. If you cannot escape or find cover and the shooter continues to shoot, your best chance is to distract, delay, or disable the shooter. Discharging a fire extinguisher; throwing a heavy object; and tackling, clubbing, or stabbing the shooter are all justified in this situation. If you have a firearm, use it. Yes, shoot the shooter in the back if you can. Aim for the head as active shooters often wear bulletproof vests. If possible, shoot from a low position so your bullets go upward and avoid hitting bystanders. Don't hesitate and don't try to get a shooter to surrender; he will just shoot you. Caution: Remember, the police will consider anyone they find holding a gun as the enemy. Once the shooter is down, you can kick his weapon(s) out of his reach but do not pick it up. Then put your weapon down and your hands up, and wait for the police.

Communicate

If not in immediate danger, use your cell phone to call for help. Provide the police with any information that you can, such as the description and number of shooters, location of shooters, type of weapons used, and the direction shooters are moving or did move. If you are barricaded or behind cover, provide your location and your own description. If nothing else, pull the fire alarm to warn others and distract the shooter.

Recovery

If you are lucky enough to initially survive a mass shooting, you are not safe yet because the police are going to be very jumpy on entry. Stay down and keep your hands up. Follow police instructions carefully. Officers will consider everyone there as a threat until they are searched, interviewed, and cleared. There may still be other active shooters at large or there may be bombs or booby traps left behind. If you are carrying a firearm (open or concealed), be sure to immediately tell the police while keeping your hands up. If you have any medical training, try to help the wounded until the medics arrive. Stopping severe bleeding and treating for shock may save lives.

While Jones provides some basic sound guidance with his model, I do disagree, as you will read later, with his advice to play dead and pull fire alarms.

Evade – Barricade – Respond

This model is presented by Rob Pincus in the very good I.C.E. Training Company DVD *Spree Attacker Response.* Pincus provides practical advice in this clear and easy to understand program. I also liked that the DVD included a bonus segment: "Using a Fire Extinguisher as a Defensive Tool." These are the key points Pincus makes with this model:

Evade

- The first thing you should do if you find yourself in the area of a spree attack is to try to evade.
- Evade means to get away from the area under attack or get to out of range of the attack.
- Evasion should include the option of leaving the building/campus/area entirely, do not limit yourself to the confines of your immediate area.
- If evading will actually put you in more danger (jumping out of a 5th story window in a building, disconnecting yourself from life-sustaining equipment in a hospital, running into sub-zero temperatures without any protection from the elements...) then it is not appropriate.
- In the event that you find yourself in the area of a spree attack and you have the opportunity to evade but your group or designated "leader" is hesitating, Take Action! The best thing you can do is get out of the area of the attack.
- Scattering and running as individuals is often a better choice than staying together as a slow-moving group or mass of potential targets.

Barricade

- If you cannot get away from an attack, your next best option is to Barricade.
- Barricading means to make it harder for the bad guy to get into a position to hurt you.

- A "barricade" doesn't need to be impossible for someone to get through, it is anything that makes it more difficult, or makes it take more time, for the bad guy to hurt you.
- Closing doors, locking doors, blocking doors, making the floor slippery or placing obstacles in the travel path of the attacker can all be ways to barricade.
- The longer it takes an attacker to get to you, the more chance that law enforcement or others will stop the bad guy before you get hurt.
- Spree attackers will be trying to reach as many victims as possible as quickly as possible. If they come up against a barricade, they may simply choose to move in another direction.
- If you work in an area that may be targeted for a spree attack, you should take measures ahead of time to set up simple ways to secure doors and/or barricade rooms efficiently.
- Depending on the construction of the building and doors, there are many options available to you. Exploring those options and putting the ones that make the most sense into practice is part of your preparation for defense during a spree attack.
- "Hiding" is a combination of Barricading and Evading. If the bad guy doesn't know where you are, it is "more difficult for them to hurt you."

Respond

- Ultimately, if the attacker reaches you, you must take direct action to protect yourself.
- There are three goals that your action can have:
    1. Prevent injury
    2. Distract the Attacker
    3. Disable the Attacker
- Preventing injury means to make it harder for the bad guy to hurt you. If they have a knife, you can block their strikes with a chair or wrap the blade in a thick coat to make it less dangerous. If the attacker has a gun, thick books held in front of you can stop bullets in some cases.
- Attackers can be distracted from their plan by throwing things at them, by scattering and/or by impact.
- Attackers can be disabled through a variety of means:
    1. Blinding
    2. Choking
    3. Taking away their mobility
    4. Overwhelming their ability to think
    5. Disabling/Removing the Tool
- Blinding can be accomplished by attacking the eyes with any type of liquid or granular substance.

- Stopping an attacker from breathing can be done through impact to the throat or chest and/or smothering.
- Attacking a bad guy's legs can keep them from being able to maneuver and make it easier to take other action or for you to evade.
- Striking an attacker's head can keep them from being able to control their body and/or make decisions.
- Taking away the attacker's tool or affecting their ability to use it may render them unable to hurt you or anyone else.
- Think ahead of time of the items you have in your environment that you might be able to use as an improvised defensive tool.

Run – Hide – Tell

In London, they promote the "Run – Hide – Tell" model. The main points of this model are:

Run – to a place of safety. This is a better option than to surrender or negotiate. If there's nowhere to go, then...

Hide– Turn your phone to silent and turn off vibrate. Barricade yourself in if you can.

Tell– the police by calling 999 when it is safe to do so.

I personally feel this is the worst of the models I've shared here because of the omission of fighting or attacking back as you'll see I call it in the *Survive A Shooting* model. I've included it to illustrate what is out there, as I have also heard "experts" on American television programs stating that your options are to run or hide and never to fight back. Obviously, I think this is nonsense and disagree with telling people they can't or shouldn't fight back to protect and save themselves or others.

Why Another Model?

All the models above, and others out there, are similar. With the exception of those that don't advocate fighting back, they are generally sound advice and definitely better than nothing. I'd much rather someone watch the *Run – Hide – Fight* video and think about where they would run or hide (even though I don't like that word), and how they would fight back, than do nothing at all and remain in denial believing it will never happen to them. Obviously, the models that have live training combined with the model will prepare people much better than just watching a video on-line. But again, anything is better than denial and nothing.

So, why another model? Through the study of vocabulary and words you find the power in the right words, and how they can create images, emotions, and actions. This is one of the reasons I don't like the word "hide" in the "Run-Hide-Fight" model. What image does the word "hide" create? One of empowerment? One of personal responsibility and capability? More often it conjures an image of cowering under a table or desk. People have been killed by active shooters as they hid under tables and desks. *Hiding and hoping is not a plan for survival!* I wanted my model to use words that were more pro-active and empowering, and that also conveyed the responses that would best increase survivability in such an extreme situation. "Escape – Deny – Attack Back" does just that.

Escape – Deny – Attack Back

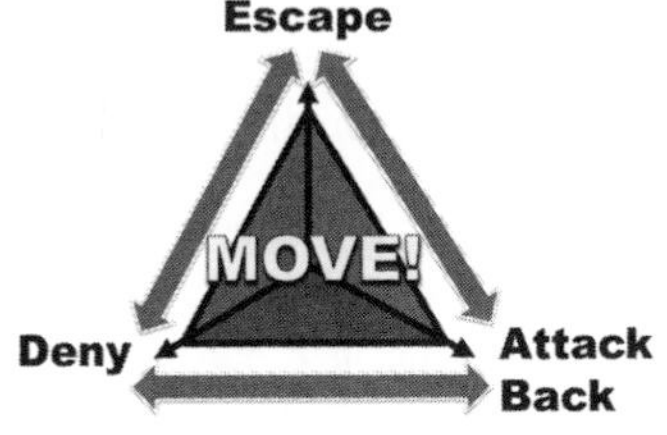

The following chapters will detail these three responses: Escape, Deny and Attack Back. In this section, I want to explain why I chose the terms I use, and then I'll go over the triangle and why it is better than the linear models.

Escape

I chose the word "escape" because I feel it better conveys the concept I want people to do. I don't want you to just "run." I want you to escape the danger zone if there is opportunity to do so. This may be running away, but it might be diving behind cover and crawling toward safety, or going out a window to effectively escape the danger. This is why I feel it is better to teach people to escape to safety over just "run."

Deny

The word deny stands for denying the killer access to kill you. This can be done in a variety of ways. Locking and barricading the entrance to your location is one way, and an effective way, to deny the killer access to kill you. Getting behind cover can deny the killer access to shooting you. If the armed intruder is armed with a knife or similar stabbing type weapon, holding a chair out between you, as I teach in my classes, is a way to deny him access to stab or slash you.

I teach this concept in my Stay Safe classes too. For instance, in the cities, sometimes muggers will pretend to beg from you to get close enough to then attack and rob you. It might go down something like this.

"You have a dollar?" said by mugger trying to get close to you.

"No," you say, but without setting any boundaries and permitting the mugger to get closer to you.

"Come on man, just a dollar?" said while getting even closer.

"I don't have anything for you," said while letting the person enter your "personal" space, even though uncomfortable, you say nothing about it.

"Give me your wallet!" said commandingly as the mugger pulls a knife, closes the distance, and sticks the knife up toward your throat.

In my classes, after demonstrating this scenario, I have people practice setting boundaries and denying the mugger access to that "personal" space. Doing this entails putting your hands up in a non-threatening manner, and being assertive (not aggressive) when telling the person "no," and not to come closer. You set your boundary and don't allow the person inside. If they persist and continue to try to enter your personal space by closing the distance, you are probably justified in physically defending yourself, but in most cases setting boundaries will cause you to fail the criminal's interview and he will go look for an easier target.

By using "deny" in all my teachings, it keeps it simple and easier for people to remember and for my messages to remain consistent. While the level of denying access is different, the concept of keeping the bad guy away from you and not allowing them to attack is the same.

Attack Back

There are a couple of reasons I use the term "Attack Back" instead of "fight." I initially used "Attack Back" when teaching self-defense programs, and then incorporated the terminology into my *Survive A Shooting* model and courses. The reasons for using it in both are the same, as well as wanting to use concepts and terms that are consistent across the different classes I teach.

I feel "Attack Back" is a stronger more proactive response than "fight," and the rhyming makes it easier to remember.

But there was much more than "it rhymes" to my decision to use the term "Attack Back." I specifically wanted the word "attack" because it is more proactive and aggressive and conjures a different emotional response than "fight." Imagine General George S. Patton out in front of his troops. Would he yell, "Fight!" as he led them into battle, or would he yell, "Attack!"

To answer that, let me share a passage from *Patton's One-Minute Messages* by Charles M. Province (p. 46):

"In case of doubt, attack

The enemy is just as ignorant of the situation as you are and perhaps more so. Instead of waiting to see what might develop, attack constantly, vigorously, and viciously. If you're standing around trying to figure out what is happening or what the enemy is up to, you are making one hell of a good target out of yourself and your men. Never let up. Never stop. Always attack. When the enemy is defending himself against your assault, he doesn't have the time to plan an offensive against you. If you were a boxer and your opponent were on the ropes, you wouldn't stop and let him rest, would you? When you get him on the ropes, keep punching. Beat the hell out of him until he's out for the count. 'L'audace, l'audace, toujours l'audace.'"

(Author's note: one of Patton's favorite quotes was said by Danton during the French Revolution – "De l'audace, encore de l'audace, toujours de l'audace!" It means, "Audacity, Audacity, always audacity.")

In an active threat situation, I want to encourage the same spirit of aggression in potential victims as General Patton did on the battlefield with his troops. I don't want victims, I want survivors, and using aggressive, ruthless, violence of action is the only option when escaping and denying access are not possible. I want people to have an offensive mindset and not one of defending. I want the killer to be worried about defending himself and not have time to hurt or kill anyone else. The term "Attack" empowers people emotionally to do this better than "fight."

So, why add "back," and not just use Escape – Deny - Attack? There was a more important reason for doing this than the rhyming and sounding cool. While it is appropriate for General Patton to lead his men during a time of war with the command of "Attack," most people I'm teaching are not in the military and preparing for war. While those of us with military backgrounds have no trouble with the aggressive "attack" mentality, many people without this background don't feel the same. Many have been taught that aggressiveness and violence are wrong and not appropriate. They don't believe in hurting others. And in normal situations, they are right. Unfortunately, an active shooter incident is not a normal situation. It calls for a response that is not normal for most people. By adding "back" to the model, I'm giving people permission to do something that is outside of their belief system.

When a person believes that attacking someone is wrong, it is easier to get them to accept it is okay when I tell them to attack back. They didn't start it. They are not being the initial aggressor, which is what their beliefs are against. They are attacking back after the bad guy started it. While some may dismiss this, or think it is just mixing words, it actually makes a psychological difference to some people. Many self-defense instructors will tell you the importance of giving some people "permission" to defend themselves. When I teach people to attack back, I'm giving them permission to do something outside of their belief system, that of hurting or killing someone else. And these words help me with that important message.

Crisis Communication

The area of crisis communications covers a variety of communication strategies and tactics for a crisis, which can be defined as any situation that is threatening or could threaten to harm people or property, seriously

- During an active threat, there is NO time to talk.
- If the threat is communicating, he is not an active shooter. Someone communicating would be a hostage taker or barricaded gunman.
- Crisis communication techniques only work with individuals interested in dialog. Active shooters are only interested in a high body count
- The recognition that talking is not an option should be very apparent.

interrupt business, significantly damage reputation and/or negatively impact the bottom line. For purposes here, discussing active threats, people usually think of de-escalating techniques or hostage negotiation techniques. Neither of which are appropriate when an active killer has begun his rampage. When a person's sole goal is a high body count, and he doesn't care if he will die (often they plan to die during the incident), the time for talking is over. You can't de-escalate or negotiate when bullets are flying, knives are waving, and people are dying. De-escalation techniques, hostage negotiation strategies, and other crisis communication skills are extremely valuable and worth learning and practicing. But they are not the tools for an active killer situation and thus beyond the scope of this book and Active Shooter Response models.

Active Shooter Triangle vs. Linear Models

This is a very important consideration that I have seen play out when teaching thousands of people in active shooter scenarios. I will admit that when setting up scenarios, we design them to elicit certain reactions and to reinforce specific training objectives. This means we may set up a scenario that will force students to Attack Back and fight the instructor in the padded suit. We may purposefully take away the Escape and Deny options to achieve the training objective. But the reality is that these options may not be there in an actual active shooter situation either.

Using a linear model, and teaching in a linear fashion, doesn't take this into account. By linear, I mean, teaching: first you run; then if you can't run, you hide; and only if you can't run and can't hide do you fight. This linear teaching and thinking doesn't fit with how situations may occur.

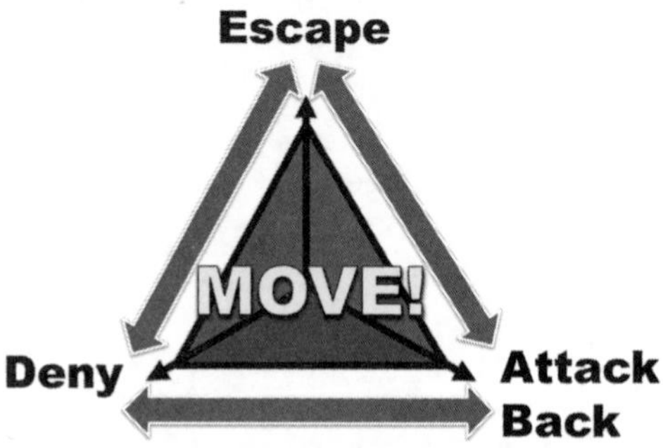

The Escape | Deny | Attack Back - Active Shooter Triangle

This is why I created the Active Shooter Triangle for my presentations, posters, etc. In the center of the triangle is the word "Move!" The worst thing you can do in an active shooter situation is to stand or sit there and do nothing. Movement saves lives. Freezing in confusion, fear, and shock is a likely response, especially with people that don't have a plan and have no training. We must act. Move!

"Move!" has arrows pointing to each of the three responses: Escape – Deny – Attack Back. Which one you do will be determined by various factors, including: your proximity to the shooter, your location and the environment, and your strengths, weaknesses, and ability to perform the three responses. Yes, escaping to safety is always preferred to physically attacking back and engaging in violence with the killer if possible. There is more risk of injury and death when you are engaged in a physical confrontation with the killer, especially if you are unarmed and have other disadvantages. (We will discuss ways to reduce your disadvantages in the Attack Back chapter.) The key here is "if possible." When escaping is not possible, nor is denying the killer access to you, attacking back may be the best and only option. I feel the triangle best represents this concept and helps me get the idea through to those I teach that they must do one of the options, but which one will depend on various factors.

The triangle doesn't stop there. While the middle "Move!" has arrows pointing to the three responses, each response has an arrow pointing to the other two responses. These are the triangle sides of the diagram. It represents another important concept. Just because you are doing one of the responses, doesn't mean you are not prepared to do one of the others as the situation changes. You must always be looking to better your position and increase your chances of survival.

When you are escaping, you must be prepared to deny access or attack back. For instance, you may be escaping and when you turn a corner you run right into a second shooter (or maybe the first shooter, as I've seen people run down hallways toward the shooter in scenarios when they were not able to identify where the shooting came from in particular buildings). If you turn the corner and run into a killer, you have to attack back and take him out.

You hear shots in the hall and immediately get up and secure the door denying the killer access to the room you are in. You then look to see if you can maybe escape out a window or different door, or you prepare to attack back if the killer breaches your locked door or barricade.

You take out a killer that bursts into your room, and now you must prepare for a second threat by locking down and barricading, or escaping to safety. We must always be prepared to do one of the other two responses even though we are currently doing one of them. We want to always be doing something proactive to better our position and increase our odds of surviving. I feel the triangle conveys this more accurately than a linear model.

A note on being proactive versus reactive. Initially, when the active shooter incident erupts, you will naturally be in a reactive state. You didn't know it was coming, and at the first sound of gunfire, you must react. The goal is to become proactive as soon as possible. That is what this model, planning, and training help accomplish.

Curling up under a desk, hiding and hoping, maybe crying and praying, is not being proactive. Remember, hiding and hoping is not a plan. Moving, escaping to safety, finding cover or at least concealment, denying the shooter access to you, grabbing a fire extinguisher, stacking at the door, and knowing when to engage the gunman to take him out are all proactive actions. Go ahead and pray, but do so while you are taking proactive action.

Being Proactive

Another way to be proactive is to make sure there is a plan in place wherever you and your family spend time away from home. If your place of employment has a plan, review it, and ensure everyone is familiar and onboard with it. (Also assess its validity with what you learn in this book, because sadly some places believe that having employees watch the *Run - Hide – Fight* video on YouTube is adequate planning and "training.") If there isn't a plan or procedure where you work, talk to the decision makers about implementing one and providing training for all employees. If you have children, do the same with their schools. Find out what the school plan is, and if they don't have one encourage them to develop and adopt one as soon as possible. Be persistent and make sure this aspect of security and keeping kids safe is addressed to your satisfaction. Sure, this will take time and effort, but it will be worth it if the unthinkable happens.

Conclusion

Many of the active shooter models provide better guidance than nothing at all. However, the "Escape – Deny – Attack Back" active shooter triangle has been carefully thought out to provide a model that accurately reflects the best possible response to an active threat. It will be covered in more detail throughout the rest of this book, and it provides the framework to increase the survivability of anyone caught in an active threat situation.

Escape to Safety

www.SurviveaShooting.com

Use the most reasonable escape route given the circumstances and building layout you are faced with. ”

Steven Remey
Indomitable Spirit: How to React and Survive in a School Shooting

TOPICS

- ✓ Getting Off the X
- ✓ Why Movement Saves Lives
- ✓ Playing Dead
- ✓ Recognizing Gunshots
- ✓ How to Tell Where Gunfire is Coming From
- ✓ Determining Opportunity and Avenue of Escape
- ✓ How to Look, Listen, and Plan Your Escape
- ✓ Leap Frog Maneuvers
- ✓ Movement Techniques
- ✓ Running Zig Zag vs. Straight
- ✓ Cover vs. Concealment
- ✓ Escaping When in a Crowd
- ✓ Separate Yourself from the Crowd
- ✓ Should You Pull the Fire Alarm?

It's simple to tell people to escape to safety or to run. But what does that mean? What does running away or escaping entail? This chapter looks at important aspects related to escaping an active shooter event. The information in this chapter is designed with one purpose, and that is to help you escape to safety when that option is available to you.

Getting Off the X

A common phrase in the military is "Get off the X." This refers to the kill zone, or X, and the fact that when gunfire erupts, you must remove yourself from the immediate vicinity (kill zone or X) without hesitation. This is why having a plan is imperative. In the chaos of such an event, it's essential to get out of the line of fire. This may mean dropping and low crawling, or it may mean sprinting as fast as you can. The key is to do whatever you can to get out of the kill zone as quickly as possible and find cover if available.

If a shooting occurs, you must move. Fortunately, it's natural for people to use the flight instinct and run during a shooting. Unfortunately, it's not always true for everyone. Some people freeze, and others want to gawk at what's happening. Others run, but without forethought. I realize there is little or no time to think, but you must move, and preferably your movement is calculated so you don't turn yourself into a more visible and attractive target.

Joining a panic-stricken mob bottlenecked at a doorway may mean you go nowhere. Running closer to the line of fire may be equally disastrous. Calculated flight gets you clear of the danger, or off the X. It's preferred to run away from the shooter and/or away from his focus without bottlenecking with a group making easy targets, or running into an area where you can't escape or barricade.

Dropping to the floor is often an instinctive reaction to bullets flying around, and it can save your life. But don't just lie there covering your head hoping for the situation to pass. Stay low and move! Move toward cover or an exit as quickly as you can.

If you know where the shooter is, immediately sprinting to safety may be the best option. If you don't know where the shooter is located, or where the bullets are coming from, drop immediately to the ground to scan for cover and where the shooter is located. Don't stay there! Determine where to move to, and that means behind cover or escaping to safety. Dropping down makes you a smaller target if the shooter is on the same plane. However, if the shooter is above and shooting down, as happened in the Las Vegas shooting of October 1, 2017, being on the ground does little or nothing to reduce target size. In that kind of situation, the only options are to get behind cover or escape the kill zone.

Once off the X and out of the kill zone, 1. continue to escape toward safety, 2. find a location you can barricade and deny the shooter access to you, or 3. prepare to ambush and fight. As stated elsewhere in this book, these options are not always in this order, nor are they always all available.

> "If you survive the first ten seconds of this type of ambush, you have a much better chance of making it out alive."
>
> *Cade Courtley*
> *SEAL Survival Guide*

Movement Saves Lives

This bears repeating: Movement saves lives. You must move to get off the 'X'. You must move to run and escape to safety. You must move to deny or barricade. You must move to fight or attack back.

If you study threatening situations, they all have this in common. Floods, hurricanes, tornados, earthquakes, plane crashes, terrorist attacks, and active shooters or threats are all the same in this matter. Regardless of the threatening situation, movement saves lives. You must not freeze. You need to quickly get yourself out of danger, and that means move. Those that move have a greater chance of surviving.

> **The Three "Fs"**
>
> The three Fs: Fight, Flight, and Freeze. During many emergencies, including shootings, those who freeze are usually added to the casualty toll. Do not freeze. You must react and move immediately.

Additionally, a moving target is much harder to hit than a stationary one. If the shooter sees you: ***be a moving target.*** You must not freeze. You must not stand there wishing you were someplace else or hoping the gunman will go away. If you have ever fired a gun, think about trying to shoot at a target that keeps moving and dodging all over the place. Your chances of hitting the target are considerably reduced, and that's what you want for the killer. Make yourself as hard to hit as possible. Mark Puddy, a Navy Veteran, police officer for more than 20 years, and an instructor with the *Emergency Response To An Armed Intruder* team, likes to tell people who don't have a clear escape route such as in the back of a room with the shooter in front of the only exit, "Be Jackie Chan. Zig, zag, dodge, and move! Do whatever you can to be a hard target." While this may sound like a futile exercise, there was a video years ago of a shooter trying to shoot an attorney outside a courthouse. The attorney dodged and hid behind a small tree as the would-be killer kept trying to shoot him as he moved (One of several videos of the incident: https://youtu.be/9tkMYoOLAhk). The attorney was shot, but he lived. Movement saved his life.

> "I've always felt that if someone is shooting at you, it's better to be a good ducker than a good fighter. Survival all comes down to your ability to make yourself a difficult target."
>
> *Neal Rawls*
> *Be Alert Be Aware Have a Plan*

An experiment that illustrates this was conducted for the 12 DVD Video Program *Active Shooter Massacre Survival Israeli Method* with Doron Benbenisty, former Israeli Special Forces member and a Counter Terrorism expert. Benbenisty took two volunteers that had no prior tactical or combative experience and had them enter a room and shoot targets representing a teacher and a class of students and it took them only 34 seconds to kill everyone in the room when no one moved. (Targets were actually stationary balloons shot with pellets.) If the targets had just gotten under the desks, they would have been just as easily killed. However, in all of the experiments with people reacting, moving, barricading, locking the door, and attacking back, the casualty rate was extremely reduced or eliminated. Movement saves lives!

Playing Dead

Playing dead is an intentional strategy that has saved people's lives. People have also been shot and killed when the strategy didn't work. The advice to play dead appeals to those who don't want to fight. They want the attacker to pass them by looking for new victims as they play dead. Sometimes it works, sometimes it doesn't.

This is what Arthur Cohen says about playing dead in his book *Surviving A Massacre, Rampage, Or Spree Killing*: "Playing dead is a variation of freezing, but unlike freezing, playing dead is an intentional strategy. You consciously decide to lie motionless on the ground, looking as if you were dead. When might this strategy be attempted? If you are too far away from reliable cover or wounded so that you can't run, dropping down and playing dead might be the only reasonable option. But remember, if you do decide to play dead, your body position must convince the gunman that you are dead. You must remain absolutely still and silent. This might work because spree shooters are pressured by time and focus more on those trying to escape. If you can fool the killer long enough for him to either leave the area in search of more victims, prepare to engage police, or commit suicide, you might survive. But not always. The Virginia Tech killer revisited a couple of rooms, searching for survivors and shooting those he found still alive in the head to make sure they were dead."

While Cohen mentioned the Virginia Tech killer, we have to note the Columbine High School shooting as well. In both of these active shooter incidents the shooters went back and shot people hiding and playing dead. Here is a very chilling piece of information: Seung-Hui Cho, the Virginia Tech killer, actually practiced shooting people hiding or playing dead on the shooting range before going on his killing spree. This is what John Giduck wrote in *Shooter Down! The Dramatic, Untold Story of the Police Response to the Virginia Tech Massacre*: "On March 14, 2007 Cho was seen at a national forest shooting range outside of town. What the range managers and other shooters recalled that was so unusual was a young Asian man putting paper targets on the ground in two long columns with a narrow aisle between them. He was walking down the aisle, a gun in each hand, shooting down into the targets on both sides of him."

People have survived shootings by playing dead, so I don't want to say *never* play dead. The run, lock, fight; or escape, deny, attack back strategies are much better options. I believe these strategies will provide a better chance of surviving a shooting. However, there may be a situation where these are impractical or have failed, and as a last-ditch measure, playing dead could save your life. I really wouldn't want to bet on it, but that is because I don't like betting against the odds when my life is on the line. If, for whatever reason, you decide that playing dead is your best bet for surviving a shooting incident, make sure you do it well. In the passage by Cohen above he mentions body position and remaining absolutely still and silent. All three are important. For a little more advice on playing dead you can look up self-defense instructor Jim Wagner's YouTube video titled "Jim Wagner my self-defense instructor: Playing dead during a shooting."

Again, I'm not really a fan, nor am I recommending this strategy, but if you are going to play dead, do it right.

> "Playing dead may work for Mr. Opossum, but it doesn't work as well for humans under attack."
>
> *Greg Ellifritz*
> *Active Response Training Blog*

Recognizing Gunshots

When a gun is fired right next to you, it is easily recognizable. When one is fired down the hall, around the corner, in a different room, or up and down stairs from you, it starts to become much more difficult to identify. In the Active Shooter Response class scenarios where we fire off blanks inside of buildings, we have students in various locations inside the buildings we train in. Sometimes students say they wouldn't have thought it was a gun if they hadn't known we were doing exercises. Other times, we have people inside parts of the building where they don't hear anything when shots are being fired in different locations of the structure.

There are various factors that may affect your hearing gunfire in the building you occupy. The distance from where the gun is being fired and where you are, corners or different floors between you and the gun shots, the caliber of weapon being fired, the type of walls and construction of the building, your hearing ability, and external noise and commotion going on. These various factors can affect your ability to hear and discern gunshots. Combine a few of them and you might not hear shots being fired at all.

Another concern is the ease that many people will attribute gun shots to some other sound that is more in line with their frame of reference. Guns are not supposed to be fired in schools, movie theaters, businesses, churches, and other peaceful places. This makes it easier to rationalize the sound of gunfire as something more explainable. People have thought gun shots were fireworks, cars back firing, construction noises, balloons popping, someone kicking a door, science experiments, and other explanations for loud noises rather than gunfire.

The problem with both situations, not hearing the gun fire, or your brain thinking up alternate explanations for the loud noise, is time. We know that seconds count. By not escaping or barricading immediately upon hearing possible gunshots, you increase the possibility of more casualties.

You can become better at recognizing gunshots by becoming familiar with them. Going to different shooting ranges to hear different caliber firearms will help. But gunfire inside a building will sound different from gunfire at the shooting range. If you have a chance to do training where blanks are fired in different locations of a building, that will help, but know that it is still difficult to locate where shots are coming from inside a building. The bigger the building, the more difficult it becomes.

Collaborating information will assist you in recognizing gunfire: People screaming and running away, seeing smoke, and the smell of smoke can all aid you in determining the noise you hear is actual gunfire.

Changing your mindset, acknowledging that shootings happen, and that one could happen to you, are also important. The loud noise may be a car backfiring or a balloon popping. But what if it is a gunshot? If you assume wrong, you could be dead. If you jumped up and shut your already locked door and prepared to deny access, escape or fight and it turns out that it was a balloon popping, what is the harm? A little embarrassment? You can live with that. The key word being *live*. If you are in a public place and hear something that might be gunshots, don't rationalize them away as something else. I'd rather you be embarrassed because you immediately exited the building in the opposite direction from the sounds, than become a victim. Better to be embarrassed than dead. The faster you can recognize the sounds of gunfire, the better your chances of survival.

What Do Gunshots Sound Like?

Many people have difficulty recognizing gunfire for what it is. This may be due to denial, or just being unfamiliar with the sound of gunshots. It is also much easier to dismiss the loud bang as something else; something less terrifying than an active shooter killing people. An excellent illustration of this comes from Andy Brown's book *Warnings Unheeded: Twin Tragedies at Fairchild Air Force Base.* Brown was the first military police officer on scene of the June 20, 1994 active shooter incident at Fairchild Air Force Base. Brown shot and killed the gunman. In his thoroughly researched book on the incident, he not only tells his story, but that of many involved. While many did recognize the gun shots immediately for what they were, many others didn't, or tried to rationalize them as something more familiar. These are quotes from the book, *Warnings Unheeded*, that illustrate people's initial mistaken thoughts when they heard the gunfire:

Medical technicians SSgt Jennifer Werder, SrA Kevin Seeley, and Airman First Class Raynes were in the audio room, Room 106, administering physicals to two young patients. They had just put the two youths inside the steel soundproof audiometric booths when they heard a gunshot from down the hall. They reasoned the sound was a door slammed closed by a summer breeze. When the sound repeated, one of them joked that it was gunfire.

Thirty-six-year-old LeDeane Stewart was a civilian data specialist. LeDeane said, "I heard the first shot....I thought a door had slammed. The annex got warm during the summer, and we had no air conditioning on the first floor. So it was not unusual for a door to be open."

Caroline Goodman was working at a computer terminal in the upper level of the annex when the shooting started. Caroline said, "I joked with my co-worker that is sounded like someone was shooting, so I said I better lock the door." Instead, Caroline opened the door. "People were running wild. An employee yelled for us to run."

Maj George Estes was a thirty-nine-year-old flight surgeon working internal medicine on the first floor east end of the hospital annex. Dr. Estes was in his office with a patient when he heard noises he associated with the wind slamming doors closed. When a group of people fled past his office, shouting, Dr. Estes looked down the hall and saw someone run out of the door with a chart. He ran with the crowd, thinking someone had stolen a medical chart. Once outside the east door of the annex, Dr. Estes realized that someone was in the area shooting.

Joneil Delrosario, a fifteen-year-old visiting his military brother, was in a Ford Bronco parked near the hospital's north entrance. He waited in the back seat while his sister-in-law ran into the pharmacy for a prescription. Joneil's four-month-old niece lay in a car seat up front. Joneil said, "I was sleeping in the car when I woke up and heard a boom. I thought it was a firecracker." Joneil closed his eyes again. He heard another gunshot and looked to see a gunman running toward the car. (author's note: the shooter ran past the car and Joneil and the baby made it to safety.)

Marlene Lee said, "I was sitting in my car when I heard noise that at first I thought was Fourth of July crackers."

Dennis Moe walked toward the north doors to investigate the sound of gunfire outside. He thought it might be an exercise until he saw the gunman trying to come in through the "out" door. Dennis yelled, "Oh my God, he's got a gun, everybody run!"

The gunman fired from the hip and moved continuously. His first shots flew toward Hap Joplin and Patrick Deaton. Deaton initially thought he heard a car backfiring until a bullet tore into him. Joplin saw the gunman but assumed it was an exercise. A bullet ripped through a computer kiosk Joplin was seated next to, splattering his face with fragments of particleboard. Joplin realized the danger was real and ran for cover down a hall behind the pharmacy.

Omar Karns couldn't hear the gunfire. He saw people running and had begun to follow them, when he felt a vibration in his lower back as a bullet splintered his pelvis.

Michelle Sigman thought it might be an exercise until she smelled the acrid gun smoke and heard people yell "He's got a gun!"

Eva Walch heard the gunfire, which she described as "pop, pop, popping" like "early Fourth of July."

Lt. Col Joe Olenoski was a B-52 navigator who worked a staff position in Fairchild's Bomb Wing. Lieutenant Colonel Olenoski sat in the clinic with his sixteen-year-old daughter, Stacy, who had just received an allergy shot. Olenoski said, "While sitting in the clinic with Stacy, I heard a banging that initially sounded like locker doors being slammed." He quickly recognized the sound to be gunfire that was growing louder.

Margaret Lum had received her allergy shot and waited in the clinic to ensure she didn't have an adverse reaction. She said, "I heard a couple of popping sounds, then again and again. I remember looking at the man next to me, and I said, 'that doesn't sound good'... and seconds later I knew it was not the backfire of a car. People were screaming, and the shots got louder. I could hear people running and screaming 'Oh my God.' I looked around the room for someplace to hide. There was nowhere to run and nowhere to hide."

Sergeant Lecker heard the shots in the hallway, and his first thought was the security police must be conducting an anti-robbery exercise at the pharmacy. That thought faded quickly as the shots and screams in the hallway intensified.

Thirty-year-old medical technician SSgt Deborah Foster worked in the family practice clinic. Foster said, "I heard popping noises down the hallway toward the pharmacy." She went to the edge of the waiting room and peered down the hall. A patient took off running, Foster heard him yell, "It's for real. He's got a gun. He's shooting people."

Terri Melton, a technician in the physical therapy department, heard shouted warnings about someone having a gun and then heard a boom. She opened her door and immediately closed it when she saw a flash of gunfire.

On the afternoon of 20 June 1994, Dave Root heard what he believed was the sound of exercise equipment being assembled down the hall. For the past few days the physical therapy techs had been working on a project. Root said, "They were just making a racket... and I told them a couple times, 'Look fellas, why don't you do it after work or something? You're just raising hell and making a lot of noise and upsetting my docs and my patients." When Root heard the noise again, he said, "That's it, I've had it," and headed across the hall. Root stopped short in the hallway. He poked his head around a corner into family practice and saw the gunman. "I really didn't see ***him*** *as much as his big-ass rifle. ... I pulled my head back, and as I did the corner just exploded."*

Once outside, Lorraine Murry and Dr. Baker realized the evacuation of the hospital was not due to a fire drill and the firecracker sounds they were hearing was actually rifle fire.

One man in a third-floor corner office above the mental health center paused at his desk. He thought he had heard a car backfire When he heard the sound again, he got up to investigate, "suspecting gunshots, but not believing it."

How to Tell Where Gun Fire is Coming From

As I mentioned above, it is often difficult to determine where gunfire is coming from inside a building. You cannot just trust your ears to determine the direction the gunfire came from. I remember one training exercise in an Active Shooter Response class when two ladies came out of a bathroom to escape to safety. They had two options when they exited the restroom, run left down the hall or run right. They chose right and ran straight toward where the shooter was located. They swore afterward that the shots had come from down the hall on the left.

Besides the sound of gunfire, look for people screaming and running away, smoke (this is less with the smokeless powder used in modern ammunition), and muzzle flashes. These can all help you determine where the shooter is located so you can escape in the opposite direction.

Opportunity and Avenue of Escape

One of the reasons I don't teach the linear approach of escape, deny, and then fight is due to needing two things to flee successfully. Without these, you should immediately be denying access or fighting. You must have both an opportunity and an avenue of escape to successfully get away.

Opportunity

The opportunity to run to safety may be immediate, or you may have to create an opportunity by doing something else first, and this could mean fighting. It may depend on your proximity to the shooter, the attention of the shooter and direction he is facing or shooting, and if you are alone or responsible for others, such as a teacher responsible for young children (there may be an opportunity for the teacher to escape, but not for the entire classroom).

Avenue of Escape

To flee, you must have an escape route. This means unobstructed pathways. If you run into a locked door that you can't exit, your escape will be halted and you may be in a worse position than if you'd have barricaded in your previous location.

Your avenue of escape may not be a door, but rather a window. I encourage everyone to know the exits and ways out of their buildings and anywhere they frequent on a regular basis. And for those places that are new to you? Get in the habit of looking for and recognizing exits and ways out. Knowing the way out is important when an emergency happens. It could be an active shooter, or it could be a fire, but knowing how to get out will save your life.

If you don't have the opportunity to flee and an avenue of escape, running may not be the best option even if it is what you prefer of the three. Without these two elements, you must barricade and deny access to your location or fight depending on your proximity to the shooter and other considerations.

> Notably, trained law enforcement professionals when under the stress of a violent encounter often achieve less than a twenty percent hit rate according to the FBI. It is the author's opinion that such statistics should not be interpreted as criticism of these departments' professionalism. Rather, these facts underscore the realities of a violent, often surprise encounter. You can therefore extrapolate that if you must run, it is a fair assumption that you may reach safety unscathed.
>
> *David Kahn*
> *Krav Maga Weapon Defenses*

Look, Listen, and Plan Your Escape

If you have the opportunity and avenue of escape from an office or room, don't just blindly run out into the hall to evacuate. Maybe an evacuation code has been triggered in your building, or possibly you heard shooting or screams from down the hall. Regardless of what triggered your action, if you decide to evacuate and escape to safety, look, listen, and plan first.

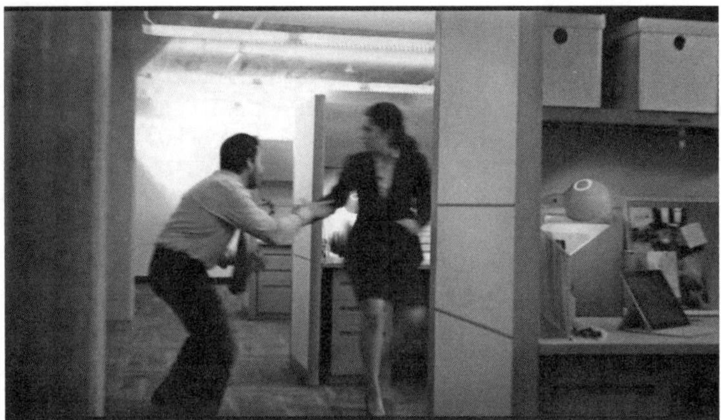

Reasons You Can't Escape

While escaping to safety is ideal, it is not always possible. There may be a variety of reasons why escaping is impossible or not the right choice. Here are a few common ones:

Physically Trapped/Unable to Escape. Physical environment prohibits escaping. An example might be in a room with only one door and no windows, and the shooter is outside the door.

Immoral to Escape/Presence of Loved Ones. This may be a parent or teacher with young children, a provider for disabled, or a medical provider for sick or injured. If there is someone with you that is unable to escape with you, you wouldn't be able to live with yourself if you escaped without them.

Physically Incapacitated. You are unable to escape because injured, sick, elderly, out of shape, etc. For whatever reason, you are unable to escape to safety.

Presence of a Long-Range Weapon. Guns reduce the options of escaping. If someone is down the hall to the left with a knife, I may be able to run out of the room to the right and escape. If the person has a gun, running out into the hall, even to the right, increases the likelihood of being shot. Staying in the room and denying access would be a preferable response when you can't escape due to the presence of a long-range weapon.

Before entering a hallway or corridor, look carefully to see if there are any threats or dangers. You are less likely to be seen if you get down and look out with your head and body closer to the floor. Don't just stick your head out, but slowly look at sections working your way around the corner. We call this "slicing the pie." Alternatively, some instructors teach the "quick peek" to clear corners where you quickly peek, not leaving your head visible for more than a second. I personally prefer and teach "slicing the pie" for corners and think it is a better tactic. Make sure you look both left and right to ensure a clear avenue of escape. Don't let any part of your body extend into the hallway to be seen, and that includes your hand grabbing the doorframe. While looking, also be listening for gunfire, screams, warnings, and instructions that can help you plan your escape.

Slicing the Pie

This technique is used at doorways and corners rather than just blindly going out into an open area. It is preferred to the "quick peek." You essentially clear each "slice of the pie" one slice at a time.

Position yourself away from the corner so you are not sticking past as you look. Move laterally, looking past the apex of the corner, moving slowly so you can clear each section before moving a little more.

Slicing the Pie

Leap Frog Maneuvers

When escaping, it is sometimes preferable to leap frog from one safe area to another. For example, you could move from a room down the hall to a corner, and then you stop to check around the corner (remember, low and slice the pie) to see if safe to continue. If safe, you move to the next corner and so on until you are out of the area and someplace safe. If outside, you may go from behind an engine block of a car to another vehicle's engine block and so forth, leap frogging from one cover to another until safe.

When escaping from a building, be wary of doorways, corridor/hallway intersections, windows, and staircases. Before crossing these open spaces, you can "quick peek," or "slice the pie," to see if safe, and then burst across the open area toward safety. When you exit the building, continue to leap frog from cover to cover to get yourself as far away from the building as possible. I remember being told of one business that had an Active Shooter Plan that included a rally point for everyone to convene in the middle of the parking lot. The location was in full view of anyone in the building. I don't think I have to explain why that wasn't well thought out. (I'm guessing it was copied and pasted from a fire evacuation plan.) In some terrorist events, the killers anticipate and expect fleeing victims to gather at common areas outside. These areas become planned secondary killing zones.

Movement Techniques

Sometimes dropping to the ground will be a better option than running. As I stated earlier, when bullets fly, some will hit the floor instinctively. This can be good to get you out of the line of fire, but you can't just cover your head and hope for the best. Remember, movement saves lives. Stay low and move toward cover or an exit as fast as you can. If you have to, use this time to determine where the shooter is and the safest direction to move. Once you've made this determination, get moving.

Another benefit of staying low is that shooters will often shoot at shoulder height. Staying low keeps you below the main stream of fire. He will have to adjust his aim to shoot at a lower target, and any change to his plan messes with his OODA Loop and can buy precious seconds for you to get further away.

During basic training in the Army, we learned to low crawl and high crawl. In sniper school, we did more of the same (see side box Crawling the Army Way). Low crawling involves pushing with your toes and pulling with your fingers. It keeps you the lowest to the ground, but it is also slower. The high crawl is faster, but you aren't as low to the ground, thus possibly being more of a target.

I recommend practicing both the low and high crawl so you know you can do them if you have to move toward cover or an exit while keeping yourself low to the ground and less of a target. If for some reason you can't perform either of these, it's good to know. You should then think about what you would do if faced with such a situation and plan accordingly.

Crawling the Army Way

While you won't be crawling with a sniper rifle, the descriptions from the Department of the Army Training Circular No. 23-14 Sniper Training and Employment provides guidance on the best way to crawl.

Crawling. There are times when it is necessary to move with the body close to the ground to avoid being seen. There are two ways to crawl, the low crawl and the high crawl. Use the method best suited to the situation, regarding visibility, cover and concealment available, and speed required.

Low crawl. The low crawl is used when cover and concealment are scarce, where visibility permits the enemy good observation, or when speed is not essential (fig. 90). The correct technique is to keep the body as flat as possible against the ground. The sniper grasps the rifle as indicated, pushes the arms forward, pulls the right leg forward, then moves with the pull of the arms and the push of the right leg. He may change the pushing leg frequently to avoid fatigue, being careful not to raise or lift any part of the body.

High crawl. The high crawl is used when cover and concealment are available, where visibility reduces enemy observation, or when more speed is required (fig. 91). Keep the body free of the ground and rest the weight on forearms and lower legs. Cradle the rifle in the arms, keeping the muzzle off the ground. Keep the knees well behind the buttocks and move forward by alternately advancing the right elbow and left knee, then the left elbow and right knee.

Low Crawl

High Crawl

Running Zig Zag vs. Straight

Many experts advocate running in a zigzag pattern when fleeing from a shooter. I've heard many state, "Don't run in a straight line." You will also hear that you should crouch down while running. The theory behind these statements is that a smaller target that is moving randomly will be more difficult to hit. In theory, this sounds good. I'll explain here why I believe "Don't run in a straight line" may be bad advice.

In the book *Staying Alive: How To Act Fast And Survive Deadly Encounters*, the authors discuss training people to run in a zigzag fashion while they are being shot at, and the troubles with this type of training. They reference a study by Ohio police officer and president of Active Response Training, Greg Ellifritz, whom I know through social media. So, I contacted Greg for his study. While not scientifically conducted, I think it does illustrate the concerns with trying to train people to run away in a zigzag fashion. This is especially alarming when the concept of running away in such a manner has not been proven to work in civilian arenas.

Ellifritz couldn't find any documented evidence to suggest that any one technique is better than any other when it comes to running away from a shooter. He concluded that the experts were just guessing. He then decided to conduct an experiment during an active shooter response class he was teaching at the Tactical Defense Institute. Using Simunitions weapons and the students as test subjects, he devised a test to see if there was any real difference between running in a straight line, running in a zigzag pattern, and running in a crouched position.

In Ellifritz's simulated active shooter event, he wanted the designated shooter to find his target and attempt to shoot it. The target (or runner) was randomly selected to either run in a straight line, run a zigzag pattern, or run in a crouch in order to get to cover. The runner had to traverse a distance of 30 feet and get behind cover to be "safe." Ellifritz ran 34 separate tests, evenly split between each of the running options.

There wasn't much difference in hit rates between the running methods. Regardless of the running method, people were shot 52% - 55% of the time. However, the straight-line run resulted in the fewest percentage of hits, and even more importantly, it also resulted in the fewest number of shots fired. In three of the test runs (25%) the shooters were unable to fire a second round due to the speed of the runners. Less rounds fired is likely to improve the chances of a successful escape.

The crouch position resulted in both the highest percentage of total hits as well as the highest percentage of center mass/head hits. At least in this test, there didn't appear to be any benefit to running in a crouched position to escape a shooter.

While running in a zigzag pattern did not reduce the percentage of hits, it did reduce the chance that the runner would be hit in the torso or head. While hit rates were similar with all three methods, there were far more extremity hits with the zigzag groups. This could be good or bad depending if the person shot was a civilian or military/law enforcement with body armor. Ellifritz suggest that we need to provide different recommendations for different populations.

> "Don't zigzag; just run hard."
>
> *Loren Christensen*
> *Surviving a School Shooting*

Acknowledging that this was a small study with specific parameters, Ellifritz provides these five recommendations:

1. I don't think there is enough evidence in the superiority of running in a zigzag for wholesale recommendation. It does not reduce total numbers of hits, but may be enough to turn what would be a fatal wound into a less serious extremity hit in some instances.

2. Zigzag running should not be recommended for people who have knee problems or who are wearing body armor. I saw several people with knee issues fall down on their zigzag runs. Falling down would likely lead to the worst possible outcome and should be avoided at all costs. People who have knee trouble or who are wearing body armor should use straight line running.

3. The crouched running position should not be used while running in the open. It may be useful to crouch if that crouch keeps you behind cover. Otherwise, the crouch has no utility in this situation. One other note with regard to the crouched position...several of the hits were to the low back. They were angled in such a manner that they would have likely slid underneath any body armor the runner was wearing. Be cautious about bending over and exposing gaps in your ballistic coverage!

4. Speed is important. The faster that the victim can get to cover or out of the shooter's range, the safer he is likely to be. Anything that slows the runner down (zigzagging, crouching) will likely increase the chances of getting hit. In my observations, I noticed that the fastest runners got hit the fewest times. If you have sprinting ability or speed, it is likely best for you to run in a straight line towards cover.

5. For those people who can't run fast, zigzagging may be a better option. They are still likely to be hit, but those hits tend to be less damaging.

Ellifritz concludes that we trainers should not be providing advice that any one escape strategy is clearly superior to any other. I agree with him, with one caveat, I do believe for the largest population of people that running away in a straight line is generally a better option than zigzagging or crouching. If I waiver at all with this, I think crouching may reduce your size as a target, but only if you can crouch and maintain speed. If your crouch is so low it reduces the speed of your escape, it's too low.

Based on watching thousands of students run during active shooter response scenarios, most don't think of zigzagging or crouching, they just run. (This is even after being given the advice to zigzag, or after a discussion on zigzagging vs. running.) If a person isn't used to running, or a trained athlete, the potential to fall while attempting to zigzag is too great (just as Ellifritz saw in his tests). And yes, out of those thousands of students, I have seen many fall, even when trying to run away in a straight line. And for these reasons, in classes that I teach to the general public, I'll continue to teach people to run in a straight line. And I'm not the only one. Loren W. Christensen, retired Police Officer and author of over 50 books, recommends not zigzagging and just running hard. Arthur Cohen, author of *Surviving A Massacre, Rampage, Or Spree Killing*, says, "I often hear experts suggest running in a zigzag pattern to prevent the shooter from getting a good shot. You had better be in good shape to do this because it requires a lot of energy. If you elect to run, select the quickest direction to get out of view." I'm sure there are many more who also advocate running away in a straight line as fast as you can, but you get the idea.

There is also another principle taught, and that is to run diagonally away from the shooter. This means if the shooter is facing twelve o'clock, you don't want to be running in the direction of twelve o'clock. The shooter will be able to hold his gun pointed at you while shooting. If you are running diagonally to twelve o'clock, such as toward ten o'clock or two o'clock, the shooter will have to track left or right with his gun while shooting, making it more difficult to hit you. You are still running in a straight line, but that line is diagonal to the twelve o'clock orientation of the shooter. This makes sense, but I don't want you stopping to try and figure out which direction is diagonal or not when seconds count. If you know, and can run diagonally, great. If you don't know, just get yourself out of the kill zone as fast as you possibly can.

Another strategy for certain situations is the leap-frog, or two-to-three-second, rule while fleeing. Run for short bursts between cover. You leap-frog from cover to cover to cover until you are out of the kill zone and somewhere safe. During the two-to-three-second sprint between objects of cover, the shooter will have more difficulty acquiring you as a target. Obviously, this is only practical if the environment provides cover to move from one location to another on the path toward safety.

Improvised Ballistic Shield

Unless you are a law enforcement officer, you probably don't wear ballistic armor during the day. Nor do you dress your kids in it when sending them off to school. You do, however, send them off with an item that could be used as a ballistic shield, and you may carry one yourself. Backpacks and different bags can offer some protection, especially against smaller firearms. A backpack filled with textbooks, folders, notebooks, etc. may stop bullets and protect vital organs. If running away from the shooter, the backpack on a person's back protects the torso from shots from behind, and if a person hugs the backpack in front of them it can help protect vital organs from the front.

Commercially Manufactured Ballistic Armor and Shields

There are now a number of commercially manufactured products on the market offered as solutions to active shooter incidents. These include removable ballistic shield inserts and panels that can be inserted into backpacks, briefcases, or computer bags; and backpacks and bags themselves that are made with bulletproof materials to stop bullets from different caliber weapons. Other products include: a wide range of bulletproof clothing, preacher lecterns, 5-gallon buckets, chair backs, tablet cases, briefcases, laptop cases, shields, roller bags, and even carry-on bags for traveling.

These products don't negate the strategies, tactics, and planning this book suggests, and they certainly don't replace the plans and drills schools and businesses should incorporate into their emergency planning. However, they may give people a greater peace of mind, and there is a benefit to that, even if some experts say these items are unlikely to be the difference between life and death.

I personally feel these products can be an extra layer in your personal security layers. You must recognize their strengths and weaknesses and weigh their benefits with your budget and how you will use them. But don't be like the young lady in one of my university safety presentations. She told me she didn't need the awareness information I was teaching because she had mace in her purse. Ballistic armor and shields are just one small piece of the whole.

Cover vs. Concealment

Cover and concealment are military terms that everyone should be aware of when it comes to surviving a shooting. These concepts are not one and the same. It is important to know the difference and how to use them. In the simplest terms, cover will stop bullets and concealment may hide you, but won't stop bullets. For example, a concrete wall can provide both cover and concealment.

You can hide behind it, and bullets won't go through it. If you are in the mall, you can hide behind a rack of clothes, which provides you concealment. However, the clothes are not cover because you can still be shot through them. Again, concealment provides visual deception but not ballistic protection, while cover provides protection from gunfire as well as possible concealment.

Materials such as steel, concrete, water, packed earth, and thick wood can all make good resources for cover. Examples of possible cover:

Examples of Cover

- Cement walls
- Car or truck engine block
- Heavy machinery
- Solid metal or wood doors
- Heavy cabinets
- Heavy metal desks
- Freezer or Refrigerator
- Copy machine
- Large Trees
- Telephone pole
- Books or large reams of paper
- A solid concrete pillar
- A stone statue
- A safe
- Sandbags

It is important to note that effective cover may depend on what the bad guy is shooting. Materials that will stop a 9mm or other pistol round may not stop a bullet from a rifle, a shotgun slug, or buckshot.

Things like foliage, netting, shadows, fabric, and non-reflective surfaces can all make good concealment. Examples of possible concealment:

Examples of Concealment

- Hollow walls
- Hollow doors
- Car doors
- Sheetrock walls
- Plywood desks
- Fabric cube walls
- Empty boxes
- Painted or shaded windows
- Window blinds
- Curtains or drapery
- Clothes rack
- Portable partitions
- Podiums
- Wooden fence
- A thick bush
- A decorative hollow pillar
- A plaster statue
- Fog from fire extinguisher

I know that I stress that movement saves lives, but when it comes to concealment, not moving is a form of concealment because motion is noticed more than anything else. This is a concept that was stressed in sniper school, and the combination of good camouflage and not moving were extremely important to sniper missions. Darkness also aids in concealment if your attacker doesn't have night vision capabilities. When effective cover is absent, concealment may be all we can obtain. If the shooter doesn't see us, it may provide us time to better our position and prepare to escape or take offensive action.

Some types of cover may cause bullets to ricochet. These bullets tend to ricochet on a path approximately parallel to, and a few inches out from, the surface they've hit. This is the reason operators don't hug corridor walls when clearing hallways. Ricochet bullets can travel along the wall. For most people reading this book, just knowing what cover is and being able to find it quickly in an emergency will be satisfactory to save lives.

Cover and concealment are both important, and they both can aid you in surviving. Take advantage of both and use them together. But if you have a choice, always go for cover which provides you with more protection. Make it a habit of recognizing potential cover when you are out-and-about. Knowing where the exits are and what will provide cover will provide you direction when you have to move and get off the X. Going toward cover and exits increases your chances of surviving a shooting.

This table does not provide cover or concealment from an active killer

U.S. Army Sniper Training Manual TC 23-14
Cover vs. Concealment

This is the introduction I had to cover and concealment when I was going through the 2nd Infantry Division Scout Sniper School. Both were expanded upon out in the field. And just as they were important to military snipers, the concepts are important to anyone caught in a shooting. This is how the U.S. Army defines the terms in the U.S. Army Sniper Training Manual (TC 23-14):

26. Cover and Concealment. The proper understanding and application of the principles of cover and concealment, in conjunction with the proper application of camouflage, will provide protection from enemy observation.

a. **Cover** is protection from the fire of enemy weapons. It may be natural or artificial. Natural cover (ravines, hollows, reverse slopes) and artificial cover (foxholes, trenches, walls) protect the sniper from flat trajectory fires and the effects of nuclear explosions. Even the smallest depression or fold in the ground may provide some cover when he needs it most. Properly used, a 15-centimeter (6-inch) depression may provide enough cover to save his life under fire. Form the habit of looking for, and taking advantage of, every bit of cover the terrain offers. Combine this habit with proper use of the movement techniques explained in paragraph 27 and the sniper can provide himself with excellent protection from enemy fire.

b. **Concealment** is protection from enemy observation. It, too, may be natural or artificial. Remember that concealment is *not* protection from enemy fire.

Escaping When in a Crowd

Bullets are not the only danger during a mass shooting. During the terror of such an incident, people will often stampede and the potential to be injured or killed by being suffocated or trampled is just as real as being injured or killed by bullets. People have been suffocated or trampled to death at concerts, sporting events, and even Black Friday sales after Thanksgiving.

Panicked crowds present a real danger. It may be a shooter, a fire, or no real danger at all that triggers a human stampede. Regardless of the trigger, a moving panicked crowd can be hard to stop and very dangerous. People are killed when trampled, and others can be killed when standing because of the pressure applied to their bodies that makes it so they can't breathe. (This is usually a front back pressure, as pressure from the sides doesn't constrict breathing the same as pressure applied from the front and back.)

Here is a list of important considerations when escaping when in a crowd:

1. Know your exits. Remember this from the earlier chapter? It's important enough to bear repeating. You always want to know your ways out and have an exit strategy in mind when you are at an event. Most people will go toward the entrance/exit they came in, so knowing alternate exits enables you to avoid bottlenecks and get out through an exit not being used. Main exits often become bottlenecked and gridlocked, so if you can't be one of the first out of the main exit, a secondary exit may be the best strategy. Positioning yourself close to escape routes makes it easier to escape in an emergency.

2. Know the terrain. Uneven or slippery surfaces can cause you to fall, especially when being shoved by a crowd. You don't want to be on the floor where you can be trampled.

3. Go sideways with the crowd if you can get out of the crowd and to an exit. However, if the crowd is too much, don't fight against the pressure. It will be too great. Establish a good stance and try to weave your way through the crowd. Zig-zag through people diagonally toward safety.

4. Keep your hands and arms in front of you like a boxer. This protects your chest and can prevent being suffocated. The danger of dying of suffocation by being squeezed together too tightly to breathe is real, and why you should work toward getting out of the crowd and not squeezed in the middle or crushed against a wall or immovable object. Keeping your hands and arms up in front of you will also help you keep your balance as you are being jostled by the crowd as you work your way through it.

5. Remain on your feet. Yes, this might be easier said than done, but it is vitally important you stay on your feet, and if you do fall onto the ground that you get back up as quickly as you can. Pick up children, and if someone with you falls help them back up quickly. Make sure they know to help you back up if you are the one who gets knocked down. You must avoid the danger of being trampled. If you can, help anyone who falls back up. Keeping everyone standing increases the odds you all make it to the exit without people being trampled.

6. If you fall, and for some reason cannot get back up, you must protect yourself. If you can, crawl in the same direction as the crowd is moving to keep from being trampled. Always be looking for an opportunity to get back to your feet. If there is something to crawl under to keep you from being trampled, take advantage of it. If these options are not possible, curl into the fetal position and cover your head with your arms. You must protect your head and your body. When an opportunity arises for you to get up and escape, do so.

Separate Yourself from the Crowd

Besides reducing the likelihood of being trampled or smashed in a bottlenecked crowd, separating yourself from the masses and putting distance between yourself and the group may have additional benefits toward your survival. It only makes sense if there are hundreds of people grouped together, and a murderer is intent on killing a lot of people and achieving the highest body count possible, he will be shooting at the group. If you can separate yourself from the crowd as you make your escape, you become less likely to become a random victim.

Should You Pull the Fire Alarm?

> “Don't pull the fire alarm if you are in a building with an active killer. You may have the best intentions, but pulling the alarm will ultimately lead to more fatalities.”
>
> *Greg Ellifritz*

We are often asked by students if they should pull the fire alarm during a shooting incident to warn others to escape the building. It would be easy enough when running out to pull the alarm and get others escaping too. While this seems reasonable, it might not be the best option.

In a short blog article, Greg Ellifritz outlined several reasons why you shouldn't pull the fire alarm during an active shooter incident. When the fire alarm is pulled, people think and move differently than they do if they know someone is shooting at them. People's thoughts turn to annoyance that there is a fire drill or wondering why they must exit while trying to determine if it's false alarm or was pulled by some mischievous kids. And ambling out of the facility via the closest exit may not get you to safety.

Ellifritz states, "When escaping an active killer, we want potential victims to get outside via the closest door that takes them AWAY from the shooter. As they move to that exit, they should be making short sprints between places of cover along their path of exit. They should be looking around and be ready to stop moving and get behind something that stops bullets as soon as they see the shooter. The normal, lackadaisical ambling toward the exits during a fire alarm is exactly the type of movement we want to avoid in an active killer event."

Additionally, pulling the fire alarm can also create more chaos for the first responders. This could cause longer rescue times. The chaos is caused at the dispatch center as well as on scene making it harder for police officers to communicate via their radios.

With all of this said, the fire alarms may go off anyway. The shooter may pull the fire alarms to get people into the hallways to be easier targets. (This is why I recommend looking before leaving, and not just ambling out into the hallway because of another fire drill.) A shooter's gunfire may also set off the fire alarm. The percussion can cause dust particles to activate alarms, and this is one of the reasons we turn off the fire alarms in the buildings we shoot blanks in for our scenario training. (Again, this is a reason you should check before leaving your room when a fire alarm sounds.)

So, besides answering the question of whether you should pull the fire alarm during an active shooter incident (you shouldn't), I hope this also gets you to think about how you are exiting buildings when a fire alarm does go off.

> “Don’t sound the fire alarm, because it could place workers in harm’s way as they try to leave the building unaware of the true nature of the threat. They will be looking for smoke and flame rather than a homicidal gunman.”
>
> Loren W. Christensen
> *Surviving Workplace Violence: What to Do Before a Violent Incident, What to Do When the Violence Explodes*

Conclusion

Escaping to safety is the best way to ensure your survival in an active threat. The information, strategies, and tactics provided in this chapter will best aid you in achieving safety when the opportunity and avenue of escape present themselves. When you have that opportunity and avenue, get yourself to safety. But don’t forget to always be prepared to stop and deny the shooter access to you, or attack back and take the shooter out, if circumstances change.

7 Deny Access

www.SurviveaShooting.com

Given the option, the killer will follow the path of least resistance.

Chris Bird
Surviving a Mass Killer Rampage: When Seconds Count, Police Are Still Minutes Away

TOPICS

- ✓ Locking Doors
- ✓ Commercial Lock Down Devices
- ✓ Improvised Lock Down Measures
- ✓ Barricading
- ✓ What to Do After You Lock and Barricade

The quote above, from Chris Bird's *Surviving a Mass Killer Rampage,* is the key to the "deny access" strategy. Active killers will follow the path of least resistance to amass the greatest body count possible within their limited amount of time. For example, the killer at Sandy Hook walked past two closed doors that had construction paper over the windows. Every minute we can deny a killer access to us, is one-minute closer to the incident being stopped by

someone attacking back and putting the killer down, preferably by trained law enforcement.

While this might sound like I'm advising you to give up personal responsibility and wait for the police to save you, after I've already stated that when seconds count the police are minutes away, giving up personal responsibility is not what I'm recommending. Let me explain. Denying the killer access to you, by locking and barricading him out, is a proactive means to keep yourself and others with you alive. It's not just "hiding and hoping," but rather choosing the survival strategy that is best for your situation and circumstances. Surviving a shooting does not mean you have to be the one to stop the shooter and eliminate the threat. This strategy has saved people's lives and it should be part of your survival plan.

There are different ways to deny a shooter access to you and keep them out. People say hide, which I've already explained I don't like, but is saying "lock" or "barricade" much better? Yes, it is better and in this chapter, we will look at the different ways to lockdown, barricade, and deny a shooter access to you.

In the previous chapter, we looked at escaping and cover and concealment. Escaping the danger zone is one way of denying the killer access to harm you. Putting cover between you and the gunman is also denying him the means of shooting you. But for this chapter, we are more concerned with when you are in a room or space that can be locked down to keep the killer out.

The information in this chapter is designed with one purpose, and that is to help you lock down and deny the shooter access to your location to keep you safe when the opportunity to deny is available and escaping isn't.

> “Whether you're using a slingshot or an assault rifle, you can only shoot what you can see and have access to.”
>
> *Chris Sutton & John Graden*
> *The Cobra-Defense Active Shooter Response Plan*

Lock Doors

This seems simple enough, but is it? Different doors and various locking mechanisms can make it extremely difficult to lock down in a time of stress. Here are two problems that most often arise:

- You have to go into the hallway to lock the door from the outside.
- You must use the key to lock the door.

Often both of these factors are present in the same door. The first issue is obvious when you think about it. Going into the hallway when gunfire has been heard may not only be dangerous, but suicidal. This was one of the factors listed in the lawsuit after the Sandy Hook shooting. The teachers there had to go into the hallway, exposing them to danger, to lock the doors.

Using a key is not so obvious. Many teachers found out during the scenario training of the Armed Intruder course that it is not so easy to put that small key into the small key hole when under the stress of gunfire. And that was in training! A real situation would be worse. We saw in the chapter discussing what happens under stress where fine motor skills deteriorate, and locking a door with a key is a fine motor skill.

One solution, if changing the locking mechanism is not an option due to financial or other reasons, is to pre-lock the door. Keep the door locked, but open slightly, at all times. In an emergency, where you need to lock down, a simple push or pull on the door will close it and it will be locked. This is probably the simplest and most practical solution for most people. The key is to get into the habit of doing it. And don't quit doing it when it becomes a nuisance when you have to get up and open the door for someone because the wind blew it closed and locked someone out. This simple tactic of keeping doors locked while you are inside increases survivability.

I'd like to see doors made with simple deadbolts that just have a handle to slide over and engage the dead bolt: shut the door and slap the handle over to lock it; simple, fast, and can be done under stress. Until they are made this way, we have to work with what we have, and keeping the door locked so all you have to do is close the door is one of the simplest ways for most people.

Locking the door may not be enough for your peace of mind if a killer is in the hall, or to actually keep him out. Depending on the door, the lock, and the door frame, some locked doors can easily be bypassed. An active threat may just break the lock, or he may push or kick the door in. ALICE Instructor Kenny Mayberry, a lieutenant with Southeast Missouri State University Police Department, was quoted in *Surviving a Mass Killer Rampage*: "'Don't rely on the lock,' he said and gave an example. A fourteen-year-old middle-school student armed with a gun broke into three classrooms, smashing the glass of the locked doors to get inside. He ran out of a back door before being apprehended without further incident. Just because the door's locked doesn't mean he can't get in."

Besides locking the door, commercial or improvised locking devices can be utilized as well as barricading methods. These will differ depending on if the door opens into the room you are in or out into the hallway. The key is to fortify the door with whatever you have available to keep the threat outside.

Commercial Lockdown Devices

In recent years, there have been a number of commercially made lock down devices that can be purchased and used to more effectively secure a closed door. There are designs for open-in and open-out doors, as well as devices that go over the hydraulic door closers on the top of many doors. However, one manufacturer, Strategos International, that makes the Barracuda Lock Down Devices and the Guardian Angel Lock Down Device, states about their product for over the door closer, "The DCS 'Door Closer' lockdown device is designed to be used in conjunction with the OPEN OUT or OPEN IN Barracuda lockdown device to provide an additional level of security. Due to the wide variety and inconsistency of door closers and their fasteners, it IS NOT recommended to use the DCS as a standalone solution."

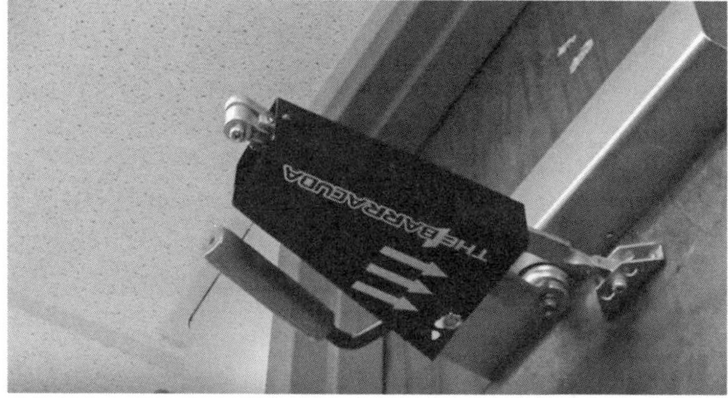

DCS Barracuda Door Closing System

Barracuda Door Lock for Outward Opening Doors

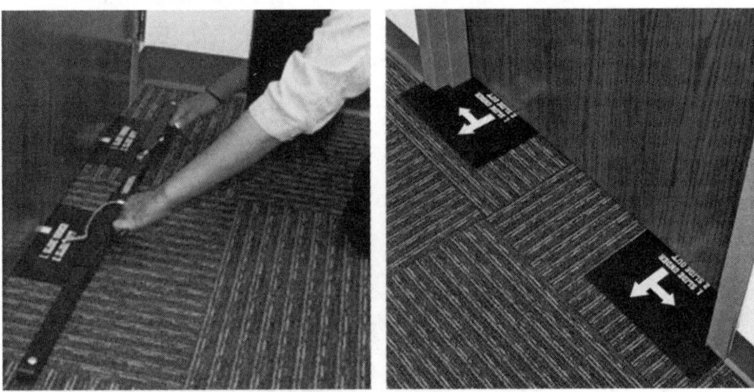

Barracuda Guardia Angel Lockdown Device

The difficulty with some of these commercially made lock down devices is the cost. Financial limitations of many security budgets prohibit organizations from purchasing such devices for widespread use. This is often the case with security measures, including training employees in how to respond to active threats and other emergencies. Organizations don't want to prioritize money for such devices and training. It is very sad that security budgets are often so underfunded. (That's for organizations that even have a security budget. It is extremely sad that some places don't have a budget for security measures at all.)

I believe in the future we will see more buildings being constructed with security measures to provide for quicker and easier lockdowns. (As I've said before, I'd also like to see infrastructure with more doors and exits to improve safety by providing avenues of escape.) Until then, some of these commercially made lock down devices provide an option to better lock down and secure doors, thus effectively denying active killers access to the people inside.

Improvised Lockdown Measures

There are less expensive ways, and improvised lock down measures, to better secure doors from being opened than simple locks alone. There are items that can help with both open-in and open-out doors. Here are a few of the ways I like to show and have people try out and practice in classes:

Door Stops: Door stops are simple, inexpensive, and effective. There are a variety on the market to choose from, and the important thing is to choose one that fits and works with your door. The gap between the door and the floor can vary considerably, even in the same building. And the floor surface can make a difference as well. Door stops range from the simple wooden and rubber varieties to the more expensive Tac-Wedge type used for law enforcement that will damage the floor when used, but definitely stop a door from budging.

The Tac-Wedge Door Jammer (left) and a Typical Rubber Door Stopper

Securing hydraulic door closers. Just like there are commercially manufactured devices to slip over the hydraulic door closers, you can tie the two arms together so it can't be opened, or only opened a small crack. You can use a belt, cord from an electrical appliance, or anything else available to tie around the closer to keep the door shut.

Securing a Door with a Belt

Tie-down for door handle. There are a number of ways to do this. You can pre-install an eye bolt next to the door and have a cable and carabiner clip ready to slip over the handle and snap the carabiner clip to the eye-bolt, thus securing the door. (Be sure to use quality materials, not the cheap keychain type carabiner clips.) This is especially good for open-out doors that you can't secure by barricading. If you don't have this pre-installed locking mechanism, you can improvise. Wrapping an extension cord around the door handle and securing it to an immovable object can keep the door from opening. I also like the tie-down straps you can get inexpensively from hardware stores. Loop around the door handle and secure the other end to something that won't give and cinch it tight. I have one of these I teach classes with and it works like a charm as long as there is something to attach it to. And if I worked in a room or office that didn't have a way to lock down and secure a door, I'd take time to make changes so it could.

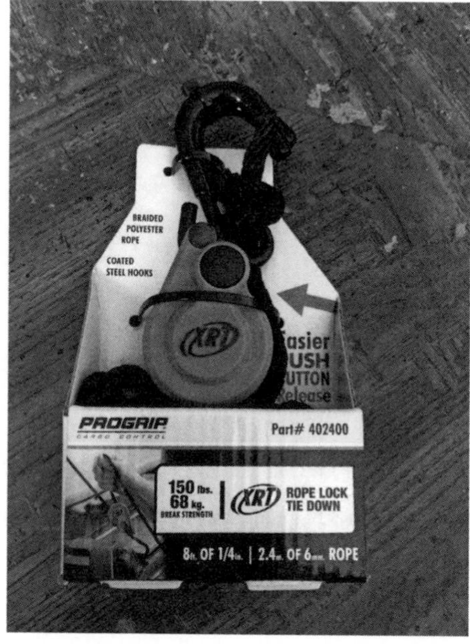

Commercial Tie Down for Securing a Door

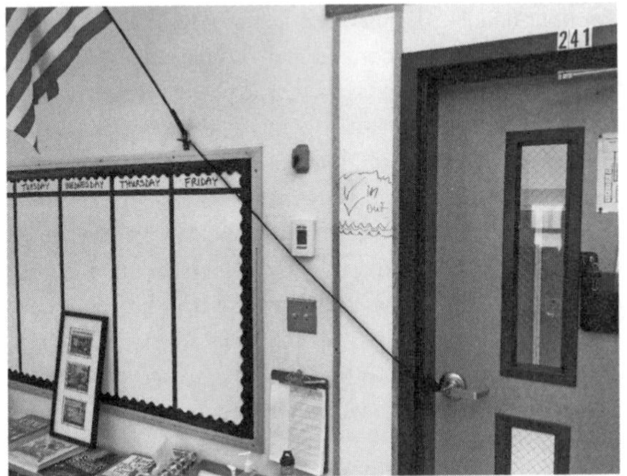

Securing a Door Handle with a Tie Down

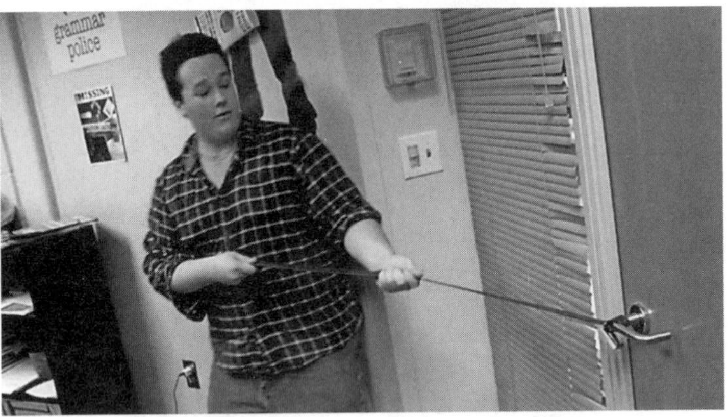

Securing a door with a belt (also: extension cord, or rope)

Barricading

Barricading is simply moving objects in front of a door to prevent the door from opening, or to prevent someone from entering the room, even if the door does open. This section will provide a few tips to help you barricade successfully.

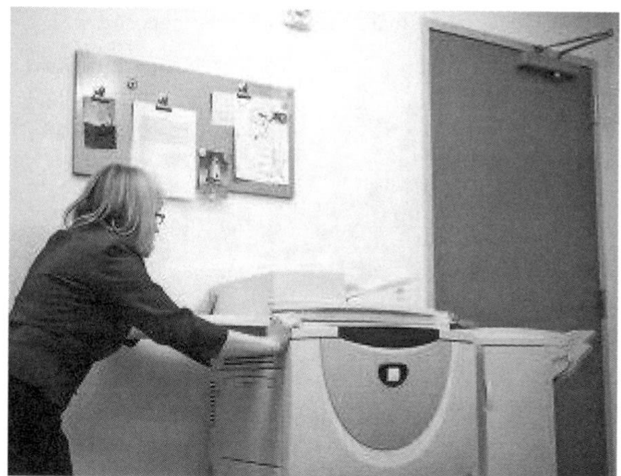

Barricading a door with a copy machine

Open-in vs. Open-out Doors

Barricading is primarily used to prevent open-in doors from opening. This is especially true if you are using yourself as part of the barricade. However, barricading can sometimes be used for open-out doors if you have the right barricading materials. If an intruder opens the open-out door and is left facing a large cabinet or an upturned table blocking the entrance, it may be enough to make him move on and look for easier targets. Even a large pile of desks, chairs, and other items that the killer would have to climb over, or through, may be enough to make him look elsewhere. So, don't discount barricading as a successful tactic to deny entry to a room with an open-out door.

Immovable Objects

The most secure barricade will be one with immovable objects. There are a couple of ways to achieve this. One, you can move something extremely heavy in front of the door that the bad guy can't move when pushing from the other side. Unless you are stronger than average, this may be difficult to do when alone. A team of people may be able to move a heavy object that wouldn't be pushed from the outside.

Another way to create immovable objects is to stack them up to something that is immovable. For instance, a desk and a table may be placed between a door and the opposite wall so that when you try to push open the door, it goes against the desk, that pushes the table, that is up against the opposite wall, creating an immovable barricade.

Barricading a Door with Desks and Tables

When there are no objects to be used, or not enough, you can make an immovable barricade with people by laying on the ground with your feet against the door, and then having the next person lay down with their feet on the first person's shoulders and create a chain to the opposite wall. I have also taught students how to do this in a bathroom by taking a garbage can and laying it against a closed door, and then laying down with feet against the can and reaching the other wall to create an immovable barricade. Sometimes you just have to think creatively.

This technique saved lives during the Virginia Tech shooting. The students in room 205 pushed a teacher's desk against the door, and then lay on the floor, holding the barricade in place with their hands grasping the bottoms of the desk legs and their toes dug into the carpet to keep from being pushed backward. Cho was unable to enter the room as he couldn't shove the barricade aside to open the door. Frustrated, he did shoot two rounds through the door before moving on. The rounds were shot high and no one was shot in room 205. This is the only room where everyone emerged unscathed.

This is important to note. Very few active shooters have shot through doors that have been barricaded. Cho shot through the door of room 205 because he was frustrated that he couldn't get in and knew there were students inside. But by being low, no one was shot.

Unfortunately, in room 204, Prof. Liviu Librescu was holding the door shut by pressing the door with his hands and body. Frustrated with another door he couldn't open, Cho shot through this door as well. He then hit the door hard and Librescu was overpowered and knocked to the floor. Investigations revealed the Librescu was probably hit by one of the bullets that went through the door. That's probably why Cho was then able to force the door open. Prof. Librescu is a hero. While he was keeping Cho outside, he directed his students to escape out the window. Almost all of them escaped. Cho killed the professor, and one other student in room 204, and shot and injured two others in the room. Ten students made it out the window while the professor was holding the door closed. Even though Prof. Librescu's barricading attempt with his body wasn't fully successful, he saved the lives of his students and can be considered a hero due to his barricading attempt.

Analyzing the different methods used in rooms 204 and 205 reveal the better way to barricade a door, especially if using your body. Stay low and preferably stack things to increase the strength of your barricade. Stacking all the way to an immovable object will be best.

Using bodies to barricade a door

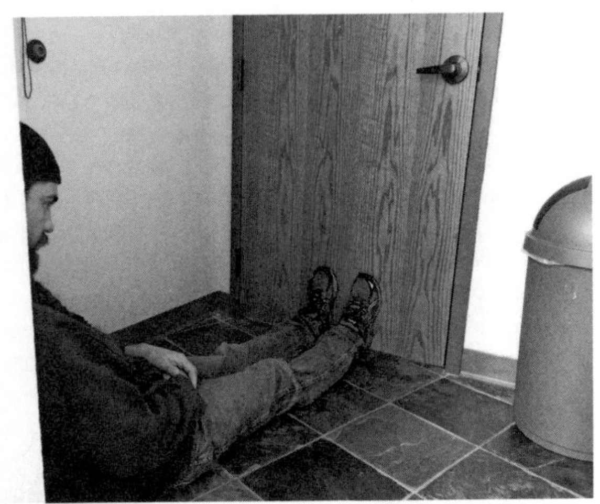

Using your body to barricade a door

Using a table to cover a window in a door

What to Do After You Lock and Barricade

Shots were fired in the hall. The door was already locked and you pulled it closed. You then kicked the door wedge under the door and pushed a cabinet in front of it. Then you slid a table between the cabinet and the immovable bookcase creating an immovable barricade. Now what?

Hiding and hoping is NOT a plan!

Do NOT go hide and hope for a good outcome under a table or desk in the back corner! We must always be bettering our position and thinking about how we can escape, deny, or attack back. After locking and barricading a door, there are many things left to do. Here is a list of things to do, in no particular order, that will vary depending on your location and the inhabitants of the room.

- Check other doors. Can you escape to safety through them? If yes, do so. If you can't escape, lock and barricade these as well.
- Turn off lights. If the room appears unoccupied and doesn't attract attention, the killer may bypass it looking for more noticeable targets.
- Pull blinds and/or cover door windows. For the same reason as we turn off the lights. If the killer can't see inside, he may bypass the room to look for other targets.
- Escape out windows if possible.
- Silence cell phones and be quiet. If the shooter doesn't know you are in the room, you don't want to alert him to you by making unnecessary noise. Gain control of your breathing. Breathing gently through an open mouth is quieter than breathing through the nose. (Yes, I realize the initial

barricading by moving furniture, etc. will be chaotic and noisy, but once this is accomplished, remain as quiet as you can.)

- Call 911 if you can do so quietly and safely.
- Prepare to attack back if your barricade is breached. Arm yourself with any weapons or improvised weapons available. Stack beside the door to ambush the killer coming into the room. Put those who can't attack back, such as young children, in the safest area of the room, behind cover and out of the fatal funnel. (The "fatal funnel" will be explained later in this book.)
- Administer first aid or trauma aid to any injured persons. This could be someone who was shot in the hall and ran inside before you barricaded, or someone who was injured during the barricading process.
- I do not advise leaving a "safe" area to go track down the killer and take him out. Once barricaded and "safe," only leave if you can escape to safety or when the threat has been neutralized and law enforcement advises you it is clear and safe to come out.
- Be alert and continue to be proactive to ensure your survival.

Conclusion

Denying the shooter access to you is a successful strategy for surviving an active shooter event. The strategy works for many kinds of threats. If the shooter comes to a locked door at a room that appears empty, he will most likely move on to find easy targets. If the room is locked and barricaded (with commercial or improvised lock down devices or measures), and the shooter can't get in, you will remain safe as he moves on for easier targets. Regardless of how you deny the killer access to you, continue to think of ways to better your position. If you can safely escape, do so. If not, prepare to attack back if your lock or barricade is breached. The "deny access" strategy has saved people in these situations, and it will save others in the future.

8 Attack Back

www.SurviveaShooting.com

Violence is rarely the answer, but when it is, it's the only answer.

Tim Larkin
When Violence is the Answer: Learning How to do What it Takes When Your Life is at Stake

TOPICS

- ✓ Legalities of Attacking Back
- ✓ Attack Back Attitude
- ✓ Armed and Unarmed Resistance
- ✓ Armed Resistance
    - ✓ Armed Resistance Tactics and Considerations
- ✓ Unarmed Resistance
    - ✓ Arming Yourself with Improvised Weapons
    - ✓ Firearm Familiarization
    - ✓ When and How to Attack Back
    - ✓ Gun Disarms
- ✓ Defending Against an Edged-Weapon Assault

The only way to stop a determined killer you cannot escape from, or deny him access to you, is with offensive techniques that disable his willingness and ability to continue with his attack. As I explained earlier, that is why I use the term "Attack Back" rather than anything with the terms "defense" or "fighting." You must attack back with offensive techniques to stop the aggressor.

Offensive techniques include punching, kicking, shoving, tackling, tripping, throwing, and anything else you can do to put the aggressor on the defensive and stop him from continuing his attack or rampage. When weapons are used, the same thing applies. You do not brandish your weapon in these situations and attempt to negotiate or reason with someone killing people. You use your weapon offensively to do whatever it takes to stop the threat, and that includes killing him. When using a firearm offensively, we don't "shoot the gun out of his hand" or any of that other Hollywood nonsense. You shoot to kill. Regardless if you tackle the shooter and pound his head against the floor, hit him in the head with a fire extinguisher, drive your pen into his eye, or shoot him center mass, your thought is the same: stop the threat from hurting or killing you or anyone else.

When attacking back, you don't stop until he is incapacitated enough that you can safely escape. There's no going half-way. You must be totally committed and use techniques that are lethal or at least severely disabling. If armed, you shoot to kill. If unarmed, or using improvised weapons, aim for vital points such as eyes, ears, and throat. Use all your strength, all your will, all your determination, and anything you can use to assist you as a weapon. Make everything count.

> "Our Police do what they can, but they can't protect us everywhere and all the time. All too often they cannot even protect themselves. Your physical safety is up to you, as it really always has been."
>
> *Jeff Cooper*
> *Principles of Personal Defense*

Angela McQueen: Hero Teacher, Takes Down Gunman at Illinois High School

Angela McQueen, a teacher, took down a gunman inside Mattoon High School, an Illinois high school, after he opened fire in the school's cafeteria on Wednesday, September 20, 2017, at about 11:30 a.m. Police say Angela McQueen's quick response saved lives. A 16-year-old student was shot and later released from the hospital, and the suspect, who the police said was a student, was arrested and placed in custody. The shooter, whose identity was being withheld since he is a minor, acted alone.

According to a CBS This Morning report, investigators were working through about 200 interviews to figure out the gunman's motive and how he obtained his weapon, but police were already pointing to the incident as an example of the value of preparing teachers to respond to active shooters.

According to witnesses, veteran math and P.E. teacher Angela McQueen grabbed the shooter's arm and subdued him after he opened fire in Mattoon High School's cafeteria.

CBS also reported: McQueen and hundreds of students were in the school cafeteria Wednesday when the student began firing. One boy was struck in the hand and chest. He's now in good condition and his mother posted on Facebook that her family was, "very blessed it's not worse." She described McQueen lunging for the shooter's arm, forcing it upward. "He fired 5-6 more rounds into the ceiling as she took him down," she wrote.

"When she saw the situation and, you know, 'Okay, this kid's going to kill somebody if I don't do something,' she just took action,'" said Angela's mother, Barbara McQueen.

This is just one more example illustrating that people don't have to be victims! Ordinary citizens, unarmed, have and will continue to stop these violent acts. No, facing a gunman unarmed is not an ideal situation, but nothing about an active shooter is ideal. It's scary. Terrifying. And something I wish would never happen again. But you can do something to prepare. It's reported that Mattoon High School employees had gone through some active shooter response training. Angela McQueen did what she learned and stopped the shooter. Another hero from the education system.

Make no mistake about this, I'm not saying attacking an armed person empty handed is easy. Nor am I guaranteeing the strategies and tactics in this book will prevent EVERYONE from dying. I can't do that. No one can. In an actual situation, you will be terrified. All those things discussed in the chapter about fear (your mind, adrenaline, and mindset) will come into play. But if you can't escape or deny the killer access to you, the only choice you have left is to attack back and take him out.

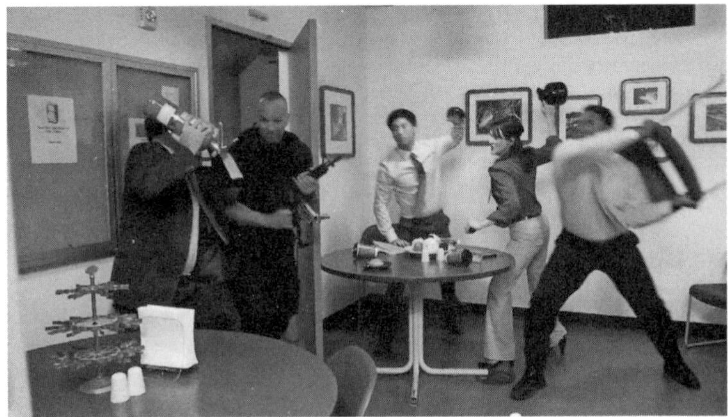

Surrendering and dying are not choices in my book. Not when you are a survivor. We must also acknowledge that attacking back, even if we are killed, may be the difference that saves other lives. The heroes on United Airlines Flight 93 on September 11, 2001, illustrated this. They attacked back. And even though they lost their lives heroically, they saved many others by preventing the terrorists from completing their mission of crashing the plane into the capitol building, which would have killed who knows how many more innocent people.

The purpose of this chapter isn't to turn you into a Ninja, or even to make you a competent martial artist or fighter. It will provide a few simple ideas that will help you attack back, and hopefully encourage you to seek out even more knowledge and training on the topic. Attacking back is the way to survive and save others when no other options are available.

Legalities of Attacking Back

Any time you hurt or kill another human being, you must be justified to use the force you used or you risk being prosecuted in a court of law. And while taking out an active shooter seems like it would obviously fall under the justified category, I still wanted to provide a little information on the legalities involved. I highly encourage you to find out more regarding the self-defense laws of your jurisdiction, especially if you carry a firearm for self-defense.

> **Are You A Warrior Or A Sheep?**
>
> By their very nature, people fall into either the warrior or sheep category, according to Lt. Col. David Grossman, the director of the Warrior Science Group and the author of the seminal book *On Killing*. Being a warrior allows you some options that won't even occur to "sheep." Sheep will inherently select running away, hiding, freezing, or avoiding direct contact with a shooter, whereas warriors might decide to physically engage the shooter if the opportunity presents itself. I believe the stress of the situation or the need to protect one's family and loved ones might bring out the "latent" warrior in some people.
>
> \- Arthur Cohen
> *Surviving A Massacre, Rampage, Or Spree Killing*

You are allowed to defend yourself if you are in imminent danger. The AOJ Triad is often used to determine this. AOJ stands for Ability, Opportunity, and Jeopardy.

Ability means that the attacker has both the physical as well as practical ability to kill or maim you.

Opportunity means your life and well-being are in clear and present danger because your attacker has the immediate opportunity to harm you.

Jeopardy or immediate jeopardy relates to a reasonable person in a similar situation should feel in fear for his or her life. It distinguishes between a truly dangerous situation and a potentially dangerous one.

A person actively hurting and killing others, which is the definition of an active threat, would meet this criteria for being imminent, and you would be justified in using the amount of force necessary to prevent him from continuing to hurt and kill people, including lethal force. (Sometimes you will find AOJP. The P stands for preclusion and is more relevant in areas where there is a duty to retreat. If you can run away from harm's way without further endangering yourself, the criteria of preclusion has not been met.)

> "No half-measures are possible when dealing with a firearm. If you do attack an armed opponent and later discover that his weapon was not loaded, or was a replica, you will not have acted unlawfully. So long as you believed the weapon was real at the time, virtually any action you could take would be lawful."
>
> *Martin J. Dougherty*
> *Special Forces Unarmed Combat Guide*

One thing people must remember though, is that once a person is no longer a threat, you must stop. I am often asked in my classes if you can shoot the person with their gun after you take it away. The answer is always, "it depends." If the person still meets the AOJ criteria for being an imminent threat, you may be justified in shooting and killing him. An example would be if you took his gun and he drew a second firearm and was about to shoot and kill you with it. Shooting him with his gun to prevent him from killing you would be justified. If, however, he is on the ground subdued and being held there by your co-workers after you took his gun, he would not meet the criteria, and you would not be justified in shooting him because of what he had previously done. You are allowed to defend yourself. You are not allowed to take revenge on a person or punish them. I recommend you read *The Law Of Self-Defense: The Indispensable Guide for the Armed Citizen* by Andrew F. Branca for a detailed look at this subject.

Attack Back Attitude

> "Skill and ability aside, there is a great deal of evidence to suggest that the attitude of the person under attack has an overwhelming impact on the outcome of the battle."
>
> *Gabe Suarez*
> *The Combat Perspective: The Thinking Man's Guide to Self-Defense*

There is no nice and tidy way to deal with an active shooter or terrorist. There is no politically correct way to stop an armed and violent predator who is out to kill innocent people. You don't have time to be squeamish or weak willed. When you attack back, you must have the attitude and willingness to do whatever it takes to stop the aggressor, and that includes responding immediately with a level of violence greater than he is using. Your goal is survival. You must be willing to hurt, maim, injure, and even kill to achieve your objective.

When faced with sudden violence, most often the only way to overcome it is with greater violence. This means being decisive, courageous, ruthless, willing, vicious, determined, and brutal. You must believe in yourself and that you will prevail no matter what. The attack back attitude is a survivor's attitude. Losing is not an option because losing means you or others might die. And this is very important when it comes to the proper attitude. *You must be willing, without question, to kill any person who is trying to kill you.* This does not mean that situations can't be resolved without killing the active threat. We all know situations have been stopped by both civilians and law enforcement with the killer being apprehended rather than killed. But you must be *willing to kill*, if you have to, because you just might.

> "If you are close to a gunman, you will need to disable him. Trying to run when very close to an armed opponent makes you an easy target. An all-out assault is the only chance, though you need to remember your goal is to escape and to take an opportunity if is arises."
>
> *Martin J. Dougherty*
> *Special Forces Unarmed Combat Guide*

In a life-threatening situation, your attitude is more important than all of your knowledge and training. Without the proper attitude, knowledge and training won't be applied effectively. This is why there are so many examples of untrained people with the proper attitude successfully defending themselves, and trained martial artists without the proper attitude that have become prey to violent criminals. Combine attitude with knowledge and training and your odds of surviving a violent encounter have just increased dramatically.

12 Attack Back Principles

> "Your best defense is a good offense; it must combine your instinct for survival and the practical application of proved principles."
>
> John Styers
>
> *Cold Steel: Technique of Close Combat*

These 12 principles should be learned, and they should guide your training and how you defend yourself. They are simple, but critical to your survival. Applying these principles can mean the difference between life and death when you have no choice but to attack back.

1. **Attack the Attacker**: The best defense is to ATTACK. You must attack relentlessly to prevail. Focus your energies on ruthless, speedy, powerful, and continuing offensive counterattacking techniques.

2. **Attack Vital Areas**: Debilitate the attacker by attacking back at any vital area that presents itself. Eyes, throat, and groin are often taught, and they can be good targets. However, you must fully destroy whatever target you can get. When possible, go for the head to inflict severe blunt trauma to render him unconscious.

3. **Continuous Attack**: Seldom will you get a single blow knockout against a determined adversary. Follow up your first technique with a series of effective techniques. Continue attacking until the attacker is completely subdued. Overwhelm his senses by attacking multiple areas, possibly at random, to overwhelm his ability to what is happening and thus shutting down his ability to react and respond.

4. **Arm Yourself**: Use any available object or item as a weapon. This isn't a sporting match. One of the things being aware of your surroundings will provide is the availability of potential weapons.

5. **Use Simple Techniques**: Keep your techniques simple, direct, aggressive, and effective. Gross movements are easier to perform under stress than techniques that take fine motor skills.

6. **Make Noise**: Yell when attacking or defending. Scream, shout, get vicious. This can startle your attacker, it forces you to breath, it lets others know

something is happening, and it can make you more powerful. It can also reverse the fear reaction and break fear paralysis and get you attacking back.

7. **Don't Hold Back**: Get rid of the psychological block of not wanting to hurt or kill someone. During a life and death encounter, you must immediately use the most deadly, crippling technique you know. Visualization practice can help you get rid of such psychological blocks and prepare you to do what you must to survive a life and death situation.

8. **Don't Go to The Ground With An Attacker If You Can Prevent It**: Being on the ground can be a dangerous place in a combat situation. However, using a swarm strategy, or tackling a shooter, can be effective. They key is to get back to your feet as quickly as you can if you go down. Real combat is not a grappling and submission bout.

9. **Fight Dirty**: Never fight anyone on equal footing. Be unfair, be ruthless, be deceptive. Don't fight empty handed if you can find something to use as a weapon. Don't hesitate to gouge, kick, stomp, knee, elbow, or bite if necessary. Do whatever it takes to survive.

10. **Do the Unexpected**: Feints, deception, and distraction can all aid you in slowing down the attacker's OODA Loop, making him adjust his mind to the situation. This provides you greater opportunity to attack with your own offensive techniques. My friend, Tim Boehlert, includes spitting in his recommendations because it is nasty, gets attention, and is great as a distraction technique when transitioning to another attack.

11. **Stay Alert Under Stress and Keep Calm**: You must be fierce, but not so enraged that you lose your alertness and ability to think. Training, practice, and breathing all help staying alert and calm under stress easier.

12. **End The Battle Quickly**: The faster you terminate the encounter, the better. The longer the battle lasts, the more chance you or others will get hurt or killed. Stop the enemy any way possible, and stop him fast.

Armed and Unarmed Resistance

For purposes in this short section, armed resistance refers to being armed with a firearm, and unarmed includes empty hands and improvised weapons. According to the statistics compiled by the FBI, and just watching news reports, both armed civilians and unarmed civilians have stopped active shooters. This is important because it proves that you don't have to be a victim. It proves that the concepts in this book and my courses, including Attacking Back, can save lives.

There are some out there that teach that you should never attack back. (They usually don't say you shouldn't attack back, they say you shouldn't fight, referring to "fight" from the "Run – Hide – Fight" model.) Never fight? I've seen them on television spouting off this nonsense with the word "expert" after their name. I vehemently disagree with this this so-called expert advice to never fight back. I just told you there is evidence that armed and unarmed civilians have stopped active shooters. The scum that are killing innocent people are cowards and they want victims that won't fight back. Surprise them and send them to their maker sooner than they anticipated without the body count they wanted.

Some claim that the only way to stop an active shooter is by an armed good guy. And while I agree that I'd rather have my firearm facing an active shooter than my cane, pen, or bare hands, the evidence shows that people without firearms have stopped active shooters. It can be done. Is it ideal? No, none of this is ideal. But it is ridiculous to say an unarmed individual is helpless and must succumb to being a victim. If the only thing you take away from this book is the attitude of, "I don't have to be a victim!" it will have been worth reading. You don't have to be a victim and I want you to do everything possible to ensure you aren't one. And I'll do whatever I can through my writing and teaching to help you. Let's get back to Armed and Unarmed Resistance.

Seven School Attacks Stopped by Unarmed Educators or Students

Thurston High School, Springfield, Oregon, 1998: Jake Ryker, seventeen, led the charge in tackling the gunman and knocking him to the ground.

South Orangetown Middle School, New York, 2009: Superintendent Ken Mitchell tackled a distraught parent with a gun and disarmed him. No one was injured.

Hillsdale High School, San Mateo, California, 2009: a former student returned to the school armed with ten pipe bombs. After setting off two and attempting to flee, he was tackled by English teacher Kennet Santana and held until police arrived. No one was injured.

University of Alabama-Huntsville, 2010: a forty-four-year-old Biology professor was attending a faculty meeting, when she pulled a 9mm handgun and started shooting at her colleagues. She killed three and wounded three before her gun either jammed or clicked on empty. Debra Moriarity, dean of the graduate program, led the rush that pushed the shooter out of the room and barred the door. Moriarity is credited with saving the lives of others in the meeting.

Deer Creek Middle School, Colorado, 2010: a thirty-two-year-old man armed with a high-powered rifle shot and wounded two students before being tackled by math teacher David Benke, a six-foot-five former college-basketball player, who led two others in disarming the suspect and holding him for police.

Snohomish High School, Washington, 2011: a fifteen-year-old female student attacked two fourteen-year-old girls in a school bathroom, stabbing them many times. Three football players intervened and stopped the attack.

Chardon High School, Ohio, 2012: a seventeen-year-old student opened fire on other students with a .22-caliber Ruger semi-automatic handgun, killing three and wounding three, before being chased out of the building by teacher Frank Hall.

(Source: Surviving a Mass Killer Rampage)

Armed Resistance

As I stated earlier, there are those that support the claim that the only way to stop an active shooter is by an armed good guy. Some of these people advocate arming not only teachers, but every person in the country. And while I support our 2nd Amendment rights, this position is neither accurate nor realistic. I have taught thousands of people who are not allowed, legally, to carry firearms while at work. These include teachers and employees of both K-12 and Universities, hospitals and medical facilities, and other occupations where carrying firearms is prohibited. In addition to the legalities, we must accept that there are people who, for whatever reason, are not comfortable with the notion of them having to carry and use a firearm. While I am not one of them, I respect that position and don't feel those people should just give up and be victims of violence. Remember, you don't have to be a victim. Because of this, and because of the increased responsibilities of carrying a firearm, this chapter will focus more on unarmed resistance and only contain a few guidelines regarding going armed with a firearm. (Arming yourself with improvised weapons will be addressed in the unarmed section.)

> “If you haven't committed to killing another human being who poses an imminent threat of death or serious bodily injury to you or a third party, you have no business carrying a gun!”
>
> Richard Nance
>
> *Gun Fight! An Integrated Approach to Shooting and Fighting in Close Quarters*

Armed Resistance Tactics and Considerations

If you are going to carry a firearm, I advise you to do so legally. In order to resist an active shooter with your weapon, the following should be a bare minimum for how you should train and things you should consider before the unthinkable actually happens.

Firearm Safety

First and foremost, I support the responsible carrying and use of firearms for sport, recreation, and self-defense. People must be responsible and use common sense when handling firearms. These four common firearm handling maxims must be followed at all times:

1. All firearms are always considered to be loaded and immediately ready to fire all the time and will be handled accordingly. Unloaded guns are handled no differently than loaded ones.
2. The muzzle of any firearm must not, at any time, be allowed to point in an unsafe direction.
3. Fingers are to be kept out of the trigger guard and out of contact with the trigger until/unless the gun is sighted on a target and it is intended that the weapon discharge at once.
4. When pointing a gun at a target, be sure it is something that you want to shoot and that the area around and behind it is clear and safe.

The Ten Commandments of Firearms Safety

(from the Remington Arms website, www.remington.com)

1. Always keep the muzzle pointed in a safe direction.
2. Firearms should be unloaded when not actually in use.
3. Don't rely on your gun's safety.
4. Be sure of your target and what's beyond it.
5. Use proper ammunition.
6. If your gun fails to fire when the trigger is pulled, handle with care.
7. Always wear eye and ear protection when shooting.
8. Be sure the barrel is clear of obstructions before shooting.
9. Don't alter or modify your gun and have it serviced regularly.
10. Learn the mechanical and handling characteristics of the firearm you are using.

(Source: *Gun Safety In The Home* by Massad Ayoob)

There is absolutely no excuse for not handling firearms in a safe manner. Additionally, make sure you meet all your state's legal requirements before getting or carrying a weapon.

Firearm Training

If you are going to carry a firearm for self-defense purposes, you should take training courses both in tactical pistol shooting and use of force and legal aspects of carrying a firearm and using one in self-defense. There are many trainers around the country that teach one or the other, or both, of these types of courses.

I encourage anyone carrying a firearm for self-defense to take classes regularly from qualified instructors as well as personal range time to keep skills sharp.

Firearm Tactics

While this book is not designed to teach tactical pistol shooting, I encourage anyone carrying a firearm for personal protection reasons to seek out qualified instruction in this area. It will better prepare you to respond to an active shooter if you are unfortunate enough to ever be present when the unthinkable happens. You may have to attend multiple courses from different instructors to adequately cover all the desirable skills to successfully survive a gunfight. While training in these areas isn't a necessity to defend yourself with a firearm, it will certainly increase your odds of being successful. These are some of the areas, tactics, and skills that you will benefit by getting training in:

Firearm Training Tactics

- Firearm Safety
- Use of Force and Legalities
- Shooting Fundamentals
- Responsible Use of Lethal Force
- Concealed Carry and Drawing Your Weapon
- Different Shooting Positions
- Reloading Techniques
- Malfunction Drills
- Combat Marksmanship
- Shooting while wounded
- Low-Light Shooting
- Weak Hand Shooting
- Shooting while Moving
- Use of Cover while Shooting
- Multiple Adversaries

It will benefit you greatly to seek out firearm training that covers the above topics and more. There are some resources listed in the back of this book to supplement your training, but nothing will beat an actual instructor and range time.

Don't Neglect Your Empty Hand Skills

Way too often, I hear people dismiss empty hand self-defense training because they carry a firearm. These flippant comments come from ignorance of actual violence. In close quarters combat, you may need to defend yourself with your anatomical weapons like fists, feet, elbows, and knees before you are able to draw your firearm.

Combining empty hand techniques with your firearm training is an important, but often neglected, aspect of firearm training. For an excellent introduction to the concepts of fighting while armed with a firearm, I recommend you read *Gun Fight! An Integrated Approach To Shooting And Fighting In Close Quarters* by Richard Nance. This is one of the few resources that covers how to integrate unarmed fighting concepts with close combat handgun techniques. It's a missing component to too many gun owner's training regimen, and one I strongly suggest you incorporate into your training if you wish to be the best you can possibly be and prepared for any situation.

Active Shooter/Terrorist Scenario Considerations

If you are carrying a firearm and believe you are proficient with it, you must realize one important fact: During an active shooter or terrorist event, *you are not on the range!* Being a good shot on the range is not the same as taking out a bad guy in a real situation. All the factors discussed about fear and adrenaline and the affects to the body, thinking, fine motor skills, etc. come into play. And I know, everyone says they wouldn't carry if they weren't prepared to use it. Easier said than done. And that is why, even if you have a gun, escaping, avoiding, or denying access may be the preferred choice of action. No shame in escaping and staying alive.

If you do choose to attack back with your firearm, I don't recommend a face-to-face shoot-out unless there is absolutely no other choice. If you can't escape and there is no cover available, you must use your weapon immediately, and hopefully your training allows you to place multiple rounds into the killer. Remember, well placed shots are more important than speed. A fast miss will not stop the threat.

If you are not immediately in the line of fire with nowhere to go when the shooting starts, and you decide to attack back with your firearm, the preferred situation would be to outflank or ambush the killer. Get to a point outside his vision, directly behind him would be optimal, and put him down with well-placed rounds. Yes, I am advocating shooting him in the back. This isn't Hollywood. If he is killing people, he needs to be stopped immediately; and if you are behind him with a gun, you are in position to do just that. If you can, get as close as possible before shooting to maximize your effective range. Again, you are not on the range and he will be a moving target. Get as close as possible to ensure you stop the threat and don't hit any innocent bystanders. If you are close enough for an accurate head shot, shoot him in the head. Shooters and terrorists have been known to wear body armor (bullet proof vests). There is also the consideration of suicide vests full of explosives under clothing. If you can't make an accurate head shot, put rounds center mass and stop the threat.

When the shooter is down, reload. There may be more than one threat. While reloading, scan the area: left, right, and behind you. Make sure the perpetrator has been neutralized. If he is still breathing and his hand is on his weapon, he is still a threat. Kick his weapon to a safe location. I advise not to pick it up unless you need it to engage another threat. (For instance, if his weapon was a rifle and provides more firepower than your handgun, you may want to use it if you must engage more shooters or terrorists. But only if you know how to operate it.) If you see that he is wearing what appears to be explosives, or he has a backpack (which might contain an Improvised Explosive Device, IED), don't touch them and leave the area immediately. Notify law enforcement when they arrive if you suspect explosives.

The final consideration I want to address for those carrying firearms and using them in an active shooter situation is becoming mistaken for the killer themselves. In the chaos of such an event, other citizens, or arriving police officers, may mistake you for the killer. It's advisable to keep your firearm holstered and concealed until you engage the threat. Running around looking for the shooter, with a gun in your hand, may get you swarmed by a mob of citizens, or shot by another citizen with a CCW or a police officer. Law enforcement are arriving looking for someone with a firearm. If they see you with one, you will be considered a potential killer. If law enforcement officers see you with a gun in your hand, they may respond with lethal force. Remember in the chapter about adrenaline when I said that auditory exclusion occurs in high stress situations? Don't think that yelling, "I have a concealed carry permit" will be enough to get the officers to dismiss you as a threat. When law enforcement arrives, drop your weapon and hold your hands up showing they are empty. Don't be offended if you are handcuffed and treated as a suspect until they have determined the facts of the matter. They are just doing their job.

Another reason to keep your gun hidden as you escape or move to confront the killer occurred during the shooting at the Thornton, Colorado, Wal-Mart on November, 2, 2017. Authorities said a few individuals drew handguns, and while they posed no physical hazard to officers, their presence slowed the process of determining who, and how many, suspects were involved in the shooting. The problem for investigators occurred when they reviewed the surveillance footage and had to follow each individual with a firearm until they could eliminate them as a suspect. When seconds count, you don't want to lengthen the time it takes to stop a murderer. Just something to think about if you carry, and another reason to keep your weapon concealed until it's time to use it.

Unarmed Resistance

> "Fight Back. Critics of this option will probably argue that you should never try to attack a shooter. But if you're in a situation where there's no place to run and no place to seek cover, what other option do you have? Most critics fall silent when asked that question."
>
> *Robert Richardson*
> *The Ultimate Situational Survival Guide*

Many people, either by choice, or because of statutes, policies, and regulations against the carrying of firearms, will not have access to a firearm during an active shooter event. This does not mean you must become a victim. I will repeat, many people have successfully stopped active shooters without a firearm. However, just because you are unarmed does not mean you can't arm yourself with an improvised weapon. Before we go empty-handed against an active shooter, we should exhaust the option of arming ourselves with whatever may be on hand to use against the killer.

Arm Yourself

> "Never fight empty-handed unless you're forced to."
>
> *Kelly McCann*

No matter where you are, there will be potential weapons for you to use to attack back. While improvised weapons may not be as good as items designed to be used to defend yourself, you must be able to see objects as more than their intended utility. This list is just a sample of what may be available to you. Read it to broaden your thinking. I want you to see ordinary items and think of how you can turn them into weapons to attack back and save your life.

Pot of hot coffee. Splash hot coffee in bad guy's face, or better yet, smash the pot into bad guy's face.

Cup or mug of coffee. Same as the pot, only smaller.

Pen/pencil. Have the pen sticking out the bottom of your hammer fist and drive it into the eye, face, ear, neck or throat. If you have one of the new tactical pens, so much the better. But a number 2 pencil in the eye works too.

Keys. Forget the garbage of having them between your fingers as you punch. Have one sticking out the bottom of your hammer fist as you strike. Alternatively, have a key between your thumb and first finger and use it to stab or scrape the eyes and face.

Aluminum water bottle, thermos, etc. Use as a striking implement and smash the bad guys head and face with it.

Wasp Spray or Hornet Spray. Some people disagree with this as an improvised weapon, but if you have nothing else, spraying it into a person's eyes may create opportunity to escape or attack back with something else. But don't plan on using these for self-defense. If you are purchasing something to be used to defend yourself, there are better options than wasp or hornet spray.

Flashlight. Many flashlights on the market today are made of aircraft aluminum and work very well as an impact weapon. Some are even sold as flashlights/improvised self-defense weapons.

Cell phone. Cell phones can be used as an impact weapon. Who cares if you damage your phone if it keeps you alive. I remember back in 2003 when I was assisting my friend Geoff Booth during a seminar and he put me down into a painful position using his cell phone and then asked, "Can you hear me now?" (Channeling Paul Marcarelli's Test Man character in the popular "Can you hear me now?" Verizon Wireless ads.)

Stapler. Use as an impact weapon.

Scissors. Stabbing weapon. Use with hammer fist or in knife fighting saber grip to stab face, eyes, throat, or anywhere else available to stop the bad guy.

Heavy book (hard cover preferably). Impact weapon slammed into bad guy's head. Repeat until he's unconscious.

Magazines. These can be rolled tight and used to strike or jab the face and throat. I must have been in high school when I first read about this in an article by Bradley J. Steiner.

Credit card. Can be used to slash and cut a person's face. You can hold it normal in your hand, or fold it.

Chairs. You can hit a person with them, you can keep a person with a knife away from you with one, and you can use one to hold a person down on the floor once he is down.

Knives, forks, and other kitchen utensils. Many "kitchen" items can be found not only in kitchens, but in break rooms and such. There are many ways to use these items to defend yourself: Knives and forks can stab, iron skillets and pots can be used to strike; what else can you think of?

Soda can. Rip it in half by twisting it back and forth and you have two sharp slashing instruments.

Tools. Screwdrivers, hammers, and other tools are found in many places. If you are in a garage or shop, your choices multiply. It doesn't take too much thought to figure out how you can use these to defend yourself if needed.

Rocks. I tell people in my classes that you can use just about anything to defend yourself. Pick up a rock and smash the bad guy's head in. It worked for cavemen and it will still get the job done today.

The Fire Extinguisher

The fire extinguisher is one of my favorite improvised weapons to teach people that work in schools, government offices, and other places where traditional weapons are not allowed. No one is going to object to more fire extinguishers being placed in these locations, and they can be used to defend against armed intruders. I've had businesses order more fire extinguishers for their locations after I taught my course and how they can be used.

When I am on the road teaching my four-hour *Survive a Shooting* class, I teach how to use the fire extinguisher, and we then simulate its use in training. During the active shooter response course I've been teaching with the team here in Missoula, we don't just mention that it can be used as an effective weapon, we take the class outside and let them actually spray and strike the training dummy BOB with one.

Spraying BOB the training dummy from a distance

There are a lot of positives regarding fire extinguishers. First of all, they are already readily available in most buildings. And while there may be objections to other security measures, especially arming teachers, I don't believe anyone would be against putting a fire extinguisher into a classroom. A principal of a nearby school that is out of the primary district we teach to came to one of our classes. He went back to his school and did put a fire extinguisher in every class room along with a simple lock down device. The fire extinguishers were mounted beside each door. No teachers or parents have a problem with it. In fact, the only thing preventing some schools from doing this is budgetary restraints. That principal had the budget to put them in, and the added security for their school was a priority.

If budgets permit, it would also be a good idea to attach a small trauma kit that includes a tourniquet to each fire extinguisher. You hope neither of them ever have to be used, but they are there just in case. It's basically a little insurance and preparation for the worst.

Using a fire extinguisher as an improvised weapon is fairly simple.

First: You must twist the ring on the pin to break the plastic band that is attached when they fill them.

The safety ring on a fire extinguisher must be removed before spraying

Second: Pull the pin out. Do not squeeze the handles together while trying to pull the pin.

Third: If you are right handed, I recommend holding the fire extinguisher under the canister with your left hand, leaving the hose attached to the side. Use your right hand to squeeze the handles together to activate or fire the extinguisher. From this position, you have good control of where you spray the fire retardant and you can then also use the canister to strike a shooter. To do this, thrust the canister at the shooter and hit him in the head with the bottom of the fire extinguisher. The metal canister with the edge on the bottom, combined with the weight of the extinguisher, makes this a very formidable weapon. Even a smaller person can hurt someone if they smack him in the head with it. A more powerful thrust could cause serious injury or death when striking a person in the head. This combined with the fire retardant in the face makes the fire extinguisher a very effective improvised weapon. Obviously, if you are left handed, switch hands.

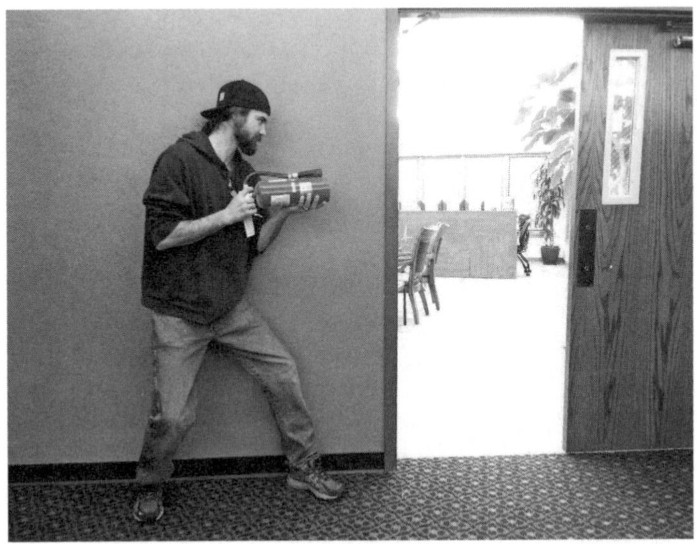

Preparing to ambush a shooter and thrust an extinguisher into his face or head

The thrusting method of striking with the fire extinguisher is preferred over swinging it at your attacker. Holding it as instructed above allows you to both shoot fire retardant or strike, or both in a controlled manner. Swinging a heavy fire extinguisher, while it would do considerable damage to a bad guy if you hit him in the head, is not recommended. You don't have as much control this way, and if you miss your intended target, you can lose your balance and not be able to recover to strike again. The way I've outlined above is the most effective way to use a fire extinguisher as an improvised weapon, and you can also use it that way to put out a fire.

Thrusting the Fire Extinguisher to the head or face

Thrusting and spraying

Often, you don't get to choose where you or your attacker are when you are forced to fight. You just have to do whatever it takes from wherever you happen to be. However, if circumstances allow you any preparation time, the ideal spot to attack back with a fire extinguisher is at the doorway or a corner. You want to be right beside the door, outside of the fatal funnel, so you can blast and strike the gunman as he tries to enter the room. You do this because it wasn't possible to lock or barricade the door or the lock or barricade failed. If you are at a corner it is because for some reason you can't run, or you are waiting to spray and strike the gunman to allow others time to escape, or maybe you are in a room that doesn't have a door. There could be many reasons why your only option is to fight, and if you have a fire extinguisher, setting up just inside a doorway or around a corner can give you the edge to prevail.

Improvised weapons are really a mentality rather than a specific tool. The examples above should stimulate thought on how you can use anything as a weapon if needed. Develop the ability to see the "weapon" attributes in ordinary things.

Armed with an improvised weapon, or empty handed, it is beneficial to be familiar with firearms to help assess the best way to neutralize the armed intruder. Before we look at attacking back, we need to familiarize ourselves with the basic types of firearms.

Firearm Familiarization

During live classes, I like to briefly go over types of firearms so people will have a little familiarity with them. While there are often people who shoot, even concealed weapon permit holders, attending the classes, there are also many who have never fired a gun and know very little about them. Some even think of guns as mystical or magic tools of death. I want to demystify firearms. They are mechanical devices that have weaknesses that can be exploited. Knowledge of firearms will better equip you to learn and perform the gun defenses presented here and learned elsewhere.

The brief introduction I provide in my classes, and this short section here, only provide minimal information on the types of guns available and their operation. Therefore, I strongly encourage everyone to seek out additional familiarization with firearms by taking a class that involves firing one or more types of firearms taught by a competent instructor. This will demystify guns for some. It will also allow people, if forced to pick up a gun that has been dropped or taken from an active shooter, to know how to handle it safely, and if necessary use it to defend themselves.

Basic Types of Firearms Handguns

> ## Gun Basics
>
> The Israeli system of Haganah, founded by former Israeli commando, Mike Lee Kanarek, predicates its gun defense on these five key points that are true of virtually all firearms:
>
> 1. A gun discharges when its trigger is pulled – provided the safety is off and a round is in the chamber.
> 2. It takes very little pressure to pull the trigger.
> 3. A gun fires the bullet in essentially a straight line toward whatever object it's pointing at when the trigger is pulled (line of fire).
> 4. A gun is extremely loud. If one discharges nearby, you'll be startled and your ears will ring – even if you expect it.
> 5. If you interfere with the normal operation of certain parts of a gun during the firing process, it'll probably jam, rendering it incapable of firing again until the problem is fixed. On a semiautomatic weapon, that involves stopping the slide from slamming backward upon discharge and then being propelled forward to chamber another round. The result is an empty chamber, which means no follow-up shot can be made without re-cocking the weapon.

Handguns are the smallest of firearms and are usually classified under two common types: revolvers and semi-automatic pistols (sometimes called "semi-autos"). Revolvers have a revolving cylinder that holds the cartridges to fire. For a single action revolver, the hammer must be pulled back before you can shoot. For a double action revolver, pressing the trigger both rotates the cylinder and cocks the hammer back allowing the revolver to fire with each press of the trigger through its mechanical action. Semi-automatic pistols use a spring-loaded magazine that holds the cartridges and feeds them into the firing chamber. Each press of the trigger fires a cartridge, and the energy of the cartridge activates the slide mechanism so that the casing is ejected and the new round is fed into the chamber to be fired immediately. Semi-automatics are in greater circulation these days.

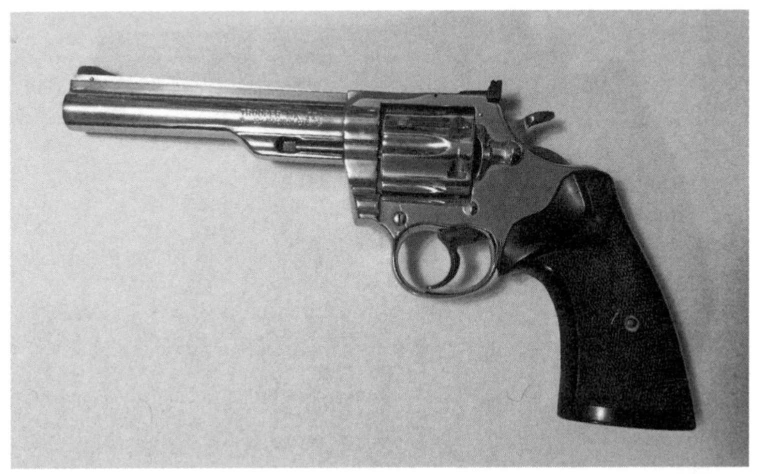

Colt .357 Revolver

Browning Hi Power 9mm Semi-Automatic

Long Guns

In general (remember I'm really simplifying it here), long guns will be either rifles or shotguns. These are larger than handguns and designed to be held and fired with both hands, usually from the shoulder. Typically, long guns have barrels between 10 and 30 inches long. (There are restrictions on minimum barrel length for certain long guns in many jurisdictions.) The receiver and trigger group is mounted into a wood, plastic, metal, or composite stock and usually there will be a foregrip, rear grip, and shoulder mount called the butt. (Note, not all long guns will have a butt.) Rifles shoot a single bullet through a barrel that has spiral fluting (rifling) that impart a self-stabilizing spin on the bullet to increase accuracy at longer distances. Shotguns are usually smoothbore (no rifling) long guns designed to fire a number of "shot," or small BBs, that vary in size. They can also shoot single slugs or specialty rounds such as bean bags, tear gas, or breaching rounds. Shotguns have less range than rifles and larger/wider fields of fire depending on the specific round or load.

There are many types of rifles and shotguns with a variety of actions, or the way they are loaded. Bolt-action and lever-action rifles are two types of manually operated rifles. Pump-action long guns are another type of manually operated firearm and this action is more common with shotguns, but is also used by a few rifles. Both rifles and shotguns also come in break-action varieties that do not have any kind of reloading mechanism. These must be hand-loaded after each shot.

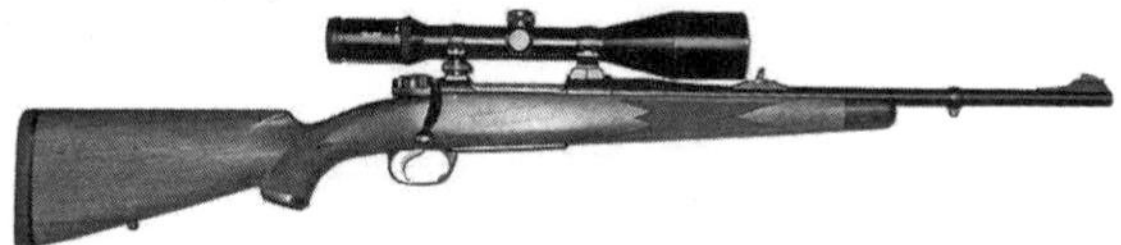

Modern Hunting Rifle

Shotgun

Both rifles and shotguns come in semi-automatic varieties too. Like the semi-auto handgun, a semi-automatic rifle or shotgun will continue to fire rounds at each press of the trigger until no more ammunition is left in the feed device or magazine. These are not "automatic" or "full-auto" as you must press the trigger for each round fired.

Automatic, or fully automatic, weapons are defined as those firearms that continue to load and fire cartridges for as long as the trigger is depressed, and until depleted of ammunition. Besides being very expensive, to purchase and own automatic weapons in the United States requires a special license from the government. Please note that a military assault rifle is defined as one that has selective fire. This means the assault rifle has the capability to be adjusted to fire in semi-automatic, multi-shot burst, and/or fully automatic firing mode. Many people mistakenly call rifles like the AR-15 an assault rifle, when it only fires in the semi-automatic firing mode. AR does not stand for Assault Rifle, it stands for Armalite Rifle, and was designated as a model name by the company that first designed the rifle and then sold the design to Colt.

Fully Automatic Rifles (top M-16, bottom AK-47)

AR-15 Style Semi-Automatic Rifle

I, again, encourage everyone to learn a little about firearms. Even if you never want to own or shoot a gun, it is wise to learn a little about them in case you ever have to handle one you can do so safely. Learning about them will also take the mysticism and fear away from them. Going one step further and firing one at a range is even better. The brief descriptions here don't do justice to all you can learn about firearms, but will suffice for our purposes in knowing the difference between handguns and long guns for ambush and disarm purposes.

> "If you don't know how to use a gun – don't"

When and How to Attack Back

If you are in a position to try and take the gunman down, or to take him out, it can be the best option for saving lives. But there are better times and strategies to increase the odds of successfully attacking back and stopping the killer. These are some important concepts and considerations to help you determine when and how to attack back. Not all of them will be used in every situation, but knowing them will help you be prepared.

The Fatal Funnel

The "fatal funnel" is a term used in close quarters combat usually pertaining to building-clearing operations. It refers to stairwells, hallways, and doorways that have a narrow or confining area. The most common "fatal funnel" is the cone-shaped path leading outward from the entry way of a room out into the larger open space. If you are standing in a doorway looking straight into a room, the funnel will be around your ten o'clock and two o'clock straight out at those angles.

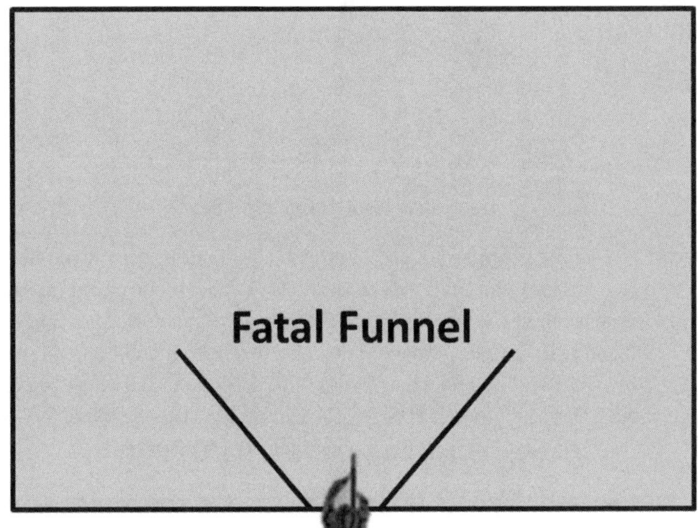

The Fatal Funnel

In military and law enforcement operations, operators are taught to minimize time in this funnel by clearing the corners and getting out of the cone-shaped funnel. It is the most dangerous place for the operator to be.

Stay Out of the Fatal Funnel

For our purposes here, we want to be outside of this funnel when a shooter comes through the entryway. This makes sense. An active shooter coming through the entryway is looking for targets. The cone that starts about ten o'clock and goes to about two o'clock (straight ahead from the shooter is twelve o'clock) is what the killer will see and focus on first. Being inside of this cone, or funnel, makes you a more noticeable target and more apt to be fired upon.

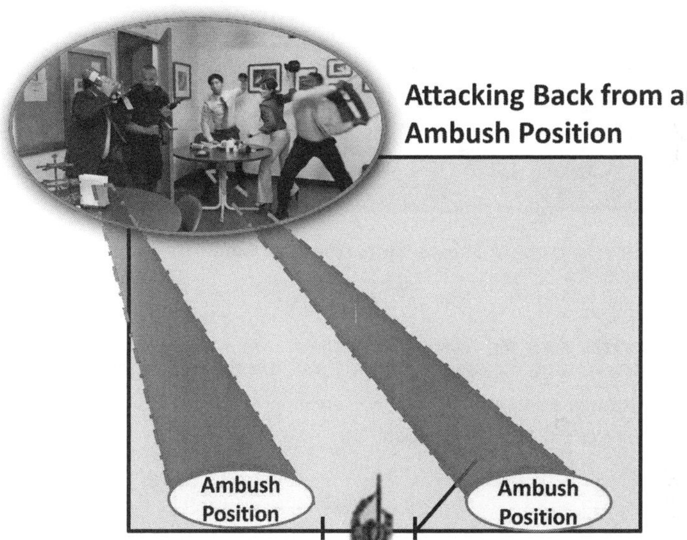

Stop the Threat in the Fatal Funnel

Just like military and law enforcement personnel are taught that being inside the fatal funnel when going through an entry way is the most dangerous place to be, it is the most advantageous place for you to attack back from to stop the killer. Most of these sick individuals don't have the training that military and law enforcement have in regard to entering and clearing buildings. If you have to attack back, ambushing at a doorway or corner as the killer enters the fatal funnel provides you the greatest advantage and chances of successfully neutralizing the threat.

A Shooter Enters the Fatal Funnel

Speed, Surprise, and Violence of Action

> "Attacking a shooter demands an uncompromising burst of savage violence on your part."
>
> *John Geddes*
> *Be A Hero: The Essential Survival Guide to Active-Shooter Events*

Three important factors taught in the military relating to violent confrontations are speed, surprise, and violence of action. Utilizing these factors when attacking back will increase your chances of success.

Let's look at surprise first. Terrorists and active shooters want easy victims. Just the fact that you are attacking back and not cowering in fear will surprise many of these murderers. If you can rush the shooter from behind him or from his flank, or ambush him at a doorway or corner, you increase your element of surprise and chances of success.

Speed comes from having a plan and knowing simple go-to defensive moves that you can default to under stress and the adrenaline dump. It also comes from being fully committed, without hesitation, once you've determined attacking back is the course of action to save you and others.

When attacking back, you must have the resolve and mindset to act with a greater degree of violence than the threat you are stopping. You must refuse to be a victim and make him the victim of your violence. That's what we mean by violence of action. The shooter has already displayed that he is willing to use violence and kill people. You must be prepared to respond with greater violence of action to stop him.

Ten Mistakes You Cannot Make When Confronted With a Violent Situation

1. Don't *hope* it goes away. Take the necessary action to end the situation.
2. Don't expect there to be even a glimmer of compassion in your attacker – there isn't.
3. Don't believe the playing field will be even when you are attacked. Conditions will be most advantageous to your attacker and you will be most vulnerable.
4. Don't apply your social restraint to their attack. The two are not compatible.
5. Don't believe you can compete normally with their level of violence. They are abnormal.
6. Don't be confrontational or challenging. The situation is bad enough; letting your anger urge you headlong into a situation won't help.
7. Don't give up, ever, if attacked.
8. Don't promulgate a lie to yourself or your loved ones. The realities of today are what they are, and they need to know hard-core facts about them.
9. Don't forget, YOU didn't start anything or ask for any trouble.
10. Never forget number 7.

Source: *Street Smarts, Firearms, & Personal Security* by Kelly McCann (as Jim Grover)

This is a quick explanation of these three principles, but the most important thing to remember is that utilizing them will increase your chances of successfully attacking back and neutralizing the threat that is attempting to injure or kill you and others.

Disrupting the Shooter

In chapter 4, I wrote the killer is also going through the same OODA Loop decision making cycle you are going through, only faster. If you can do something to disrupt the shooter and his OODA Loop, you can buy precious seconds to escape or attack back. You want to mess up his observation and orientation. You can do this by distracting his vision and attention or by overwhelming his senses. This can be done by screaming and yelling, throwing things at him (be accurate and aim for the face, throwing things at his feet won't do much), a strobe flashlight into the eyes as he comes into a darkened room, chairs or tables placed in his natural path as he comes through the door, a mirror or reflective surface placed in the path as he comes through the doorway, and anything else that can disrupt his thought process and killing cycle.

Using a table as a distraction during an ambush at the door

Stack by the Door

As mentioned in the fatal funnel section, if a threat comes into a room you are in, the most advantageous place to attack back is at the door. If you are across the room, under a table or desk, or hiding in the far corner, you are an easy target. Right beside the door, where you can attack as he enters, provides the greatest chance of successfully taking him out. This ambush position is outside of his vision (fatal funnel). Don't have your back flat against the wall, as you will have to turn to be able to attack. Do lower into a crouch and be ready to spring into violence of action.

If you are alone, this is where you want to ambush the shooter. Use a fire extinguisher if you have one, or any other improvised weapon. If you are empty-handed, I've included disarms that can be done alone from this position beside the door.

A lone defender ready to ambush a shooter as he enters the fatal funnel

If there are more than one defenders, you can stack together and work as a team to take the threat out. I've also included disarms for when there are more than one attacking back.

Multiple defenders stacked at the door to ambush

Stacking and ambushing an active threat from a corner is essentially the same as ambushing at a doorway if the shooter is walking near the wall and corner. If the shooter is walking down the middle of a wide hallway, or on the other side of the hall from your ambush, you may have a much greater distance to cover to effectively attack back. This distance will make ambushing the shooter much more difficult, and your physicality and training will be important factors in whether you will be able to successfully take the shooter out in this scenario.

Swarming the Shooter

One strategy that can, and has, worked against an active shooter is to rush or swarm him to bring him down. What this means is for a group to tackle him, weigh him down with numbers, and immobilize him. While doing this, they should be trying to inflict the maximum damage possible with anything at hand until the shooter is no longer a threat. This can be very effective by a group or crowd of potential defenders that decides to attack back, rush the shooter, and immobilize and stop him with numbers and ferocity. It can also be achieved by one or two people with the determination, viciousness, ferociousness, and brutal savagery needed to stop a stone-cold killer from murdering more people. (Yes, I recognize that people have stopped shooters with less than this attitude, but it's the attitude I want you to have to be a survivor.)

> **Dog Pile**
>
> For our purposes, a dog pile is when two or more coworkers leap on the perpetrator, knock him to the floor, and restrain him by holding him down with their body weight. Think of a football game where several players pile on the man with the ball.

While the swarm tactic can and may work, it does not guarantee there will be no casualties. But it almost certainly will reduce the number of people killed. People closing in and tackling the shooter will interrupt his actions and OODA Loop. Tackling him and smashing his head will keep him from killing others. But please note, the likelihood of someone being wounded or killed in the rush is high, especially if rushed from the front. I do not recommend rushing the shooter head-on. Those rushing from outside of the ten o'clock and two o'clock of the shooter's vision have a greater chance of being successful with reduced likelihood of being injured or killed by the shooter. Remember, attack back from behind or the sides unless you have no other choice.

> "The Israeli authorities advocate this swarm technique, and it has been used with success there...With the increase in random terror attacks in our society, perhaps it's time to take a leaf out of their book."
>
> *John Geddes*
> *Be A Hero: The Essential Survival Guide to Active-Shooter Events*

Swarming an active shooter isn't easy. Rushing a person shooting and killing people when you are terrified will go against everything you want to do. Add the fear that no one else will follow you and help, and it's even more difficult to lead the charge. While people have taken down shooters by themselves, this tactic works much better when the entire crowd joins in to pile on him with you, or at the least a few of them. The shooter will not be able to resist a group of people rushing him from behind, or the flanks, when all of them are also striking him with whatever they have available, hammer fists if that's all they have, along with some of them wrestling his gun away. It will work best in enclosed situations like nightclubs, theaters, trains, or planes. Areas where those swarming can reach the shooter quickly. Yelling, "Get him!" and leading the charge for a swarm is a desperate strategy, but it has been proven to work. It could be the last thing a person ever does, but it may also be successful without more casualties. However, when doing nothing certainly means more people being killed, swarming the shooter may be the very thing that saves lives.

Swarming Works

On January 8, 2011, Jared Lee Loughner shot U.S. Representative Gabrielle Giffords and eighteen others. Six people died, including federal District Court Chief Judge John Roll; Gabe Zimmerman, one of Rep. Giffords' staffers; and a nine-year-old girl, Christina-Taylor Green. A swarm attack overwhelmed the shooter and stopped the killing. An unidentified person in the crowd struck the back of the shooter's head with a folding chair. Loughner was then tackled to the ground by Bill Badger, a 74-year-old retired United States Army Colonel who was shot and wounded, but still rushed the shooter in righteous fury after seeing little Christina-Taylor murdered. Others joined to help subdue Loughner. These people were Roger Sulzgeber, Joseph Zamudio and sixty-one year old Patricia Maisch. Zamudio, a carry-concealed weapon (CCW) permit holder, who was carrying a weapon, arrived after the shooting had stopped and did not draw his firearm.

This illustrates that a swarm or rush can work effectively. While the mechanics of a swarm or rush are spontaneous, there must be a human ignition to set it off. Someone must take the initiative like the person with the chair and Bill Badger. Others will often follow after someone starts the attack. These individuals saved lives.

Disarming the Shooter

In the next section, I will teach a couple of disarms to use when you ambush the shooter, or during an opportunity when the shooter is reloading or clearing a malfunction. However, disarming an active shooter doesn't always mean taking the gun from his hands.

If you have a gun, you will shoot the killer center mass to stop him. As he goes down, he will drop his gun and be disarmed. If you have a knife, there are ways to cut and stab to make him drop the gun and/or kill him. In both situations, he is disarmed. If you have a baseball bat, you can hit his arm to make him drop the gun, but you could also swing for the fences at his head, knocking him cold, which would also cause him to drop the gun. Spray him in the face with the fire extinguisher you grabbed from the wall and then bash him in the head until he goes down unconscious. He'll drop the gun as he goes down, disarmed. I hope you are getting the picture here. Disarming an active shooter doesn't necessarily mean taking the gun from his hand with a technique learned from this book or in a martial art or combatives class. Smashing an armed intruder in the head with a fire extinguisher after filling his eyes, nose, and mouth with chemical spray is also a disarm. Learn and practice the disarms, but don't forget there are alternative methods to stop an active shooter.

Gun Disarms

There are a plethora of gun disarms. You can find books, DVDs, and seminars teaching a variety of ways to disarm both handguns and long guns from different positions. Many of these begin with the bad guy holding a gun pointed at you. The bad guy may be in front of you, behind you, or to a side, but the gun is always held pointed at you within arm's reach. This is because you can't take a gun from someone without the gun being close enough to grab. (That or hit him so hard he drops the gun. Remember, this is also a disarm.)

There is a big difference between a person threatening you by holding a gun pointed at you and an active shooter who is actively killing people. While any gun disarm is a risky endeavor, and something that should only be attempted as a last resort, trying to disarm an active shooter from the front is even riskier. My advice is to never try to disarm an active shooter from the front unless there is absolutely no other choice. (Or possibly in the event of a gun malfunction, or when the shooter is trying to reload.) Therefore, the only disarms I'm going to include in this chapter are from the side. They can be used to attack back from outside of the shooter's vision, or preferably from an ambush at a doorway or corner.

Again, gun disarms, or any counter-weapon techniques, are risky and not 100%. There are many variables with weapons that make them extremely dangerous and very difficult to perform counter-weapon techniques against. The ambush attacks presented here have a better chance of success than attempting to disarm someone right in front of you, but they still are not 100%. No one can guarantee that. Additionally, when practicing these techniques, or any counter-weapon techniques, never use actual weapons. Train safe and use training weapons only.

Are Disarms Realistic?

There are people who dismiss gun disarms as being unrealistic, and who believe that an unarmed person can't take a firearm from a criminal or killer. I'd like to share what Col. Rex Applegate pointed out years ago in his book, *Kill Or Get Killed*, that, "there are many cases on record in which prisoners of war and criminals have escaped, killed, or seriously injured men who were holding them at gun point." Col. Applegate also pointed out, "many military and police organizations have cases on record in which their own men have successfully disarmed armed individuals." There are many who have successfully disarmed and/or stopped criminals and killers who were armed with firearms. That does not mean it is easy. But it is possible.

Handgun Disarm by Yourself

With the arm closest to the shooter (this means if you are on the shooters left side, you will use your right hand, and if you are on his right side, you will use your left. It does not matter which hand the shooter has the gun.) grab the top of the handgun. If it is a revolver, your hand will be over the backstrap and holding the cylinder. If it is a semi-automatic, your hand will be over the slide and covering the ejection port.

When you grab a revolver's cylinder and don't allow it to turn, the revolver won't fire if the hammer is forward in the double action position. If the hammer is cocked back in the single action position, it will fire once, but won't fire again if you prohibit the cylinder from rotating. When you grab a semi-automatic, it will still fire. However, your hand covering the ejection port will cause the weapon to malfunction and it will not fire again until cleared and put back into operation.

Your second hand will grab the firearm under the barrel, being careful not to put any part of your hand in front of the muzzle. Now, you can do one of two things, both involve turning the muzzle back toward the shooter.

1. Turn the muzzle up toward the shooters face, turning the gun in a vertical circle, while pulling down. This will rip the firearm from the shooters hands and keep the muzzle always pointed in a direction away from you.
2. Alternatively, twist the firearm away from you and back toward the shooter in a horizontal circle. This also will wrench the firearm from his grasp while always keeping the muzzle pointed away from you.

Remember, just because you have taken the shooter's firearm does not mean he is no longer a threat. He may have more weapons on his person. Escape or continue to attack back to neutralize the threat.

Single defender grabs the top of the handgun to gain control

Grab the weapon underneath the barrel with the second hand for more control

Step closer, bringing the weapon toward you while keeping muzzle pointed away from you

Lower your body weight, pull weapon down while twisting the weapon toward the shooter in a vertical circle, to remove it from his hands

Alternatively, twist the firearm away from you and back toward the shooter in a horizontal circle to remove the gun from his hands

In both variations, rip the firearm from the killer's grasp!

Handgun Disarm with Others on Your Side

This is a simple strategy when you have two or more people ambushing the shooter. It doesn't require remembering a disarm, and it can be used against a handgun or a long gun. It requires two or more people stacked at the doorway or a corner to ambush, or two or more people rushing the shooter from the rear or side.

The first person in the stack, or closest to shooter, will grab the gun immediately as the shooter enters the room. When grabbing, the person will force the gun toward the floor. Right after the first person grabs the firearm, the second person will tackle the shooter, taking him out at the knees. The combination of the first person forcing the gun toward the floor and the second person tackling at the knees should take the shooter down to the ground. Proceed with pounding on his head until the first person has wrested the firearm from his grasp. Get the firearm away from the shooter and continue to do whatever is necessary to subdue or neutralize the killer. Remember, he may have more weapons on his person.

Two people stacked beside the door to ambush the killer

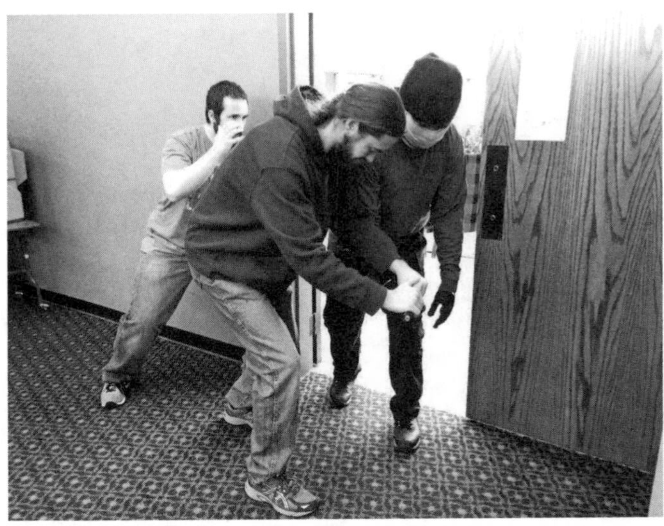

First Defender: grab, control, and redirect the barrel away from you as force the weapon downward!

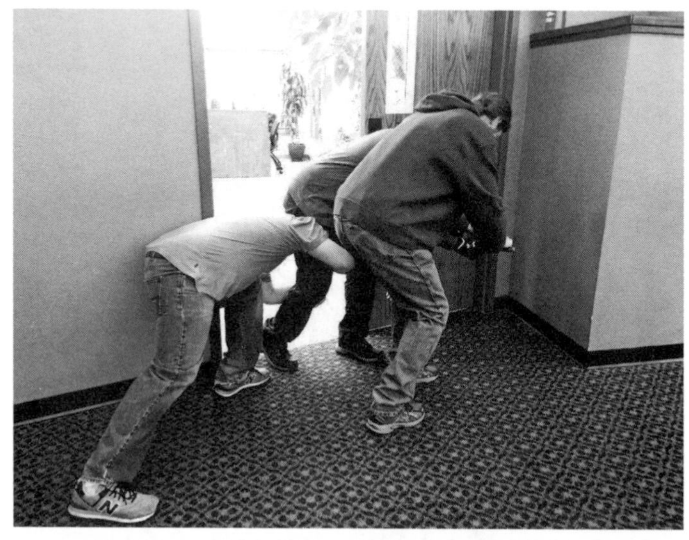

Second Defender: tackle the shooter at the knees to take him down

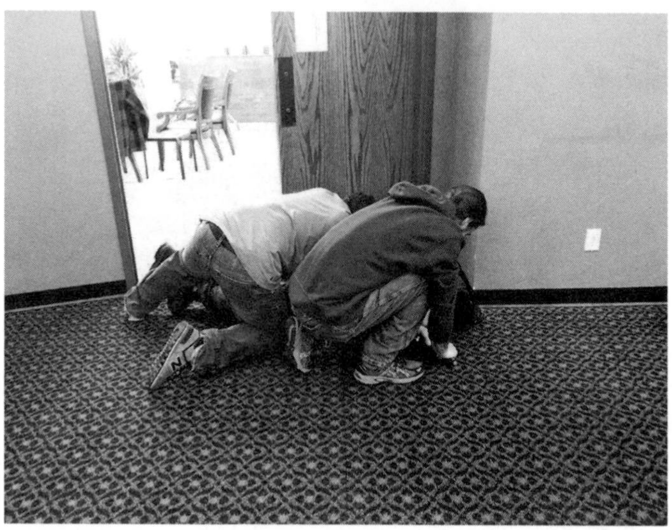

Both Defenders: subdue and control the shooter and his weapon

Rifle Disarm by Yourself

This disarm, like the handgun disarm, is being taught from the side. It can be done with a person holding a rifle on you while standing in front of you within arm's reach. However, as I said earlier, your greatest chance of taking a gun from an active shooter is to ambush him at a corner or doorway, or to attack from the rear or flank.

As the rifle barrel comes into the doorway, or appears from behind the corner, grab the barrel with the arm farthest from the shooter (this means if you are on the shooters left side, you will use your left hand, and if you are on his right side, you will use your right). Push the barrel up and away. With your other hand, grab the butt of the rifle (the part up against the shooter's shoulder). If you grabbed under the person's arm, rotate the rifle in a vertical circle, and if over the arm, in a horizontal circle, to twist the gun out of the shooter's hands. By grabbing the outside ends of the firearm and using circular motion, you gain leverage and strength to twist the gun out of an even stronger person's hands.

Taking the weapon does not necessarily neutralize the threat. The person may have another weapon, or he may decide to fight empty handed. Use the rifle as a striking instrument or as the gun is intended if you know how to operate it, and defend yourself as needed.

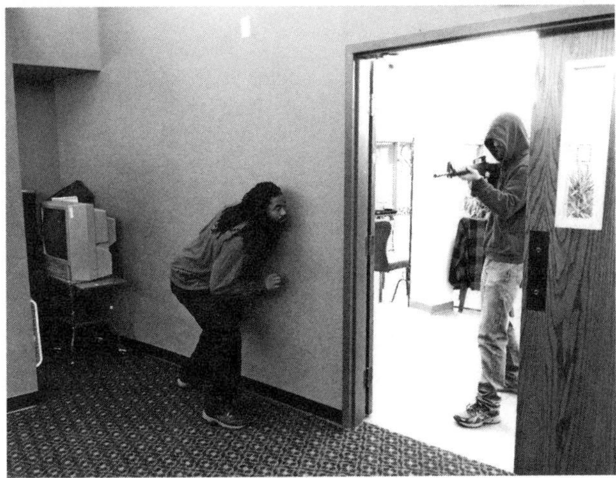

A lone defender prepares to ambush the killer beside the doorway

The lone defender begins the disarm by pushing the barrel upward

The defender pushes the barrel away while pulling the stock forward (twisting motion) in a violent manner to rip the rifle from the killer's hands

The defender has now twisted the rifle away from the shooter

Rifle Disarm with Others on Your Side

To keep it very simple, we will use the same simple strategy when you have two or more people ambushing the shooter as we did with the handgun. As I said earlier, it doesn't require remembering a disarm, and it can be used against a handgun or a long gun. It requires two or more people stacked at the doorway or at a corner to ambush, or two or more people rushing the shooter from the rear or side.

The first person in the stack, or closest to the shooter, will grab the gun immediately as the shooter enters the room. When grabbing, the person will force the gun toward the floor. Right after the first person grabs the firearm, the second person will tackle the shooter, taking him out at the knees. The combination of the first person forcing the gun toward the floor and the second person tackling at the knees should take the shooter down to the ground. Proceed with pounding on his head until the first person has wrested the firearm from his grasp. Get the firearm away from the shooter and continue to do whatever necessary to subdue or neutralize the killer. Remember, he may have more weapons on his person.

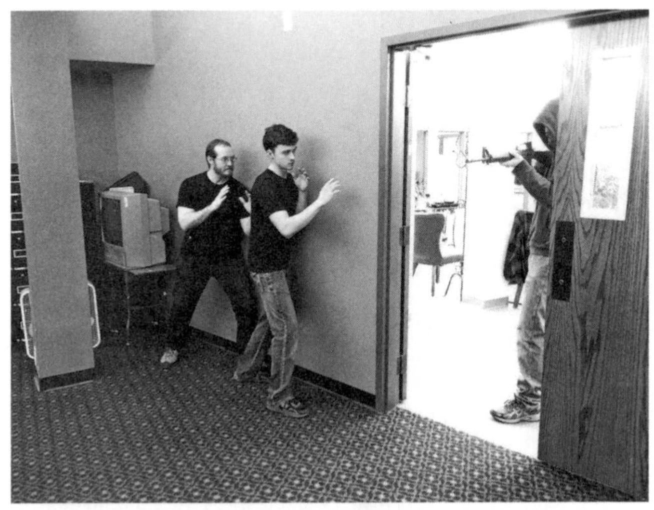

Two defenders stacked in wait for the shooter

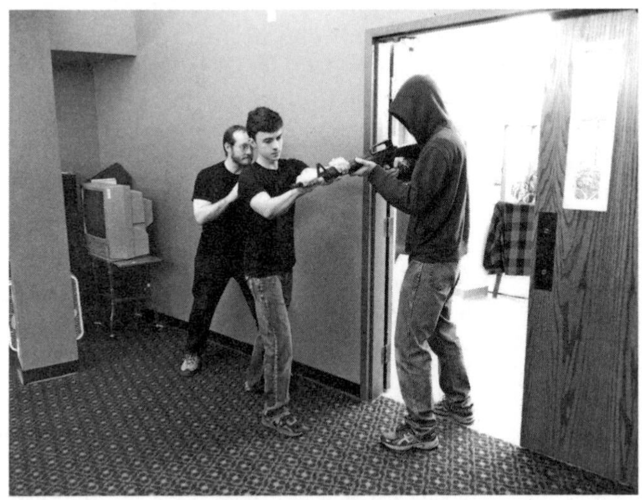

First Defender: grab, control, and redirect the barrel away from you as force the weapon downward!

Wrapping an arm around the weapon adds control for the defender

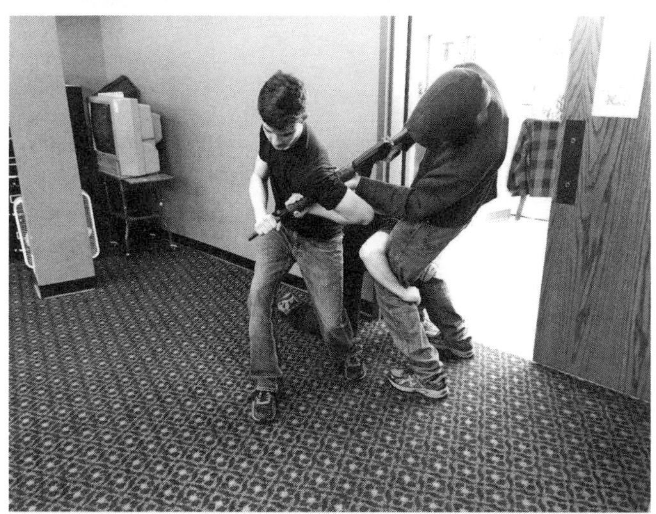

Second Defender: tackle the shooter at the knees to take him down

After the shooter is tackled, do whatever is necessary to subdue or debilitate the shooter and remove the firearm from his possession

How Hot Will the Barrel Be?

I'm often asked in classes if the barrel will be hot, and if so, will it burn your hand? I don't know. It might be. It will depend on how many rounds the shooter has fired, and how long it has been since the last shot was fired. Barrels can get extremely hot when shooting a large number of rounds in a short amount of time. If you are not wearing gloves, there is a high chance of getting burned if you take a weapon from someone who has been firing it at people. It's a terrible horrific situation, and the only reason you are attempting to take a firearm from someone is because you have no other alternatives. A burned hand is better than being shot or having others shot and killed. There's a chance you will be so jacked up with fear and adrenaline that you hardly feel it until afterwards, and then it is going to hurt like crazy. If you do feel it, you must drive through with taking the gun away and stopping the threat. Then administer first aid to your injury and get medical attention as soon as possible.

Active Shooter Weapon Malfunction is an Opportunity

There have been a number of active shooter incidents where the killer experienced a malfunction or jam with their weapon. Additionally, there have been multiple active shooter events where the killer has reloaded a firearm that ran out of ammunition. These situations, malfunction or reloading, can be opportunities, both for escaping or attacking back.

Let me repeat that by sharing a quote from Greg Ellifritz, "Weapon malfunctions give victims time to escape. They also provide opportunities for unarmed victims to violently resist the killer with less danger. Similar opportunities are presented when shooters reload their empty weapons as well. In looking at past active shooter events, it is exceedingly rare to find one where the killer didn't have either a malfunctioning or empty weapon at some point in the engagement." (Article: "Weapon Malfunctions in an Active Shooter Event")

Greg also did some research on this topic and here are some of the incidents he found and listed in his article:

1988 – Atlantic Shores Christian School. Shooter subdued by a teacher after his gun jammed. He had hundreds more rounds on his person.

1999 – Columbine High School. The two shooters reloaded several times each.

1999 – Fort Gibson Middle School. Shooter shot until his pistol was empty. He was then taken down by a teacher and school safety officer.

2004 – Al Rosa Villa Concert shooting. Killer had a malfunction with his Beretta 92 handgun.

2007 – Virginia Tech. Shooter reloaded several times.

2007 – New York, New York Casino in Las Vegas. Shooter was tackled by bystander while attempting to reload his handgun. He had more than 100 additional rounds on his person.

2009 – NVCC Woodbridge College. Shooter's gun jammed after two rounds.

2009 – Bridgeville Fitness Club. Shooter reloaded at least twice.

2009 – Fort Hood Army Base. Terrorist reloaded several times and had a pistol malfunction.

2009 – First Baptist Church Maryville, Illinois. Killer's .45 pistol jammed after he fired four shots. He continued to attack with a knife.

2010 – University of Alabama Faculty meeting. Shooter's gun jammed and she was locked in a closet by coworkers until police arrived.

2010 – Deer Creek Middle School, Littleton, CO. Teacher tackled the adult male shooter as he reloaded his rifle.

2011 – Tucson Shooting. Shooter had to reload and had a jammed gun at one point. He was tackled as he fumbled reloading and trying to pick up his dropped magazine.

2011 – Norway shooting. Killer reloaded multiple times.

2012 – Chardon High School, OH. Shooter fired 10 rounds with .22 pistol and then ran out of ammunition.

2012 – Oikos College. Shooter reloaded several times.

2012 – Clackamas Mall in Portland, OR. Shooter fired 17 rounds and attempted to reload his AR-15 rifle but was unable to do so.

2012 – California Chicken Plant shooting. Killer fired until his pistol was empty.

2013 – Sandy Hook Elementary School. Killer had to reload, and live rounds were found on the ground that may indicate malfunctions.

2013 – Ross Twp. Pennsylvania Municipal Building. Shooter fired 28 rounds out of a Ruger Mini-14 and ran it dry. He transitioned to a .44 magnum revolver and continued to attack.

2014 – Pacific University in Seattle, WA. Student safety monitor stopped the shooter by spraying him with pepper spray as he reloaded his double barrel shotgun. Suspect tried to continue his attack with a knife while being restrained.

2014 – Marysville-Pilchuck High School in WA. Teacher confronted student as he was reloading, prompting the student to shoot himself.

2014 – Second Ft. Hood Shooting. Multiple reloads of a Smith and Wesson .45 semi-automatic pistol.

2015 – Charlie Hebdo Shooting in Paris. Multiple reloads. Live 7.62 X 39mm rounds on the street indicate possible malfunctions.

2015 – Thalys France Train Shooting. Islamic terrorist fired on train passengers until his rifle jammed. He was then tackled and choked out by three traveling Americans. The shooter was also armed with a 9mm handgun and a box cutter. He transitioned to the box cutter when his rifle jammed and slashed several people.

2016 – Kansas Lawnmower Plant. Shooter fired weapon until he was out of ammunition.

2016 – Orlando Pulse Nightclub. Killer reloaded multiple times.

I've stated many times on the radio, in classes, and in writing, that the Orlando Nightclub shooter should not have been able to kill 49 people. If those 300 patrons of the club had gone through one of the classes I teach, they would have stopped him before that many were killed. The reason I can say this is because they would have learned to attack back, and they would have learned how to recognize the opportunities to attack back (ambushing at doors and corners, attacking when the gun can't shoot because of being empty or malfunctioned, etc.).

When attacking back with a firearm, your tactics won't change much. You want to shoot the killer as quickly as possible. Stop the killing. This is how law enforcement are trained, and those that take civilian firearms courses dealing with active shooter situations are trained similarly.

However, when unarmed, knowing that active killers often reload or clear malfunctioning weapons, and how to recognize an empty or malfunctioning firearm, is very important. This can provide an opportunity to stop the killer.

Rushing an active shooter with a functioning firearm is not recommended unless he is so close you can reach him before he can shoot at you. Or, in the rare instance when there just isn't any other option. (And remember, one option is to play Jackie Chan and move and be a hard target.)

If the gun can't fire because of a malfunction or being empty, rushing the shooter is not as bad an idea. Yes, this short gap in the violence, when the shooter is trying to reload or clear the malfunction, is also an opportunity to possibly escape, but it is also the time to attack back and take the killer out. Most healthy mobile people can cross a room or hallway faster than these killers can reload. The opportunity is there, especially if there are several people. If nothing else, tackle him and pound on his head with anything you can get a hold of. The window of opportunity will be short, so you can't hesitate. When you recognize the shooter can't fire his weapon, you must immediately act. If you hesitate, he will have time to reload, clear the malfunction, or possibly draw another firearm or knife.

Because of this, it is important to know how to identify a jammed or empty gun. Besides the pictures here, if you don't know how to tell if a gun is jammed or empty, have someone who owns firearms show you what it looks like. This knowledge can make the difference when it is time to escape or attack back.

Slide locked back when empty

Stovepipe malfunction

Always Check for Secondary Weapons

After disarming an active threat, you must also check for secondary weapons. Many of these killers have carried and used more than one firearm. They may also be armed with knives and possibly explosives.

Never think that a person is no longer a threat just because you took his primary weapon from him. Always check for additional weapons and be sure to debilitate the threat or restrain the person so they can no longer injure anyone else.

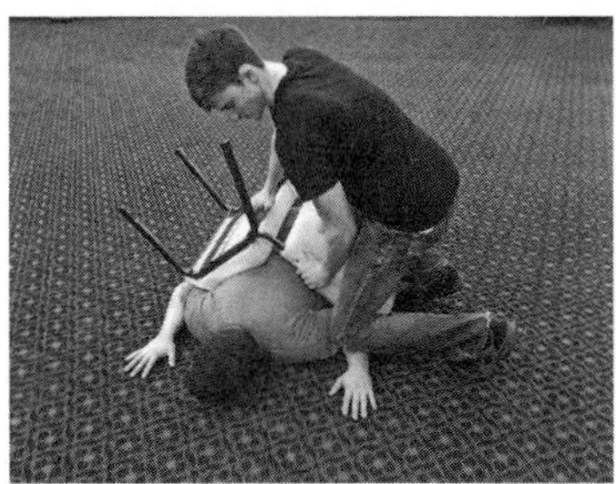

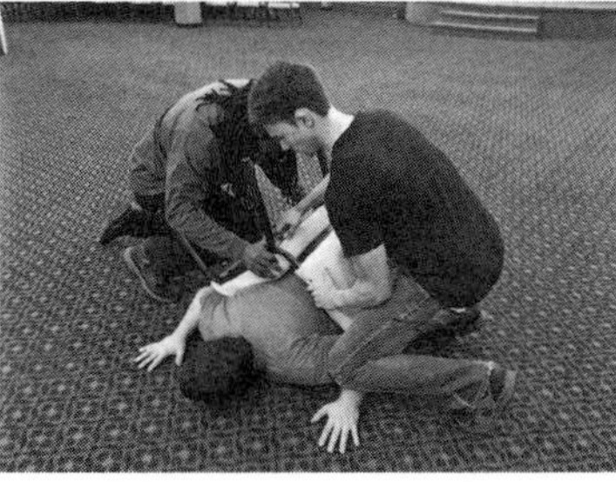

One method to restrain a person who has been completely disarmed is by using a chair. Work as a team and have multiple people hold and restrain the perpetrator until law enforcement takes over.

Always Be Prepared for a Second Threat

After you attack back and stop the threat in front of you, you must prepare for a second threat. This means escape, deny, or if necessary, attack back and neutralize the second threat too. It's easy to stop after subduing a threat as the rush of adrenaline is fueling through your body and forget that there may be another threat or tasks to perform to keep you and others safe or save lives. After any violent encounter, not only do you need to be aware of additional dangers, you must assess yourself and others for injuries, and administer first aid and trauma aid as appropriate and needed.

It's not over until law enforcement have arrived and cleared the entire area, or you are blocks away after escaping to safety. Believing you are safe and the incident is over just because you stopped one gunman can be a fatal mistake. Always be prepared to take action to keep yourself and others safe from an additional threat.

Defending Against an Edged-Weapon Assault

> “Remember, even if your assailant has no idea about how to use a knife in a scientific sense, his only objective is to cut you any way he can.”
>
> Lee Morrison
>
> *The Complete Book of Urban Combatives*

While most of the active threat incidents that have occurred have been with firearms, hence the name of this book, *Survive a Shooting*, there have been active threats with edged weapons, both here in the United States and in other countries around the world. While space won't allow me to provide a full treatise on defending against knives and other edged weapons, I wanted to at least present a few guidelines when faced with such an attack.

Escape

The threat from an edged weapon should not be underestimated. Blades can be easily concealed and are extremely dangerous. People killed by a knife are just as dead as those killed by a firearm. Our escape, deny, attack back framework works when facing an edged weapon just like it does when the active threat is armed with a gun. If escaping is possible, do so. *I repeat, if at any time during a knife assault escaping to safety is possible, do so immediately.* Under no circumstances should you ever engage a person with a knife empty handed unless you have no other option. Always escape to safety if you can.

>  The most important goal you have in your knife defense strategy is preventing yourself from getting hurt. ”
>
> *Michael I. Kaplan*
> *Edge of Freedom: Knife Defense Tactics for a Changing World*

Deny Access and Create Distance

Locking and barricading a person outside of the room you are in is a successful strategy against a knife wielding attacker, just like it is against a gunman. But with a knife, creating distance between you and the killer also denies him access. While a gunman can shoot you from across the room, a person attacking with a knife must be within arms-reach of you to stab or slice you. The more space between you and the knife, the better.

However, don't believe you are safe just because the knife-wielding attacker is across the room. A person with a blade can cover ground quickly and be on top of you before you know it. Experiments show that an attacker with a knife can cover 21 feet in 1.5 seconds. Many law enforcement agencies enacted policies stating that a person with a knife within 21 feet is considered to be in the zone of "imminent danger of death or great bodily harm." (If you would like to learn more about this concept, research Dennis Tueller and the Tueller Drill.) Creating distance allows you to further look for an avenue to escape to safety, look for alternate means to deny access, or to prepare to attack back.

Using a chair to create distance between you and an attacker with a knife is a sound strategy when you have limited options

Alternate means of "deny access" may include getting behind a table or desk and keeping it between you and the attacker with a knife. You may be able to pick up a chair or stool and hold it so the legs are pointed at the attacker to keep him at bay. A broom or mop may be used to keep him away. A backpack full of books may be used as a shield. Anything you can use to keep the knife from stabbing or slicing you is denying access.

Attack Back

If it is absolutely unavoidable, attack back to save yourself or others. If you are armed with a firearm, you may be justified in using it against a knife-wielding attacker. As I stated earlier, if you are carrying a firearm, you should be educated in the responsible use of lethal force. If you are unarmed, arm yourself with improvised or makeshift weapons. Those that provide you distance from the knife such as chairs, long handles, and fire extinguishers; or those that can shield you against stabs and slashes like backpacks, briefcases, or metal trashcan lids can all be good choices.

> Although Krav Maga clearly favors **combining the defense and counterattack simultaneously**, there are situations where this may be difficult to accomplish, e.g., when the attack is sudden and unexpected. Under these circumstances, you may only be able to respond with a defense. It is therefore extremely important to regain your composure immediately and **counterattack forcefully at the first opportunity**, and as soon as possible neutralize (and control) the hand that is holding the knife. **Remember:** Even though the defense prevents the initial attack, it is mainly your counterattack that saves lives and prevents the assailant from achieving his (or her) objective.
>
> *Imi Sde-Or (Lichtenfeld) and Eyal Yanilov*
>
> *Krav Maga: How To Defend Yourself Against Armed Assault*

Attack from the rear or the flank. Ambush at a doorway or corner. Just like attacking back against a gunman, if we can surprise the knife-wielding attacker and hit him from a location he can't see, it increases our odds of success. Spraying the threat in the face with a fire extinguisher and smashing him in the head when his eyes, nose, and mouth are full of fire retardant can be very effective. One more reason I advocate ample fire extinguishers throughout buildings.

If you must attack back empty handed, control the weapon hand, not the weapon. A firm grab on the hand and wrist will avoid your being cut like grabbing the blade may do. Preferably you are doing this with others, and as you control the weapon hand, someone else hits the attacker in the head with something hard and heavy, or with hammer fists if that's all you have. Controlling the weapon hand alone does not stop the attack. It must be combined with someone neutralizing the threat. Up close, a knife can be worse than a gun. The firearm only shoots one direction, and if you keep the muzzle pointed away from you, it won't kill you. It's not the same with a sharp blade. This is why you are better off to use something like a stool or chair to keep the threat away from you until someone from behind can stop him with blunt trauma to the head.

People have stopped knife-wielding attackers with improvised weapons and empty handed. It's not easy, but it can be done. If you attack back, it must be done with ferocity and commitment. Stop the threat with anything and everything available to you. Make sure you are the one who goes home at the end of the day. Be a survivor.

Conclusion

This is the longest chapter in the book and I still wish I had room to write much more. Too many of the resources that advocate fighting back fail to provide information on how to do so. I've attempted to share simple, practical tactics and strategies to increase the odds of being successful when attacking back during an active threat situation. Obviously, there is more learning and training to be done. I highly encourage everyone to take responsibility for their own personal safety and seek out safety and self-defense training. You are doing that by reading this book, and I hope you continue with further study and live training with me or any of the other trainers out there working diligently to help people stay safe and defend themselves if needed.

> “You don't have to take on an active shooter to be a hero, but you are a hero if you do. Simply making a decision in the face of such danger is courageous. Being decisive is being heroic.”
>
> John Geddes
> *Be A Hero: The Essential Survival Guide to Active-Shooter Events*

The things I wrote about here and teach in my classes are serious and only for dire circumstances. And make no mistake about it, if you ever encounter a situation where you have to do the things outlined in this book, it will have lasting consequences. I encourage all survivors to seek out the professional help they need to deal with the aftermath of such an event. I do want to share a comment by Kit Cessna from his book *Equal Or Greater Force*, where he discusses living after a lethal encounter, "During your ordeal and forever after, remember this: you are still alive and that beats the alternative. The alternative in this situation was to have been killed, and death will last forever."

One last time, remember, *Attacking Back* against an active shooter demands an uncompromising burst of savage violence on your part. You must be decisive, ruthless, and committed to doing whatever it takes to stop the shooter. You must have a Survivor's Attitude!

For instructional videos of the techniques shown in this chapter, please go to:

www.surviveashooting.com/bookbonus

Enter your name and e-mail. You will be taken to a page with video instruction and the updated resource list.

Stop the Bleeding

www.SurviveaShooting.com

Don't get caught on the blood or injuries which can be horrific – our goal as first responders is to stop the bleeding!

Laura J. Kendall, MCIP
Active Shooter Response Training: Tactical Trauma Care for First Responders

TOPICS

- ✓ Terminology
- ✓ Actions Before Approaching the Casualty
- ✓ How to Check the Casualty for Responsiveness
- ✓ Controlling Hemorrhaging
- ✓ Treating Open Chest Wounds (Sucking Chest Wounds)
- ✓ Treatment for Shock
- ✓ Your Personal First Aid/Trauma Kit

Casualties during an active threat, especially an active shooter incident, most resemble casualties during combat. To prepare, individuals should be familiar with trauma aid, or tactical combat casualty care, as opposed to general first aid taught by the local Red Cross, YMCA, or other such organization. This is not to say you shouldn't take CPR and First Aid classes. You should! I strongly urge you to attend a hands-on first-aid or basic life support course as well as keeping your CPR certification current. The components of an open airway, effective breathing and circulation (the ABCs of Airway, Breathing, Circulation that are taught in most courses) are still essential for survival, but they won't be the focus of this chapter.

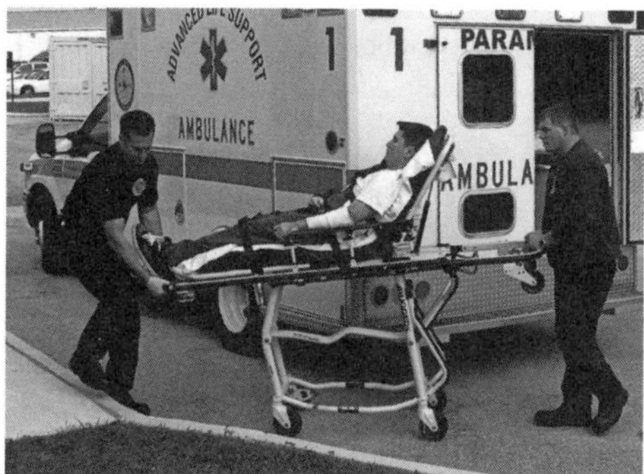

Military studies indicate that extremity hemorrhage (severe bleeding from an arm or leg), tension pneumothorax, and airway obstruction are the primary preventable causes of death in modern combat, with extremity hemorrhage resulting in the most deaths. These conditions can be treated on the battlefield, and this treatment can be the difference between being a combat death on the battlefield and a recovering soldier in a medical treatment facility. It has been estimated that proper use of self-aid, buddy-aid, and combat lifesaver skills can reduce battlefield deaths by 15 to 18 percent.

This chapter focuses on a similar type of casualty care. The goal is to keep wounded alive until they can receive medical care from an EMT or a doctor at a hospital or an appropriate facility. Treatment will usually consist of using a tourniquet to stop life threatening bleeding from wounds on the extremities and moving the casualty to safety. We do everything we can for a casualty until someone with more training takes over. It is important to remember that there may be no one to help you, and you should be able to administer self-aid and put a tourniquet or pressure bandage on your own limbs.

Remember, how you react and the actions you take can make all the difference between life and death. The situation will require a rapid assessment and urgent medical attention.

Terminology

These are basic terms used by the U.S. Army in the Combat Lifesaver Course to help you better understand this chapter. I also encourage you to consult a medical dictionary for unfamiliar terms.

Casualty. The casualty is a person who is injured.

Rescuer. The rescuer is the person who is attempting to aid the casualty (provide treatment and/or move the casualty to safety).

Self-Aid. Self-aid is care (treatment) you give yourself when you are the casualty.

Extremity. The term extremity refers to one of the limbs.

- **Upper extremity.** Upper extremity refers to the arm (located between the shoulder and the elbow) and the forearm (located between the elbow and the wrist). Often, the term "arm" is used to refer to the arm, forearm, and hand. The terms "upper arm" and "lower arm" are sometimes used to refer to the arm and the forearm respectively.
- **Lower extremity.** Lower extremity refers to the thigh (located between the hip and the knee) and the leg (located between the knee and the ankle). Often, the term "leg" is used to refer to the thigh, leg, and foot. The terms "upper leg" and "lower leg" are sometimes used to refer to the thigh and leg respectively.

Hemorrhage. Hemorrhage is another word for bleeding. It usually refers to serious bleeding.

Dressing. The term "dressing" refers to the material that is placed directly over the wound. The dressing absorbs some of the blood and helps a clot to form. The clot "plugs" the wound to stop the bleeding. The dressing also protects the wound from additional contamination and injury.

Bandage. A Bandage is the material used to hold (secure) the dressing in place so the dressing will not slip and destroy the clot that is forming. The ends of the bandage are called the tails.

Field Dressing. The field dressing consists of a pad of sterile (germ-free) white dressing with a bandage (usually olive drab) already attached to the dressing pad. The field dressing is wrapped in paper which is then sealed in a plastic envelope. The field dressing is also called the field first aid dressing and the combat dressing. It is being replaced by the Emergency Bandage, but may still be encountered.

Emergency Bandage. The Emergency Bandage consists of a sterile white pad with an elastic tail and a pressure device used to apply continuous pressure to the wound. This bandage is also known as the "emergency trauma dressing," "emergency trauma bandage," "Israeli pressure dressing," and "Israeli bandage." It is replacing the field dressing in the military's individual first aid kits.

Combat Gauze. Combat Gauze is also called the hemostatic bandage. It uses pressure and a chemical to help stop the bleeding. A hemostatic agent is an agent that arrests the flow of blood.

Tourniquet. A Tourniquet is a device for compressing the blood vessels of an extremity in order to stop blood flow distal (see definition below) to the tourniquet band.

Combat Application Tourniquet. The Combat Application Tourniquet (CAT) is a device developed specifically to be used as a tourniquet. It is a component of the military's Improved First Aid Kit.

Distal. Distal means away from the point of reference. For what we are dealing with in this chapter, the heart is the central point of reference. The hand is distal to the elbow because the hand is farther from the heart than is the elbow. (Follow the path of blood flow from the heart through the arteries as a guideline.) It is the opposite of proximal.

Proximal. Proximal means toward the point of reference (heart). The knee is proximal to the foot because the knee is closer to the heart (following blood flow) than is the foot. It is the opposite of distal.

Artery. Arteries are blood vessels that carry oxygenated blood to the tissues of the body from the heart.

Vein. Veins are blood vessels that carry blood from the parts of the body back to the heart.

Actions Before Approaching the Casualty

Before you can provide assistance to a casualty, you must first determine that you can do so safely. I understand that this can be counterintuitive, especially if the casualty is someone you care about. But you must remember, if you become a casualty attempting to provide assistance, there may be no one else to help either of you.

I'm often asked when teaching groups of teachers, "What if we are barricading in the classroom and a student is out in the hall?" Sometimes the student is mobile, other times the student is injured, and sometimes it is a co-worker and not a student when teaching at medical centers or businesses, but it always involves going into danger to help someone else. My answer is usually the same, "I can't answer that."

I then explain that each situation is different, and there is no "absolute" or "correct" answer. In an active shooter incident, I'm going to react differently if I am with my wife and daughter than if I am alone. I will respond differently if I am working and responsible for the safety of other people than I would out by myself. But, I also point out that even by myself or working, I have a responsibility to make it home to my family. We will all have conflicting interests during an emergency.

If you are a teacher, do you risk opening a door where an armed intruder could come into a room filled with students to help a single student in the hall? Do you risk leaving your children parentless to attempt to help a co-worker? I don't know, and I can't tell you what you should do. I will say that you need to be able to sleep at night, and it is important to think about these things before they ever happen so if they do occur, you are better prepared to respond.

If you determine you can provide assistance to a casualty, remember to protect yourself.

1. Scan the area for potential danger.
    a. Survey the area for the armed intruder.
    b. Survey the area for fire or explosive devices.
    c. Survey building for structural stability.
    d. Determine if there is a threat of chemical or biological agents.
2. Determine the best route of access to the casualty and the best route of egress. If you need to move the casualty to a safer area, be sure to select an area that you can deny the threat access to you, this could be with optimum cover and concealment, or a room that can be locked and

barricaded. Plan your evacuation route prior to exposing yourself to possible gun fire.

3. If you need to move the casualty to a safer area, request help if available. Two people can move a person much easier than one.
4. Anticipate the type of injuries the casualty may have received and what care will probably be needed. Was the person shot or stabbed? Was there an explosion where the casualty may have blast effects? Was the person hit with something that could have broken bones?
5. Anticipate how your actions (movement, noise, light, and so forth) may affect the armed intruder's attack.
6. Decide what care you can administer when you reach the casualty and what care will have to wait until you have moved the casualty to a place of safety. Note: a soldier may have to provide care under fire, but I strongly recommend civilians facing an active threat *always* move the casualty to a place of safety before administering any care.
7. If you need to move the casualty to safety, determine how you will move the casualty.
8. If your own life is in imminent danger, you may need to wait until there isn't the imminent threat before providing assistance to others.

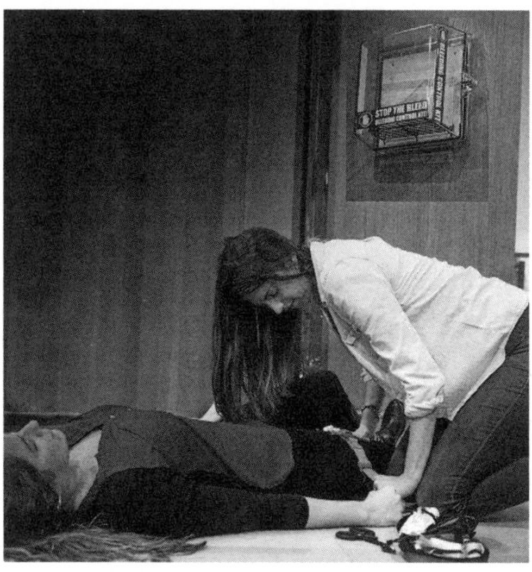

The MARCH Algorithm

The MARCH algorithm, which appears to originate from the UK military, is being used with Tactical Combat Casualty Care (TCCC) and advanced trauma life support courses. It is a simple acronym for remembering the necessary steps in priority for saving lives in combat. It can also be useful in prioritizing care during an active shooter event. MARCH stands for:

M – Massive hemorrhage
A – Airway
R – Respiratory
C – Circulation
H – Hypothermia (can also add Head injury)

Because stopping the bleeding is so critical during an active shooting event, I want focus on the M – Massive Hemorrhaging and share the four Ds to address massive hemorrhaging from an article by Rom Duckworth for *Rescue Digest*:

Detect: find the source of the bleeding.
Direct pressure: hold pressure on the source of the bleeding until the clot forms.
Devices: if necessary, use equipment such as tourniquets, hemostatic gauze, and pressure bandages to supplement direct pressure.
Don't dilute: use the concept of hypotensive resuscitation to avoid thinning the blood or pumping established clots.

How to Check the Casualty for Responsiveness

Once you are in a safe place, and this may mean you had to move the casualty, you can check for responsiveness. This is the same procedure taught in the U.S. Army.

1. Upon reaching the casualty, check the casualty for responsiveness.
   a. Ask in a loud, but calm, voice: "Are you okay?" Gently shake or tap the casualty on the shoulder.
   b. If the casualty is conscious, ask where it hurts or where his body feels different from usual. This helps to determine the level of consciousness

and provides you with information that can be used when treating the casualty.

2. Ask the casualty questions to determine his or her level of consciousness. Ask the casualty questions that require more than a "yes" or "no" answer. Examples of such questions are: "What is your name?", "What is the date?", and "Where are we?"
   a. The AVPU (Alert, Verbal, Pain, Unresponsive) scale is used in determining the casualty's level of consciousness. The four levels used in the AVPU scale are given below:
      1. A – The casualty is *alert* (knows who he or she is, the date, where he or she is, and such.)
      2. V – The casualty is not alert, but does respond to *verbal* (oral) commands.
      3. P – The casualty responds to *pain*, but not to verbal commands.
      4. U – The casualty is *unresponsive* (unconscious).
   b. The following are some guidelines to use when assessing the casualty's level of consciousness:
      1. A casualty who is yelling at you, telling you where the threat is, or performing similar actions is alert.
      2. If the casualty is alert or responds to voice, *do not* check the casualty's response to pain.
      3. To check a casualty's response to pain, rub his breastbone (sternum) briskly with your knuckle.

Controlling Hemorrhaging

Bleeding from a wound on the extremity is the greatest cause of preventable death in an active shooter incident. You must quickly check the casualty for potentially life-threatening hemorrhaging (severe arterial bleeding) from an extremity. You may notice the shirt sleeve or pant leg is red from bleeding. If severe bleeding is found, quickly apply a tourniquet high on the injured limb over the clothes and tighten it to stop arterial bleeding.

Three Types of Bleeding

1. **Capillary Bleeding.** Smallest blood vessels that deliver oxygenated blood to the tissues and take back deoxygenated blood to the veins. Capillary bleeding is slow and oozes out. It stops quickly with direct pressure.

2. **Venous Bleeding.** Veins carry blood with little to no oxygen in them which explains the dark red color. They are not under pressure and bleed slow and steadily. Deep cuts have the potential to cut open veins. The best way to stop most cases of venous bleeding is to put direct pressure on the wound. This is when a Pressure Bandage would be applied to help slow and stop the bleeding. But remember we are not trying to stop the pulse in the affected area so not too tight!

Check for Entrance and Exit Wounds

It is important to check the victim, or yourself, if shot, for not only an entrance wound, but an exit wound as well. Entrance wounds tend to be smaller. Exit wounds can be huge blow out wounds. You must treat both if there is an arterial bleed. Sometimes the bullet will stay inside the body and there won't be an exit wound.

3. Arterial Bleeding – the deadly killer! Arteries carry freshly oxygenated blood (which is why arteries have bright red blood in them) from the heart to be distributed to the tissues of the body. Because they carry rich oxygenated blood that must go throughout the body, they are under pressure. This is why arterial bleeds are so deadly.

Arterial bleeding is the least common but the deadliest type of bleeding. In an arterial bleed the blood is bright red and spurts out each time the heart beats. Picture a garden hose on at full blast. This is what a bleed of a major artery looks like. Literally the victim will be dead in 3-5 minutes if no first aid is given. In most cases of arterial bleeding, direct and extremely firm pressure on the wound is the best way of stopping it.

If direct pressure is not applied, a severe arterial wound can cause you to bleed to death within minutes. Arterial bleeding may be hard to notice right away if the victim is wearing dark clothing or if it's a dark environment. You will need to look at the clothing and watch for pooling of blood in one spot that seeps through the clothing.

If you have attempted to control the bleeding with direct pressure and it will not stop, you must immediately apply a tourniquet to stop the bleeding. The benefit of tourniquet use in patients with massive hemorrhage has been proven and is now the standard of care.

(Source: *Active Shooter Response Training: Tactical Trauma Care For First Responders* by Laura J. Kendall, MICP.)

If the bleeding (hemorrhaging) from an extremity isn't severe, or you don't have a tourniquet, the bleeding can usually be controlled by applying a dressing and bandage, applying manual pressure, elevating the injured limb, or applying a pressure dressing. If the casualty is bleeding from a limb and these methods do not control the bleeding, then a tourniquet must be applied to stop the loss of blood from the limb.

If there is an amputation of the arm, forearm, thigh or leg, a tourniquet must be applied immediately since the other measures are inadequate to control the bleeding. If you are in doubt and a tourniquet is available, use it to control the hemorrhaging. It is the surest way to stop life threatening bleeding from a limb. Remember, high and tight, just like the Army Ranger haircut.

Now let's look at the different methods of controlling hemorrhaging in a little more detail.

Applying a Tourniquet

A tourniquet is a constricting band placed around an extremity to stop arterial bleeding by stopping blood circulation to the part of the limb below (distal to) the tourniquet. They are used for arms or legs when there is a danger of the casualty bleeding to death. They are not used for wounds to the head, neck, or trunk (chest and abdominal area).

Bleeding from a major artery that can't be controlled by a pressure dressing or firm hand pressure requires a tourniquet. An amputation, either complete (the limb is completely severed) or partial (the two parts of the limb remain connected by some skin or other tissue), requires a tourniquet.

The military uses the Combat Application Tourniquet (CAT), and those are the ones I am most familiar with as well. There are other brands that are also good quality tourniquets. The important thing is to buy one from a reputable manufacturer and not a cheaper knock off. When someone's life is on the line, I want to spend a few extra dollars to ensure the product is going to do what it is designed to do. I'm going to explain the procedures for applying the CAT. Most others are similar, but if you carry another version, just be sure you know how to use it.

Amputations

A person who has suffered an amputation of the arm or leg may not be bleeding severely when first discovered. A tourniquet should be applied anyway. Lack of bleeding is due to the body's normal defenses (contraction and spasm of blood vessels) because of the amputation. Bleeding will usually start when the blood vessels relax or if the clot is knocked loose while moving the casualty. Put a tourniquet on an amputation immediately.

The CAT is usually stored in the one-handed application configuration. If you are using an older CAT, the end will already be through one half of the friction buckle. (On an arm, you don't always need to use the friction buckle, but on a leg, the complete buckle should be used.) If the loop isn't already formed, put the end through the buckle. Then slide the wounded extremity through the loop formed by the tourniquet band. If you have the newer GEN7 CAT tourniquet, they have a single routing buckle designed for simpler and faster application with more efficient slack removal. Make sure you know how to use the tourniquet you are carrying.

You will see some instructions that tell you to place the band two inches above the wound. The Army taught that too. However, based on the recommendation of a friend and fellow trainer who was a combat medic in Iraq and Afghanistan, I'm recommending you put the tourniquet on as high as you can on the limb. Put it as close to the arm pit or groin as possible. This will ensure you stop bleeding of a second wound you may have missed, and it places the tourniquet where it can most readily stop arterial bleeding.

Pull the band tight and fasten it to itself. Make sure the windlass is on the outside so you can access it easily. Twist the windlass rod to tighten the tourniquet band. Continue tightening until the bleeding stops. Place the windlass rod inside the rod-locking clip to keep it in place. If you have tightened it as tight as you can and the bleeding has not stopped, put another tourniquet on proximal to the first tourniquet, or use a pressure bandage or direct pressure if another tourniquet is not available.

Marking a Casualty

The military teaches to write a "T" and the time of application on the casualty's skin with an indelible marker. The "T" alerts medical personnel that a tourniquet has been applied. The CAT and other tourniquets have a place where you can record the time of application, but putting the "T" and time on the forehead will insure medical personnel don't miss it.

In combat zones, soldiers have been saved with their limbs with tourniquets being on for up to six hours. In active shooter or active threat situations, the likelihood that it will take that long to receive medical attention is rare. When in doubt about severe hemorrhaging, use a tourniquet to stop the bleeding. Put it on high and tight and you can save a life.

Monitor Tourniquet

If the situation permits, check the casualty for a pulse distal to the tourniquet. If a pulse is present, attempt to tighten the tourniquet more or apply another tourniquet side-by-side and proximal (above) to the existing tourniquet. This measure will help to prevent a compartment syndrome or expanding hematoma from threatening the viability of the extremity.

Do not cover the tourniquet. Leave the tourniquet in full view so medical personnel can locate it quickly. And any time you move the casualty, recheck the tourniquet to make sure it is still controlling the bleeding.

CAT Generation 7 Tourniquet

Improvise to Save Lives

Improvisation saves lives. In an emergency, you may have to think outside-the-box and improvise when the ideal tools are not available. Towels, blankets, or clothing can be ripped into strips to be used to tie splints, act as bandages, or even used for tourniquets. During the chaos of the October 2017 Las Vegas shooting, belts became tourniquets, folding tables and barricades were used as stretchers, and personal pickup trucks became ambulances. Normal people were improvising and saving lives.

An improvised tourniquet can save a life. However, it's not as simple as some want to believe. Thinking you will just use your belt as a tourniquet during an active shooter incident or other emergency isn't proper planning. Many belts are too stiff to be tightened enough to compress the arteries enough to stop all the bleeding. (But if it is all you have, use it. Slowing the bleeding may be enough to save a life.)

If you are going to improvise and make a makeshift tourniquet, you want something between one and two inches wide, and that is pliable enough that a windlass can be inserted to tighten the material until the bleeding stops. A strip of denim, a triangular bandage, a wide neck tie, or anything similar will often work better than a stiff leather belt.

Don't use electrical cords, paracord, shoelaces, and other narrow items. These are more likely to cause tissue and nerve damage rather than stop arterial bleeding.

With this said, it is much better to have a manufactured device available. Tourniquets such as the CAT and other reputable devices are easily available. There really is no reason to not have a tourniquet in your personal first aid kit, in your vehicle, and in your home. I think it should be standard for every school, government building, and private business to have tourniquets in first aid kits readily available.

Yes, knowing how to improvise is important. But planning to improvise because you don't carry or stock the correct equipment in your first aid kits isn't very prudent or wise.

Flatpack Tourniquet Carrier

There are a variety of ways people carry tourniquets, and if in a larger medical kit, that doesn't have to be carried, it isn't as big a problem. But for those that carry a tourniquet with their EDC (Every Day Carry), compactness is a priority. With the windlass on tourniquets, this makes it a bit more difficult.

There are a number of pouches available, but another option I found that I like is the Flatpack Tourniquet Carrier. You need to fold the tourniquet in a particular way, and then the carrier keeps it flat and ready for immediate use.
Sure, you could fold it the same way and use tape or rubber bands to keep it in the flat shape, but then it will take too long to access when needed. If you are looking for a carrier for your EDC tourniquet, this carrier might just be the best option for you.

Controlling Bleeding Without a Tourniquet

Bleeding (hemorrhaging) from an extremity can also be controlled by applying a dressing and bandage, applying manual pressure, elevating the injured limb, and applying a pressure dressing. The military type Emergency Bandage serves as a dressing and bandage. It can also be a pressure dressing.

Expose the Wound and Check for Entrance and Exit Wounds

If possible, expose the wound by pushing or cutting away loose clothing around the casualty's wound. If clothing or anything else is stuck to the wound, it should be left alone. Do not attempt to clean the wound. During the emergency, we are concerned with stopping the bleeding and saving lives.

Carefully examine the casualty to determine if there is more than one wound. A bullet or piece of shrapnel may enter one place and exit another. Exit wounds are usually larger than the entrance wound. If there are entrance and exit wounds, both need to be dressed and bandaged.

Gauze and Bandage

Most first aid kits will have some gauze and a form of bandage (not the little band-aids, but an ACE Bandage or similar). These are inexpensive, and I recommend adding extra of both to all of your first aid kits.

Find the source of the most active bleeding and pack gauze tightly into the wound and directly onto the source of the bleeding. Quickly apply manual pressure to get the bleeding to stop. If the situation permits it, it is recommended that you apply continuous pressure for at least three minutes. Apply the bandage to the wound to secure the gauze in the wound. Tuck the end of the bandage under the final wrap to keep it in place.

Pressure Dressing

If blood continues to seep from the dressing after you have applied manual pressure, apply a pressure dressing. The military's Emergency Bandage or the Israeli Bandage are built to use as a pressure dressing. If you don't have one of these, you can improvise.

To use the Emergency Bandage, remove it from the pouch and packaging and place the pad (dressing) directly on the wound. Wrap the elastic bandage around the wounded extremity and insert the elastic bandage completely into the pressure bar. Pull the elastic bandage back over the top of the pressure bar, reversing direction. (This forces the bar down onto the pad.) Wrap the elastic bandage tightly over the pressure bar. Continue to wrap the elastic bandage around the limb so that all edges of the pad are covered. Secure the bandage.

If you don't have a bandage with the built-in pressure bar, you can improvise by taking a wad of padding and placing it over the dressing that is on top of the wound. You can make this wad from folded muslin bandage, a rag, material torn from clothing, etc. Wrap with a bandage or something improvised such as a handkerchief, sock, or strip of clothing. If all you have is an elastic bandage, twisting it to go the other direction as you wrap will also form a type of pressure dressing.

Don't use narrow materials such as a shoestring as it would likely damage blood vessels and nerve tissue. Use something that is wide. If bleeding appears to be controlled, continue to check the distal end of the wounded extremity (fingers and toes) periodically to ensure that adequate blood circulation is maintained. If the area below the dressing becomes cool, blue, or numb, loosen and reapply the pressure dressing.

Digital Pressure

Absent of a tourniquet or dressing and bandage, applying digital pressure to pressure points is another method of controlling bleeding. You use fingers, thumbs, heel of the hand, or knee to press at the site or point where a main artery supplying the wounded area lies near the skin surface or over bone. This pressure may help shut off or slow down the flow of blood from the heart to the wound. Here are two of these pressure points that are taught in the Army's Combat Lifesaver course:

1. Arm (Brachial Artery). Digital pressure is used to control severe bleeding of the lower part of the arm and elbow.
    a. The pressure point is located above the elbow on the inside of the arm in the groove between the muscles.
    b. Using your fingers or thumb, apply pressure to the inside of the arm over the bone.
2. Groin (Femoral Artery). Digital pressure is used to control severe bleeding of the thigh and lower leg.
    a. The pressure point is located on the front, center part of the crease in the groin.
    b. Using the heel of your hand or your knee, apply pressure to press the artery against the bone. Lean forward to apply pressure.

Treating Open Chest Wounds (Sucking Chest Wounds)

Having to treat a penetrating chest trauma, or an open chest wound, is another possibility during an active shooter event. Knowing what to do can save a person's life. An open chest wound can be caused by the chest wall being penetrated by a bullet, knife blade, shrapnel, or other object. If you are not sure if the wound has penetrated the chest wall completely, treat the wound as though it were an open chest wound.

Here are a few signs and symptoms of an open chest wound:

1. Sucking or hissing sounds coming from chest wound. (When a casualty with an open chest wound breathes, air goes in and out of the wound. This air sometimes causes a "sucking" sound. Because of this distinct sound, an open chest wound is often called a "sucking chest wound.")
2. Casualty coughing up blood (hemoptysis).
3. Frothy blood coming from the chest wound. (The air going in and out of an open chest wound causes bubbles in the blood coming from the wound.)
4. Shortness of breath or difficulty in breathing.
5. Chest not rising normally when the casualty inhales. (The casualty may have several fractured ribs and the lung may be deflated.)
6. Pain in the shoulder or chest area that increases with breathing.
7. Bluish tint of lips, inside of mouth, fingertips, and/or nail beds (cyanosis). (This color change is caused by the decreased amount of oxygen in the blood.)
8. Signs of shock such as a rapid and weak heartbeat.

Steps to Treat an Open Chest Wound

Check for Open Chest Wounds

Check for both entry and exit wounds. Look for a pool of blood under the casualty's back. Open the clothes to look for penetrating wounds. Use your hands to feel for wounds. If there is more than one open chest wound, treat the initial wound you find first.

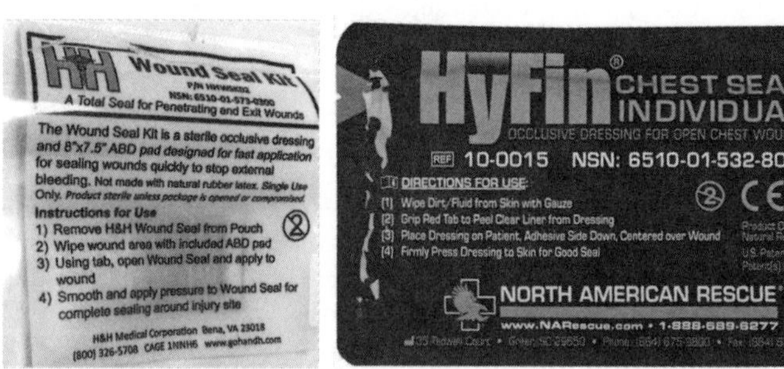

H & H and HyFin Open Wound Seals

Expose the Wound

Expose the area around the open chest wound by removing, cutting, or tearing the clothing covering the wound. If clothing is stuck to the wound, do not try to remove the stuck clothing as this may cause additional pain and injury. Cut or tear around the stuck clothing. Do not try to clean the wound or remove objects from the wound.

Seal the Open Chest Wound

Since air can pass through most dressings and bandages, you must seal the open chest wound with plastic, cellophane, or other nonporous, airtight material to prevent air from entering the chest and collapsing the lung.

Applying a Chest Seal

What do you do if the person you are trying to help has a lot of chest hair, and you can't get the chest seal to actually seal tight to the skin? A buddy of mine who was a combat medic in Iraq and Afghanistan teaches people to stick it on, rip it off, removing the hair in the process, and then put another seal on that you can secure tight and prevent air from escaping.

Ideally, you have a commercially available chest seal. There are different kinds of these, but basically, they are made of a nonporous material with a sticky side to stick the seal onto the person over the wound. I have some H&H Wound Seal Kits in my gear. The nice thing about the commercially available chest seals is they are sterile, quick, and they have directions on them to help you if needed.

If you don't have a commercially available chest seal in your first aid kit, you can make an improvised seal using any plastic, cellophane, or other nonporous, airtight material you can find. Cut the edges if needed so you make a flat plastic surface of whatever wrapper or material you are using.

Protruding Objects

If an object is protruding from the chest wound, do not try to remove it. Place airtight material (such as Vaseline gauze) around the object to form as airtight a seal as possible. Stabilize the object by placing a bulky dressing made from the cleanest material available around the object. Apply improvised bandages to hold the sealing material and dressings in place. Do not wrap the bandages around the protruding object.

Tell the casualty to exhale (breath out) and hold his breath. This forces some of the air out of the chest wound. The more air that can be forced out of the chest before the wound is sealed, the better the casualty will be able to breathe after the wound is sealed. The casualty can resume normal breathing after the wound is sealed. If the casualty is unconscious or cannot hold his breath, place the plastic wrapper over the wound after his chest falls but before it rises.

Place the cleaner surface of the plastic directly over the hole in the chest to seal the wound. Try to ensure that it extends at least two inches beyond the wound edges in all directions. If you don't have a two-inch margin, it may not form an airtight seal and may even be sucked into the wound. If the plastic you are using is not large enough, or is torn, find something else to use that will ensure the airtight seal.

Once you have it over the hole, tape down all four edges of the plastic to the casualty's chest. The airtight seal will keep air from entering the casualty's chest through the wound. It used to be taught to leave an "escape" valve on one of the corners, and some of the earlier commercially manufactured seals had a valve built in. This is no longer the standard. Just tape down all four sides and make a complete seal.

You may ask the casualty to help hold the seal in place, or you may place a dressing over the seal and wrap a bandage around it as added insurance that it will stay sealed.

If there is more than one open chest wound, apply an airtight seal over the other wound and tape all four sides of the airtight material.

Place a conscious casualty in the sitting position or on his side (recovery position) with his injured side next to the ground. Pressure from contact with the ground acts like a splint to the injured side and helps to reduce the pain. Place an unconscious casualty in the recovery position on his injured side.

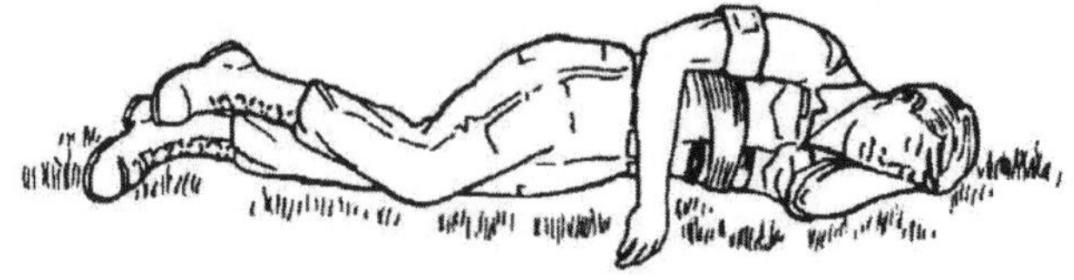

Casualty recovery position

Treatment for Shock

You should anticipate shock in all injured personnel. Shock is a condition caused by the critical reduction in the effective volume of blood circulating in the casualty's blood vessels. It can be the result of loss of blood through bleeding; loss of blood into the tissues, such as with a broken thigh; and loss of fluids through sweating, vomiting, and diarrhea. A few signs indicating shock include if a person has pale, cold, and clammy skin; a fast and weak pulse; and fast and shallow breathing.

To treat, ensure the airway is open and treat any other injuries. Then keep the casualty warm and still. Any rough handling of a casualty suffering from shock is dangerous.

Here are some guidelines for treatment for shock from the U.S. Army. Not all of these will be applicable in all situations:

- If the victim is conscious, place him on a level surface with the lower extremities elevated 15 to 20 centimeters (6-8 inches).
- If the victim is unconscious, place him on his side or abdomen with his head turned to one side to prevent choking on vomit, blood, or other fluids.
- If you are unsure of the best position, place the victim perfectly flat.
- Once the victim is in a shock position, do not move him.
- Maintain body heat by insulating the victim from the surroundings and, in some instances, applying external heat.
- If wet, remove all the victim's wet clothing as soon as possible and replace with dry clothing.
- Improvise a shelter to insulate the victim from the weather.
- Use warm liquids or foods, a pre-warmed sleeping bag, another person, warmed water in canteens, hot rocks wrapped in clothing, or fires on either side of the victim to provide external warmth.
- If the victim is conscious, slowly administer small doses of a warm salt or sugar solution, if available.
- If the victim is unconscious or has abdominal wounds, do not give fluids by mouth.
- Have the victim rest for at least 24 hours.
- If you are a lone survivor, lie in a depression in the ground, behind a tree, or any other place out of the weather, with your head lower than your feet.
- If you are with a buddy, reassess your patient constantly.

Remember, getting you and the casualty to a safe place is paramount. Next, ensure the person is breathing and stop any bleeding. Once you are both in a safe place and injuries have been treated, treat for shock. Since most active threat situations are over rather quickly, it shouldn't be that long before professional first responders will be on-site to take over for you. But the actions you take in those first few minutes can make the difference if a person will live or die. These basic skills save lives.

Moving a Casualty

It may be necessary for you to move a casualty to a safe location before you will be able to treat the injuries. Once treated, it may become necessary to move a casualty because your "safe" location becomes compromised. The military organizes different techniques to move casualties into four categories:

1. Individual movement techniques.
2. Drags.
3. Manual Carries (one-person and two person).
4. Litter carries.

In most active threat situations, you are not going to have all of these options. And the brutal fact of the matter is that it's difficult to move a person, especially when they are bigger than you. Sometimes all you can do is grab an arm or a leg and drag the person to safety. And often that is enough to save a life.

If the casualty is able to move on his own, he needs to assist you by moving himself. You may need to encourage the person, or even order the person, to move and help you get them to a safe place.

While there are manual carries, they are not easily executed. You will most likely need to practice these beforehand and be in good physical condition with adequate strength levels to be able to perform them. These include the fireman's carry and the easier Hawes Carry.

Fireman's Carry

Hawes Carry

Stop the Bleed

Launched in October of 2015 by the White House, Stop the Bleed is a national awareness campaign and a call to action. Stop the Bleed is intended to cultivate grassroots efforts that encourage bystanders to become trained, equipped, and empowered to help in a bleeding emergency before professional help arrives.

Here are the basics taught in this campaign:

No matter how rapid the arrival of professional emergency responders, bystanders will always be first on the scene. A person who is bleeding can die from blood loss within five minutes, therefore it is important to quickly stop the blood loss. Those nearest to someone with life threatening injuries are best positioned to provide first care. According to a recent National Academies of Science study, trauma is the leading cause of death for Americans under age 46.

Remember to be aware of your surroundings and move yourself and the injured person to safety, if necessary.

Call 911

You may be able to save a life by taking simple actions immediately, here are three you can take to help save a life:

1. **Apply Pressure with Hands**. EXPOSE to find where the bleeding is coming from and apply FIRM, STEADY PRESSURE to the bleeding site with both hands if possible.
2. **Apply Dressing and Press.** EXPOSE to find where the bleeding is coming from and apply FIRM, STEADY PRESSURE to the bleeding site with bandages or clothing.
3. **Apply Tourniquet(s).** If the bleeding doesn't stop, place a tourniquet 2-3 inches closer to the torso from the bleeding. The tourniquet may be applied and secured over clothing. If the bleeding still doesn't stop, place a second tourniquet closer to the torso from first tourniquet.

Source: Department of Homeland Security

The Stop the Bleed national awareness campaign also sponsors and provides local training in many communities throughout the United States. These classes teach the basics of trauma aid and stopping bleeding. It is well worth attending these classes.

No matter how rapid the arrival of professional emergency responders, bystanders will always be first on the scene. A person who is bleeding can die from blood loss within five minutes, so it's important to quickly stop the blood loss.

Remember to be aware of your surroundings and move yourself and the injured person to safety, if necessary.

Call 911.

Bystanders can take simple steps to keep the injured alive until appropriate medical care is available. Here are three actions that you can take to help save a life:

1. Apply Pressure with Hands

EXPOSE to find where the bleeding is coming from and apply **FIRM, STEADY PRESSURE** to the bleeding site with both hands if possible.

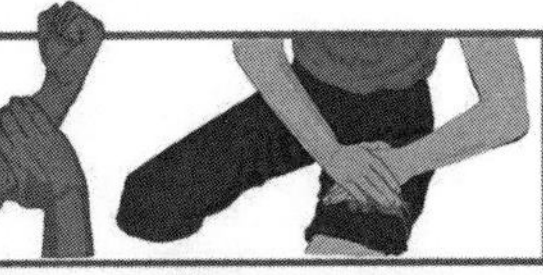

2. Apply Dressing and Press

EXPOSE to find where the bleeding is coming from and apply **FIRM, STEADY PRESSURE** to the bleeding site with bandages or clothing.

3. Apply Tourniquet(s)

If the bleeding doesn't stop, place a tourniquet 2-3 inches closer to the torso from the bleeding. The tourniquet may be applied and secured over clothing.

If the bleeding still doesn't stop, place a second tourniquet closer to the torso from first tourniquet.

PULL the strap through the buckle, **TWIST** the rod tightly, **CLIP** and **SECURE** the rod with the clasp or the Velcro strap.

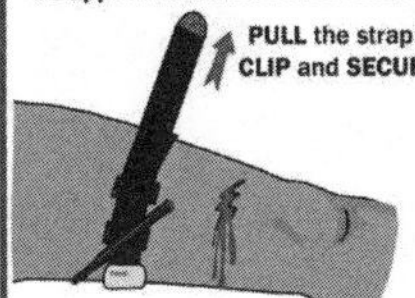

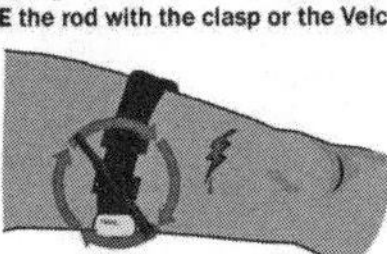

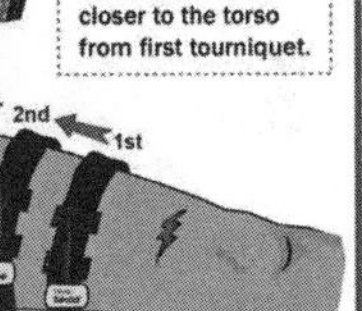

The 'Stop the Bleed' campaign was initiated by a federal interagency workgroup convened by the National Security Council Staff, The White House. The purpose of the campaign is to build national resilience by better preparing the public to save lives by raising awareness of basic actions to stop life threatening bleeding following everyday emergencies and man-made and natural disasters. Advances made by military medicine and research in hemorrhage control during the wars in Afghanistan and Iraq have informed the work of this initiative which exemplifies translation of knowledge back to the homeland to the benefit of the general public. The Department of the Defense owns the 'Stop the Bleed' logo and phrase - trademark pending."

Office of Health Affairs

Your Personal First Aid/Trauma Kit

I strongly encourage everyone to have a first aid and trauma aid kit. I differentiate those because most of the commercially sold first aid kits lack things such as tourniquets that are necessary to save lives after severe trauma. You will find commercially made "trauma kits" that contain items you will need in these major emergencies.

I actually encourage people to have more than one, as well as different kits for organizations, businesses, schools, churches, and so on. Remember, these are like insurance. You never want to use them, but in an emergency, you are certainly glad you have it. And overlap is also good. What I mean by this is, if your business has a large commercially purchased Mass Casualty Response Kit, that's great. But it is also prudent for you to have a smaller kit in your classroom or office, and maybe your personal every day carry kit on you as well. These may contain the same or similar items, but in different quantities, and that overlap is good.

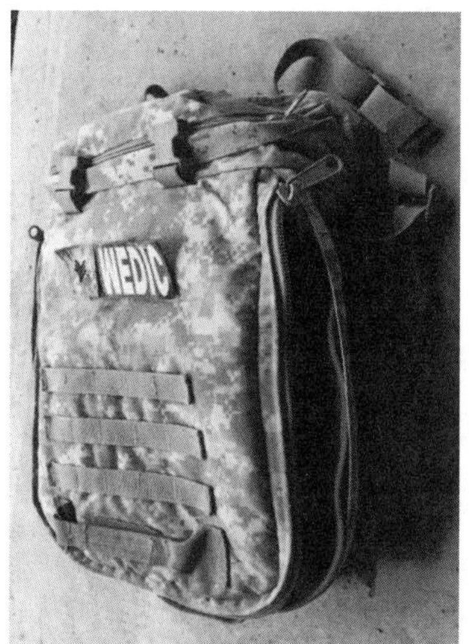

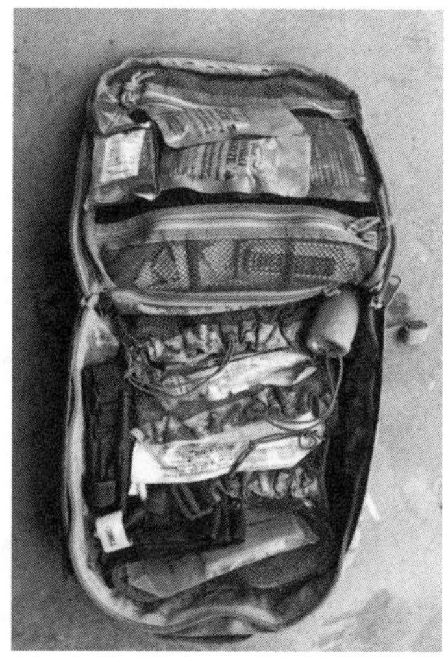

Personal First Aid/Trauma Kit

A business may have the large Mass Casualty Response Kit, but also smaller kits located in different areas of the building. One good suggestion is to have a small kit along with every fire extinguisher in the building. And individuals may have a small every day carry kit, a larger kit in the vehicle, and a different kit at home. You may also want a different kit in your outdoor gear if you hike, camp, fish, or hunt, and another if you have a go-bag ready for quick evacuations.

Group Size Trauma Kit for Mass Casualties

The size and contents of these kits will depend on your knowledge of how to use certain gear, budget, space, and your level of preparedness. I personally feel that some people go overboard with their doomsday prepper activities and hoarding of survival supplies. But there are also way too many people that don't do anything or not nearly enough. You need to determine for yourself, what education you will receive when it comes to first aid and trauma aid, and what gear you will make available at your home, in your vehicle, at your place of work, and on your person. Just remember, the odds are that the life you save with this knowledge and your kit will be your own or someone else you care about.

There are many good commercially available first aid and trauma aid kits available. They come in many different sizes from individual kits to the larger mass casualty kits and all sorts of sizes in between. You can also create your own kits with contents that are most applicable for you and your situation. The following are items often found in first aid and trauma kits:

Trauma Kit Supplies

- Tourniquet
- Personal Bandage (military)/Pressure Bandage/Israeli Bandage
- ACE Bandage
- Triangular Bandage
- Bleedstop Bandage
- Bandage Strips
- Gauze
- HemCon Dressing
- Vaseline Gauze Pad
- Abdominal Pads
- Chest Seal
- Sterile Sponges
- Standard Size 3 Airway Device
- EMT Shears
- Scalpel
- Stainless Steel Tweezers
- Safety Pins
- Tape
- Butterfly Closure Strips
- Hemostatic Agents: Quik-Clot, Celox
- Ammonia Inhalants
- Pain Relievers
- Antiseptic Wipes
- Iodine Wipes
- Burn Aid
- First Aid Cream
- Rubber Gloves/Latex Examination Gloves
- Mylar blanket
- First Aid/Trauma Aid Book or Guide

Your kit may or may not include everything listed here, and it may contain additional items not listed. This is just to provide an idea of the kinds of items you may wish to have available in an emergency. There are many good resources, including hands-on courses, to further your education in this area and help you stock the right equipment for your situation. The investment in education and gear related to trauma aid just may save a life.

Public Access Bleeding Control Stations

Something I'd like to see in more public locations are Public Access Bleeding Control Stations. The ones I am familiar with are from North American Rescue, and The University of Montana has put them at various locations on campus. These stations contain essential medical supplies to stop bleeding during an emergency. While the cost may be prohibitive for some organizations, I hope that people will allocate resources to install these life-saving supplies in more locations. This includes schools, universities, public venues, churches, government buildings, corporate offices, large and small retail shopping centers, and anywhere else large groups of people gather. When you are noticing exits and fire extinguishers as part of your situational awareness, be looking for these too. Knowing the stations are there, and being able to use the contents, just may save a life during an emergency.

Station features according to North American Rescue:

- Designed to provide bystanders and initial first responders in public buildings and populated public areas with quick, easy access to essential medical equipment for stopping life-threatening bleeding
- Includes easy-to-open nylon carrying case containing eight (8) Individual Bleeding Control Kits packaged in red nylon bags and one (1) NAR QuikLitter™ for moving injured casualties
- Each Basic Individual Bleeding Control Kit contains intuitive and easy-to-use tools proven to help to save lives such as the most effective, easiest to use, fastest to apply C-A-T® Tourniquet
- The rugged wall mounted clear storage case provides high visibility access as well as physical and environmental protection of medical supplies
- Stations are available in Basic, Intermediate, Advanced, and Advanced BCD care configurations
- Alarm available upon special request. Contact Customer Service for details

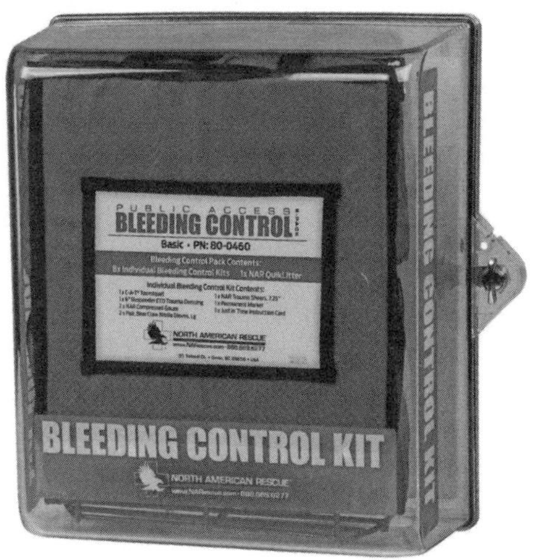

The Basic Bleeding Control Kit by North American Rescue

Conclusion

Learning first aid and trauma aid is one of the most important things you can do to save lives during an emergency. Combat First Aid, or Tactical Combat Casualty Care, teaches the critical life-saving skills needed during an active shooter or terrorist event. Knowing how, and having the tools, to stop bleeding, seal sucking chest wounds, and treat for shock are the most important skills for these horrendous situations.

While you may be able to save the life of a stranger, most often these skills will enable you to help yourself or save someone you know and care about. The information contained in this chapter, along with any further study you do on the topic, will allow you to save lives and keep people alive until professional medical personnel can take over.

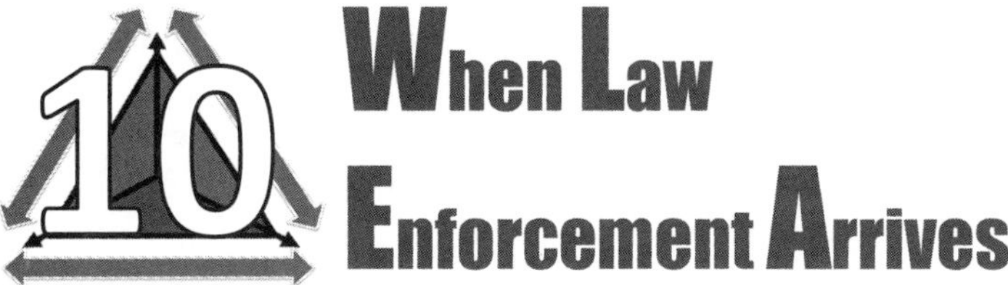

10 When Law Enforcement Arrives

www.SurviveaShooting.com

On April 20, 1999, at Columbine High School in Littleton, Colorado, two deranged students initiated a long-planned attack on their school. Using rifles, shotguns, and homemade improvised explosive devices (IEDs), the suspects forever changed the way patrol officers and other first responders would respond to ongoing, immediately life-threatening incidents.

J. Pete Blair, Terry Nichols, David Burns, John R. Curnutt
Active Shooter: Events and Response

TOPICS

- ✓ Law Enforcement Priorities
- ✓ Call 911
- ✓ Interacting with Law Enforcement in General
- ✓ Interacting with Law Enforcement When Escaping
- ✓ Interacting with Law Enforcement When Barricaded
- ✓ Interacting with Law Enforcement When You Have Attacked Back and Taken the Intruder's Firearm
- ✓ Interacting with Law Enforcement When You Have Attacked Back with Your Own Firearm

The purpose of this chapter is not to provide a detailed outline of law enforcement response strategies and tactics to mass shootings, but rather to provide a brief overview of law enforcement priorities and guidance on how you, a civilian, should interact and help law enforcement responding to the active threat incident.

Law Enforcement Priorities

The shooting at Columbine High School on April 20, 1999, significantly changed the law enforcement response to mass shootings. No longer would police set up a perimeter and wait for SWAT to come and attempt negotiations or entry into a location. This outdated strategy was replaced with more aggressive tactics to be used by the first officers on the scene of any active shooter event.

Law enforcement continues to examine each active shooter or mass killing event to learn how to better prepare and respond in the future. National training programs, along with standards and procedures, have been implemented across the country to ensure that all first responding law enforcement personnel are properly and consistently trained to address the active threats we continue to see in the headlines.

The primary goal of the law enforcement personnel responding to an active shooter is to **Stop the Killing** of innocent persons. This is the number one goal of most law enforcement active shooter training courses. This simple directive can be accomplished in a variety of ways depending on the totality of the circumstances surrounding the event. In most cases, the shooter will likely dictate what must be done to stop the killing. The response will normally be to neutralize, isolate, or distract the armed aggressor.

The second goal of the law enforcement personnel responding to an active shooter is to ***Stop the Dying***. After the shooter has been stopped, law enforcement may provide medical aid to those most seriously injured, while also working at clearing the remainder of the building of any potential threats. In most cases, emergency medical personnel will not be allowed on scene or allowed to enter the building until it has been secured by law enforcement. (There are some medical emergency responders that are training to enter with law enforcement to provide faster medical attention to those most seriously injured.)

It is really important for you to realize that law enforcement works off of these priorities during an active shooter event. Their first priority is to move in, bypassing wounded, to confront and neutralize the shooter. A friend and fellow instructor is a member of the MPD, and he often tells people attending the Response to an Armed Intruder class, "when I'm moving toward the threat, I may drop my tourniquet for you to use as I pass by, but that is all I'm going to be able to help until the threat is stopped." Only once the shooter is down, and the killing has stopped, will law enforcement turn to providing medical aid to those most seriously injured, and toward clearing the rest of the area.

Another thing to know is that an active shooter call will be an "all come," which means multi-agencies will respond. Uniformed officers will normally be the first on scene, but not always. A detective or plain clothed officer may arrive first after responding to the radio call. Or, an off-duty officer may arrive first. Look at the person's waistband or around the neck for a badge or identification.

During the chaos, try to understand where the officers are coming from. They do not who you are, and their training is to treat everyone as "unknown" until they have positively identified the person as no threat. Officers will also be experiencing high levels of stress, and their ability to deal with this will vary depending on their experience and training. They will be guided by their priority of stopping the killing, and it is important for you to remember to respond to officers appropriately. It is also important to understand, and respect, that the law enforcement officers are willingly advancing toward danger, risking their lives, to help others. Note what Doss and Shepherd wrote in their book *Active Shooter*, "In the FBI report 'A Study of Active Shooter Incidents in the United States between 2000 and 2013' data indicated that in twenty-one, or 46.7 percent of, incidents in which law enforcement officers engaged the active shooter, nine officers were killed and twenty-eight wounded. These statistics illustrate how dangerous an active shooter is and how important it is for responder officers to take the necessary precautions and safety measures when responding to this threat." The following sections will provide guidance to assist you in assisting the responding law enforcement officers with one of the most extreme situations they have probably encountered.

25 Tasks to Consider When Developing a Response Plan for Armed Assaults

While a police officer's primary mission when arriving at an active shooter incident is to stop the killing, there are so many other responsibilities and considerations law enforcement must deal with. This list, by Lt. John M. Weinstein for *Campus Safety* magazine, will give you a better understanding of some of the things law enforcement must consider when planning for and responding to such an event:

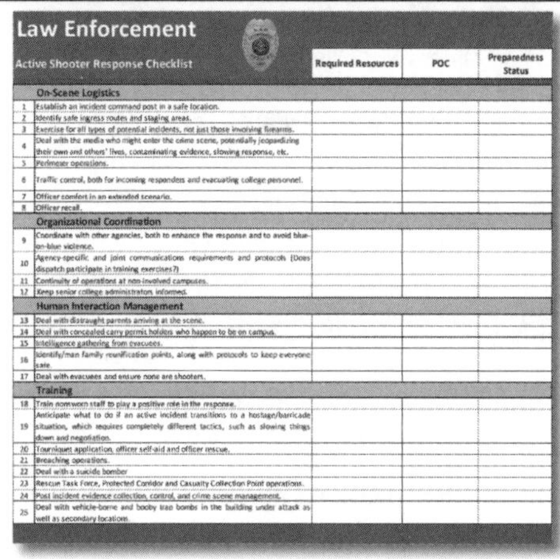

Law Enforcement

Active Shooter Response Checklist

		Required Resources	POC	Preparedness Status
	On-Scene Logistics			
1	Establish an incident command post in a safe location.			
2	Identify safe ingress routes and staging areas.			
3	Exercise for all types of potential incidents, not just those involving firearms.			
4	Deal with the media who might enter the crime scene, potentially jeopardizing their own and others' lives, contaminating evidence, slowing response, etc.			
5	Perimeter operations.			
6	Traffic control, both for incoming responders and evacuating college personnel.			
7	Officer comfort in an extended scenario.			
8	Officer recall.			
	Organizational Coordination			
9	Coordinate with other agencies, both to enhance the response and to avoid blue-on-blue violence.			
10	Agency-specific and joint communications requirements and protocols (Does dispatch participate in training exercises?)			
11	Continuity of operations at non-involved campuses.			
12	Keep senior college administrators informed.			
	Human Interaction Management			
13	Deal with distraught parents arriving at the scene.			
14	Deal with concealed carry permit holders who happen to be on campus.			
15	Intelligence gathering from evacuees.			
16	Identify/man family reunification points, along with protocols to keep everyone safe.			
17	Deal with evacuees and ensure none are shooters.			
	Training			
18	Train nonsworn staff to play a positive role in the response.			
19	Anticipate what to do if an active incident transitions to a hostage/barricade situation, which requires completely different tactics, such as slowing things down and negotiation.			
20	Tourniquet application, officer self-aid and officer rescue.			
21	Breaching operations.			
22	Deal with a suicide bomber			
23	Rescue Task Force, Protected Corridor and Casualty Collection Point operations.			
24	Post incident evidence collection, control, and crime scene management.			
25	Deal with vehicle-borne and booby trap bombs in the building under attack as well as secondary locations.			

1. Establish an incident command post in a safe location.
2. Identify safe ingress routes and staging areas.
3. Exercise for all types of potential incidents, not just those involving firearms.
4. Deal with the media who might enter the crime scene, potentially jeopardizing their own and others' lives, contaminating evidence, slowing response, etc.
5. Coordinate with other agencies, both to enhance the response and to avoid blue-on-blue violence.
6. Agency-specific and joint communications requirements and protocols (Does dispatch participate in training exercises?)
7. Deal with distraught parents arriving at the scene.
8. Deal with concealed carry permit holders who happen to be on campus.
9. Deal with vehicle-borne and booby trap bombs in the building under attack as well as secondary locations.
10. Deal with evacuees and ensure none are shooters.
11. Train nonsworn staff to play a positive role in the response.

12. Perimeter operations.
13. Traffic control, both for incoming responders and evacuating college personnel.
14. Anticipate what to do if an active incident transitions to a hostage/barricade situation, which requires completely different tactics, such as slowing things down and negotiation.
15. Intelligence gathering from evacuees.
16. Tourniquet application, officer self-aid and officer rescue.
17. Breaching operations.
18. Deal with a suicide bomber.
19. Officer comfort in an extended scenario.
20. Officer recall.
21. Continuity of operations at non-involved campuses.
22. Keep senior college administrators informed.
23. Identify/man family reunification points, along with protocols to keep everyone safe.
24. Rescue Task Force, Protected Corridor and Casualty Collection Point operations.
25. Post incident evidence collection, control, and crime scene management.

Call 911!

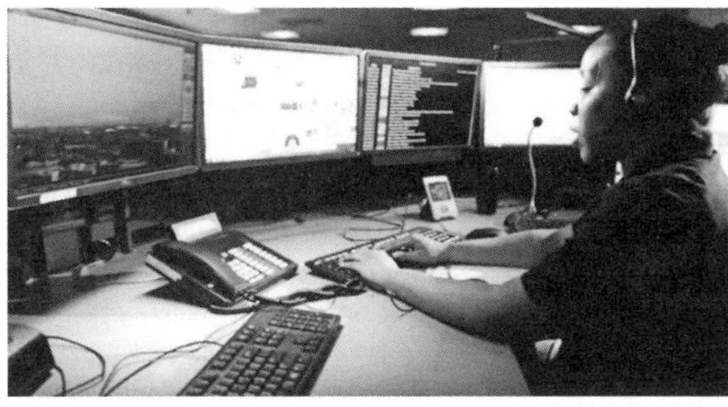

Regardless if you Escape, Deny, or Attack Back, there will be a time when appropriate to call 911 to alert law enforcement of the emergency and summon their help. This is a crucial step in responding to an active threat. In live trainings, this is always one of the responses to an active shooter or threat we cover and practice. While it is not the first and immediate thing you must do, it is something that needs to be done as soon as safely possible. And it is something that should be planned for and practiced in your visualization, practice, and training. Many people are surprised at the difficulty they have calling and talking to instructors, who role play as 911 operators, when they are under stress. But like all aspects of training, we see improvement as people practice and become more inoculated to the stressful scenarios. The following will help you when making 911 calls to report your emergency.

Carry a Cell Phone

I know, I'm always telling people to get their heads out of their apps and pay attention. I'm also annoyed at people who text and talk in the movie theater or talk loud on their phone in restaurants and other public places. But if you don't have a phone, you can't call 911. When distracting you at times you should be paying attention, especially while driving, the phone can be one of the most dangerous things you own. Please don't text and drive. In an emergency, your cell phone can be one of the most important things you own. Carry a cell phone. Just use it responsibly.

> "Just as you never see a police officer without his portable radio, you should never go anywhere without your cell phone."
>
> Loren W. Christensen
> *Surviving Workplace Violence: What to Do Before a Violent Incident, What to Do When the Violence Explodes*

Make the Call!

It is easy to become distracted with escaping, denying, and attacking back (and the huge adrenaline dump and jitters afterwards) that you forget to call. In scenario training, we see people forget all the time. Once reminded by instructors, people start calling 911 and proceed through that part of the role-play. Others might think there isn't a need to call because others surely have called already. This assumption may be wrong. What if every single person assumed this very thing? No one would call. It's better for 911 to have too many calls than none. And maybe it's just the Type A personality I have, or the insistence on being proactive, but I want to be sure someone is coming, and the only way I'm sure is if I do it myself or actually see and hear someone else calling.

Additionally, you may have information other callers didn't have. Each and every piece of intelligence provided to the responding officers and medical responders helps them do their job more efficiently and effectively. The information helps keep the first responders safe and may save other victims. If you can safely call 911, do so.

When Do You Call?

The quick answer is, as soon as it is safe to do so. Sooner the better. If a police officer wasn't present at the time of the shooting, one won't be there until 911 has been called to dispatch all available responders to your location. We know that the longer an event takes place, the more casualties occur. The sooner law enforcement officers are dispatched, the sooner they will arrive prepared to neutralize the threat.

Your safety must come first! You won't be able to call 911 if you are dead. If a shooter bursts into an auditorium, and you can escape out of a near exit, do so. After you have escaped to safety, you call 911. If you are in a classroom and hear shots in the hall, you first close your already locked door, barricade, turn of lights, etc. and then call 911 if you can do so safely without alerting the shooter of your presence. If you shut that locked door but the shooter smashes his way through it before you have a chance to barricade, you grab the fire extinguisher and spray him in the face and then smash him with the canister of the extinguisher until he's down and not getting up; then you secure the door in case of a second armed intruder and make the call to 911 when safe to do so. If you are in a safe location, but a person is shot and bleeding profusely, you put the tourniquet on, and then call 911. The important thing to remember is that you must call 911 as soon as you can, but there may be things you must do first to ensure your and others safety and survival.

What Do You Tell the 911 Operator?

You are going to be scared. Terrified. Your heart will be pounding, and it will most likely be hard to breathe. So, breathe! Remember the four-count Combat Breathing. This will help you make the call. If nothing else, you need to tell the operator the location and what happened. But remember, the more information (also called intelligence) you can provide, the more help it will be to those responding. Screaming "help me" or "I'm scared" doesn't provide information that will be usable to those rolling up on the scene. They know you want help and they know you are scared. You want to help them by providing usable information. The more help you can provide, the more lives you can possibly save.

911 will probably be receiving multiple calls about the incident. The operators will be attempting to sort information and relay usable information to those responding to the scene. These operators know that you are scared, and they are

trained to walk you through the ordeal and elicit useful information. Some operators are better than others at this, and sadly I have heard some recorded 911 calls where the operator wasn't that good at calming the caller down and gaining valuable information. The good news is, if you practice what you would say during your training, you will be better prepared to provide the operator needed information regardless of the operator's skill at working with people under duress. Also note that if you have no further usable information, the 911 operator may go to another caller that does. This is another reason we want to provide usable information as quickly and succinctly as possible.

The responding law enforcement officer's primary duty is to stop the threat. Any information you can provide to help with their mission will be helpful. Keep the information you provide to what you know. If you don't know something, don't speculate or guess. Good information is accurate information. Things that will be helpful:

- **Description of Bad Guy.** If you saw the bad guy, or bad guys, provide the information you could identify and remember. Tell how many armed intruders you identified. Describe what the intruder looks like by clothing, head gear, height estimate, weight estimate, color of skin, and any other descriptors. Describe any weapons such as rifles, hand guns, explosives strapped to body, etc. Tell the operator if you saw any bags, backpacks, or other cases carried by or with the intruders. Provide information on the intruder's behavior if possible (calm with the 1000-yard stare vs. running around erratically) and anything you may have heard the intruder say or yell.
- **Location of Bad Guy or Bad Guys.** It takes a long time to clear a large building or school. Knowing the location of the bad guy inside saves a considerable amount of time for those responding to the threat. The more specific the location provided to law enforcement, the quicker they can stop the shooting. Law enforcement most likely won't be familiar with the building and its layout. Use descriptions they will be able to understand and follow. Floor numbers, specific room numbers, cardinal directions (North, South, East, and West), and so on. One thing the schools in our community did was to put room numbers facing outside in the classroom windows. If you say room 123, the police will be able to identify room 123 from the outside of the building. Another thing we discuss with schools is that young students often remember the room as Mrs. Smith's room rather than room 123. Putting the name and number may be prudent in case of someone calling and only remembering what teacher's room it is, and not the actual room number. (Having the number on the inside of the classroom, as well as out in the hall, makes this easier for callers too.) Be as specific as possible. Also, be sure to provide every bit of information that can be helpful to the responding officers. Even if you don't know the room, say, "he came in the entrance on the West end of the building and the shots are coming from a classroom on that end." That at least narrows it down

some and will make it easier for the police to know where to start looking. Obviously, before you can tell them the West end of the building, you must be able to tell them the address you are located, and if you don't know the cardinal directions, provide something that will assist the officers in finding the correct location. For example, "I'm at the Southgate mall and a man wearing jeans and a black t-shirt is shooting at people with a semi-automatic handgun near the Clock Tower in the middle of the mall."

- **Your location and description if relevant.** If you have escaped to safety and are calling from a safe location away from the shooting, your description and location isn't going to be that helpful and you probably don't need to provide it. Information that is not helpful is best left out of the communications. If you are barricaded in a certain room, that could be relevant as it at least provides a location police don't have to search and clear. You may say, "I'm barricaded in room 132 with three other people and we are safe right now." If you had to attack back and stop the attacker, you will want to provide this information. Describe the bad guy, but also give a description of yourself as the good guy. Tell them your exact location to the best of your ability. I'll provide some additional information regarding this scenario in one of the next sections.
- **Location of injured and type of injury.** As I've said, the first priority of the police is to stop the shooting. The second priority is to ensure there are no other shooters or additional threats. Only after they have accomplished these tasks will they turn to helping the wounded. That's why it is critical that you know how to stop bleeding and have tourniquets and pressure bandages available in first aid kits. It is still important to provide the 911 dispatcher information on those injured. This information will also help the paramedics who will come in to treat wounded once cleared to do so by the police. Focus on life-threatening injuries. If John twisted his ankle while barricading in a room, he is going to be okay until everyone else is treated. The 911 dispatcher needs to know about life-threatening injuries, those that need immediate treatment or they may die: How many injured? How bad and what kind of injury? Where are they? You may also add what treatment has been provided, and if the injured person is mobile or not.

When you are scared, it is easy to want to talk and ramble. Remember to breathe, and try to limit what you say to information that will help the responding officers stop the threat in the quickest time possible, and then help those that are wounded once all threats are neutralized and the location is deemed clear of all threats. Like anything else, practicing 911 calls will enable you to perform better under a high-stress situation.

Know Your Cardinal Directions

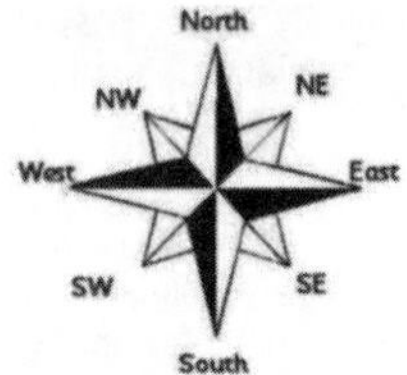

Many people don't know North, South, East and West. Don't be one of them! It's important for you to know these cardinal directions.
How are you going to tell the police you are in an office in the northeast corner of the building, or that you saw the shooter enter the cafeteria in the southwest corner of the building if you don't know cardinal directions? How can you tell the police which direction the shooter is heading or on which side of the building you saw him if you don't know directions?
Get a compass, or use an app on your phone, and learn the directions related to where you work and other places where you spend more time. Teach your kids this skill too. And then use these directions when giving directions, or determining where you will meet, etc. In an emergency, this information can be critical for law enforcement to save your life and the lives of others.

How to respond to a 911 operator or when law enforcement arrives

Initial Response

- Remain calm and follow officers' instructions
- Immediately raise hands and spread fingers
- Keep hands visible at all times
- Avoid quick movements, pointing, or yelling towards officers
- Do not stop, proceed in direction of law enforcement

Provide Information

- Location of the victims and the active shooter
- Number of shooters, if more than one
- Physical description of shooter(s)
- Number and type of weapons held by the shooter(s)
- Number of potential victims at the location

Source: Homeland Security

Interacting with Law Enforcement in General

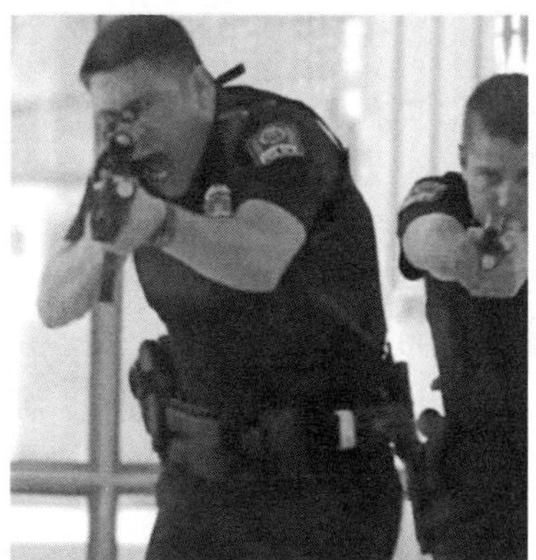

The most important considerations for you to remember when interacting with law enforcement in an active threat situation are to keep your hands visible at all times, unless otherwise ordered, and to follow all commands immediately.

The officers' commands trump any policies or procedures the building or organization may have. The commands might seem unreasonable, and innocent people may be treated as a threat, and even handcuffed or restrained at times. Remember, this is all done for everyone's safety, the officer's and all others. Their primary goal, remember, is to ***stop the killing***. If there is any doubt, they will error on the side of safety.

If you have knowledge of any threat, or anything that can compromise the officer's safety, notify them as soon as practical. You may be put to work if you have knowledge that will assist them. They could ask you to draw a map of the location or provide other intelligence. Cooperate and do as instructed.

In his DVD, *Active Shooter Survival*, Alon Stivi points out these four considerations when interacting with first responders:

1. COMPLY with instructions – Do not resist
2. REPLY when asked to provide information
3. RELAY only factual information – not emotions
4. REPEAT the instructions you receive to avoid misunderstanding

Stivi also points out what to expect when First Responders arrive:

1. You may have guns pointed at you
2. You may be treated as a suspect
3. You may be handcuffed
4. You may be yelled at

Realize that under these extreme circumstances, the police are concerned with their safety as well as everyone else's, and you need to forget about being offended and comply with their commands. Follow instructions and provide Essential Elements of Information (E.E.I.).

How to Respond When Law Enforcement Arrives

- Remain calm and follow instructions
- Put down any items in your hands (i.e., bags, jackets)
- Raise hands and spread fingers
- Keep hands visible at all times
- Avoid quick movements toward officers such as holding on to them for safety
- Avoid pointing, screaming or yelling
- Do not stop to ask officers for help or direction when evacuating

Source: *U.S. Department of Homeland Security Brochure*

Interacting with Law Enforcement When Escaping

When escaping a building, you may encounter law enforcement running toward the shooting as you run from it. Let that sink in for a moment. These brave men and women are running toward the gunfire to stop the killing and save innocent lives.

The basics apply. Keep your hands visible and follow commands. You might initially be treated as a threat until proven otherwise. Do nothing that will alarm law enforcement and have them think you are a threat.

If by chance you happened to disarm a shooter, and are escaping the building, do not carry the weapon in a threatening manner. Hold the gun out away from your body with the muzzle pointing toward the ground. You will be ordered to drop it. Do so! You may also be ordered to get on the ground. Do so! Remember, follow all commands.

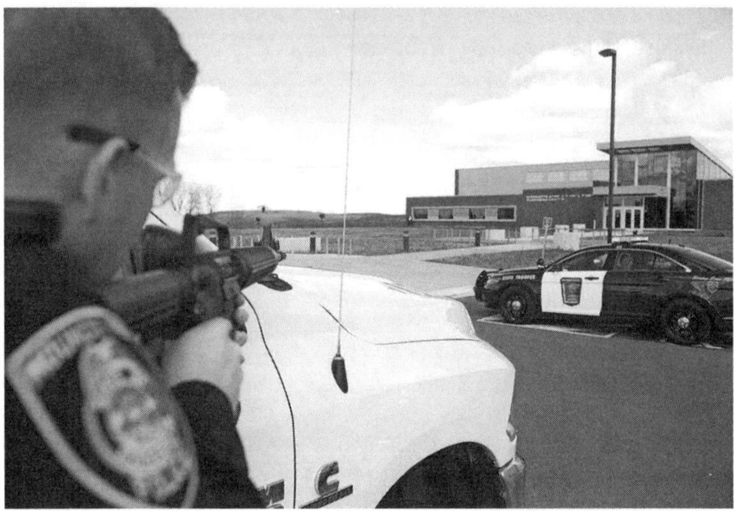

If you have escaped with a firearm you have taken from an active shooter, and law enforcement has not arrived, put the gun in a secure or safe place and tell law enforcement where it is when they arrive.

Law enforcement will also be looking for terrorist "sleepers." These are terrorists who throw away their weapons and infiltrate large crowds in order to blend in to attempt to escape the area. If there was a hostage situation before the shooting, law enforcement will also be looking for terrorists being protected by the victims. "Stockholm syndrome" is a real concern.

Interacting with Law Enforcement When Barricaded

If you are barricaded safely in a room when law enforcement arrives, stay put and let them stop the shooter and clear the building. If they contact you, tell them as briefly as you can that you are safe, and any information that may help them stop the shooter, and let them move on. Don't ask questions, and only tell them information that can help them do their job. If you say anything else, you may want to tell them how many wounded are in the room if there are wounded present, but realize that they won't be helping until their primary mission of stopping the shooter is completed.

I'm often asked in classes if you should remove the barricade and open the door if you don't know for sure it is actually law enforcement. Concerns of a killer trying to gain access by lying and saying they are the police are often brought up. If you are locked and barricaded in, and safe, and you have concerns of who is on the other side of the door, don't remove the barricade or open the door. There is nothing wrong with verifying the identity of the person on the other side before giving them access to the room. If that means you stay in your location for hours after the killer has been stopped and the building cleared, and everyone is searching for you, so be it. You survived the incident and are alive, and that is most important.

There are some locations where law enforcement and schools/businesses have developed cards that can be slid under doors to communicate. For instance, a teacher could slide a card out into the hall to inform police officers that everyone in the room is okay. If these procedures have been established where you work, be aware of the set procedures and how to use such cards if available.

When barricaded in, you are always ready to escape to safety if an opportunity arises, and you are prepared to attack back if necessary because an intruder breaches your lock or barricade. But if you are safe, there is nothing wrong with riding out the incident until you are absolutely positive it is safe to come out.

Interacting with Law Enforcement When You Have Attacked Back and Taken the Intruder's Firearm

You attacked back and neutralized the shooter. He may be dead, unconscious, or restrained depending on what you did to stop him. You now possess the shooter's firearm because you took it from him, or you picked it up to secure the gun when the killer dropped it while being neutralized.

It's at this point in most live classes that I'm asked, "Can I shoot him?" The answer is, "it depends." While I'm not providing legal advice with this book, and statutes differ in various jurisdictions, in general you would be allowed to use the gun to protect yourself or others from immediate serious injury or death. The same laws apply to defending yourself with lethal force regardless if the weapon you possess was taken from the killer. If, and only if, the shooter is still a threat (and he might still be a threat as many active shooters carry more than one weapon, or his physical size and strength might justify him being a threat), you may be justified in using his weapon against him. If he is subdued, or restrained, and no longer a threat, you cannot legally play judge, jury, and executioner. You are not allowed to take revenge for someone the killer shot. You can only defend yourself as defined by your jurisdiction's justifiable use of force statutes.

Back to the scenario of you possessing the shooter's firearm. Keep the muzzle pointed in a safe direction, and if you are familiar with firearms, make the gun safe. Secure the weapon in a safe location where no one else can access it. If you are not familiar with the firearm and how to make it safe, just secure it in a safe location where no one else can access it. When the police arrive, notify them of what you did and where the gun is located.

If you believe you might need the weapon to protect yourself. This could be because of a second armed intruder on the premises, or maybe because your co-workers are restraining the shooter and you believe there is a chance of him escaping and becoming an active threat again. It doesn't matter why, if you believe you might need the weapon to protect yourself, this is probably the best practice to keep you from being mistaken as the shooter by responding police. Place the weapon on a table, counter, etc. where you can access it quickly if you need to. You should be within arm's reach of the weapon so you can immediately pick it up and use it if needed. The downed bad guy, whether dead, unconscious, or being restrained, should be at a distance that he could not get up and get to you before you could pick up the weapon and defend yourself. If necessary, you can pick up the weapon to defend yourself or others. When police arrive, you can step back from the weapon with empty hands raised informing them of the location of the killer's weapon. This allows you the protection of the firearm if needed, but also reduces the likelihood you will be mistaken by law enforcement as the active shooter.

Interacting with Law Enforcement When You Have Attacked Back with Your Own Firearm

I briefly addressed this in Chapter 8, but because of its importance, I want to address it here too. Once you have stopped the killer, there is another very real danger you must consider. **You don't want to be shot mistakenly by the police.** Remember, the responding officer is also under a lot of stress, and what do you think the arriving cop will think when he sees dead bodies and you holding a gun? What would you think?

As soon as the threat is neutralized, and you have confirmed there is no additional threat, get the gun out of your hand. Holster it, or you may choose to place it on a table as described above when you have taken the active shooter's weapon. You don't want to be in a high-profile shooting stance when the police arrive, and better yet, you don't want a weapon, or anything else, in your hands.

If you choose to remove the shooter's gun, make it safe and place it in a secure location that you can keep an eye on if need be, and that no one else can access to use against you or anyone else. As soon as possible, inform police of its location.

When police arrive, be prepared to drop your gun, show your hands, and get down on the ground. You may be treated as a threat until police discern who did what and who the bad guy is versus you, the good guy. They are doing this for everyone's safety. *Follow all orders explicitly and immediately!*

Conclusion

The first priority for law enforcement is to stop the killing. Comply with instructions and provide any intelligence that will assist them with that priority. Don't do anything that would make them believe you are a threat. Don't be offended if you are treated as potential threat until proven otherwise. Law enforcement officers are just doing their job, and an extremely difficult one at that. Remember, as everyone is running away from the gunfire, they are running toward it to stop the killing and save lives.

11 Develop Your Plan Now

www.SurviveaShooting.com

Failing to plan is planning to fail.

Alan Lakein

TOPICS

- ✓ Why A Plan Is Important
- ✓ File Not Found
- ✓ The Importance of Multiple Plans
- ✓ Develop Your Plans
- ✓ Visualize Your Plan
- ✓ Practice Your Plan
- ✓ Discuss Your Plan with Loved Ones and Get Them On Board
- ✓ Talking to Kids

One of the most important things you can do is develop a plan of action that you will take in the case of an active shooter or terrorist attack. You should do this for your home, business, places you frequent on a regular basis, and for when you are out-and-about in public. You will want to consider all of the elements from this book: When and how you will escape, where and how you will deny, and when and how you will attack back, where first aid kits are located and what they contain, and so forth. Planning separates professionals from amateurs. When you have a plan of how you will deal with a hostile situation if it happens, you will know what you need to do and how to react when chaos and confusion raise their ugly heads and everyone else is frozen in panic. Some don't believe in planning, saying that real incidents are nothing like what you plan for. I understand that real incidents are seldom like what you have planned for, but I agree with Dwight D. Eisenhower, who said, "In preparing for battle I have always found that plans are useless, but planning is indispensable."

Why a Plan Is Important

In the business and productivity world, many authors write about how feeling out of control is one of the quickest ways to feel stress. And while the high-stress of an active threat event is different from the stress induced by being out of control with your e-mail, office, and work projects, there are similarities. The fact is, being in control can reduce or eliminate stress and the effects it causes within our mind and body.

Having a plan helps us remain in control and thus eliminate or reduce the effects of stress. This is true for high-stress events as well. In a previous chapter, I discussed Mike Day, the Navy SEAL who survived being shot 27 times. He not only survived, he continued his mission by killing a couple of the insurgents who shot him. Remember his thoughts at the time, "God, get me home to my girls," extreme anger at being shot, and then he just went to work doing what he was trained to do. There's a key. What he was trained to do. He had a plan. That plan was ingrained within him through the rigorous training SEALs undertake and continue throughout their enlistments.

I'm not suggesting you need to train like a Navy SEAL or any other military special operator. Nor will your plan resemble the "seek and destroy" plans of these highly trained military specialists. Without the same equipment and training, such a plan is not reasonable for civilians in boardrooms, classrooms, and offices. But you must develop a plan that prepares you for the likely situations you may encounter that takes into effect your own personal strengths, weakness, and environment. Having a plan, combined with breathing, practice, and training will reduce or eliminate the "freeze" response of high-stress and allow you to move and take action toward surviving the active threat. The first step to escaping, denying, and attacking back is knowing your options and having a plan to do so.

Reasons People Don't Prepare

While the rise of active shooters or active threats is relatively new, fires and natural disasters have been occurring since the dawn of time. Yet, thousands of people perish each year in fires and natural disasters when they could have survived if they had prepared. Again, planning and preparation save lives. Looking at natural disaster research we see a few reasons why people don't plan and prepare:

It Won't Happen

Many people just don't think it will happen to them. But the truth is, these things do happen, and even if the odds are low that you will be the one it happens to, how can anyone really know the odds of an unthinkable event occurring. Many law enforcement officers have stopped saying, "if an active shooter event occurs." They now say, "when an active shooter event occurs."

If we look at natural disasters, FEMA says that 91 percent of the U.S. population lives in a place that is in moderate to high risk of natural disaster. But FEMA surveys found that only 46 percent of the people they surveyed think that they do. In a survey of floodplain residents, 40 percent of respondents didn't think they were at risk of future floods. If people don't think natural disasters will occur, they probably don't believe an active threat will ever occur where they are at either. Sadly, way too many people after an active shooter event are heard saying, "things like this just don't happen here."

It Might Happen, But I'll Be Fine

People underestimate events and overestimate their response to emergencies. With a natural disaster, we see people refusing to evacuate, and in a study done at the Harvard School of Public Health, they found that 25 percent of all respondents reported that they would not evacuate even after a mandatory evacuation order had been issued before a major hurricane. We see people commenting on social media of how they would just take out an active shooter if they were there. That would be one thing if it were a trained military operator such as a Navy SEAL or member of Delta Force, but when said by someone who's out of shape and hasn't even been to a firing range in months or years, it lends itself to overestimating capabilities.

The Government Will Rescue Us

Many people believe and expect the government will rescue them in the event of a fire or disaster. This equates to people believing the police will save them from an active shooter. I was in a University Forum one time discussing the Armed

Intruder Training that was being offered to different university employees, and one person stood up and told the Captain of the police department, "Why should anyone need this training. That's your job." The Captain replied, "Yes, and we will get there as fast as we can. But we want to give people options and tools that will help them survive until we get there."

You can't rely on the police, fire department, or any other government agency to be there to save you. They will do their best, but you must take responsibility for your own personal safety and do some planning and preparing.

Preparing Doesn't Help

One FEMA survey showed that only 68 percent of respondents believed that preparing for natural disasters helps. I would speculate that it would be an even higher percentage if people were asked about preparing for an active shooter as it is a much more terrifying occurrence for so many. Too many believe that those who prepare won't be any better off than those who don't.

The fact is, preparing helps. If all the stores were closed because of a natural disaster, would you rather have stored food and water or bare cupboards? If a loved one was shot and bleeding out, would you rather have a tourniquet and have practiced using one, or nothing to stop the bleeding? If an active shooter was kicking in your door, would you rather be hiding under a table at the back of the room making an easy target, or stacked at the door with a fire extinguisher ready to take him out?

If you have read this far, you are not the person I need to convince that planning and preparation save lives. But I will ask you to help me get this message out to others. Make sure your family, friends, and co-workers are prepared along with you.

File Not Found

Captain Ben Gladwin, of the University of Montana Police Department, is one of the Safariland certified instructors on the Missoula Armed Intruder Response team. He uses an analogy that I really like and want to share with you as it makes this concept easy to understand.

When you are on your computer looking for a file, and it is not there, the computer sort of freezes and the little symbol will spin, and you finally get a message, "File not found." Nothing else happens. Our brains do the same thing (Remember the OODA Loop from earlier). When an active shooting or terrorist threat occurs, our brains look for a file to tell our bodies what to do. If there's no file in our brain to find, we'll sit there with a blank look on our face, frozen in the "file not found" zone.

Developing a plan of action to these events is simply putting the right files in your brain so they can be located in an emergency. Reading this book has already put a file in your brain that the person completely oblivious to active shooter events and what to do doesn't have. However, going a step farther and taking the information in this book and developing a personal plan will make your files much more useful. If you do even more and include visualization, drills, a live class, and scenario training, you will not only have files for your brain to go to, you will have files that can save your life.

The Importance of Multiple Plans

Multiple plans? It's hard enough to develop and form one plan, and now you are saying we must have multiple plans? Yes, that's what I'm saying, but it's not as difficult as you might think.

All of your plans will contain the three basic elements. We only have three responses to an active threat: Escape, Deny, or Attack Back. You don't have to make long complicated plans, and like I've mentioned, short and basic is better anyway.

But we do need to have different plans for different locations. A plan at home with an infant will be different than if you have teenagers or no kids with you. A high school teacher's plan will be different from a kindergarten teacher's plan. Your plan at work will be different if you are in a cubicle than if you have an office with a locking door. Your plan at the mall with your family will be different than if you are out-and-about by yourself, or at work with a dozen or more co-workers. Now you realize why you need more than one plan, even if they do contain the same basic elements of escape, deny, and attack back.

Not only will you have multiple plans, but your plans will change over time. If you have kids, or as your kids grow up, your family plan will change. Your plan may change if your co-workers, job, office, etc. change. Maybe you decide to carry a concealed firearm. This may change how you will attack back if forced to do so. Injuries or aging may also change how you can escape or attack back. Any change that affects how you would escape, deny or attack back should prompt you to review and revise your plan accordingly. This doesn't have to take much time. Make simple changes to your simple plan. But it should be done. You want to make sure your brain finds the right file.

Develop Your Plans

It's important that you develop plans that will work for you. This chapter will assist you, but you still need to put in the work. I could provide a generic plan, but that's not necessarily going to help you in your situation with your strengths, weaknesses, and environment. My goal here is to one, encourage you to actually develop a plan; and two, to provide some guidance to assist you in developing your own plans for your own specific locations and circumstances.

Each plan should have two parts. First, you want a plan of what to do in an actual active threat situation. This plan will be devised around the "Escape - Deny - Attack Back" model. For example:

Plan for my office:

- If a shooting occurs in my building, but not the immediate hallway outside my door, I will exit my office, turn right, and escape out the exterior door. I will leave the entire area and call 911 once I am at a place of safety.
- If the shooting is in the hallway outside my office, I will quickly close the door that is already locked, push the file cabinet in front of the door, turn off the lights, and prepare to attack back with the fire extinguisher in my office by ambushing at the door. I will call 911 if I feel safe to do so without alerting the intruder I am in the office.
- If an armed intruder enters my office before I can shut the door, I will attack back with anything and everything I can. I will throw things, yell, strike, tackle, or whatever else is needed to stop the threat and survive.

The second part of your plan should incorporate things you need to do to better prepare yourself for an active threat event. For example:

Things to prepare my office:

- Have company purchase, or purchase myself, a fire extinguisher to have in case of fire or active threat.
- Once a month practice closing door and pushing file cabinet in front to increase my speed in performing the task.
- Bring a first aid/trauma aid kit, including a tourniquet, to keep in my office.
- Send request to my employer that they arrange a *Survive a Shooting* class for all employees on an annual basis to teach and reinforce the survival principles, strategies, and tactics to keep everyone better prepared to survive an active threat.

As you can see, some of these things may be on-going, and other things once done, such as the fire extinguisher and trauma kit, can be checked off when completed. Your plans don't have to be extravagant or complex. Simple and easy to do will be more beneficial and something you will more likely follow.

Again, the most important thing is for you to develop a plan that is going to work for you. Do it. And I mean do it now. It's not paranoia. I just want you to be better prepared to survive. And I guarantee if you have a plan, you will not only be better prepared, you will feel less stress and anxiety regarding active threats, whether on television, in casual conversation, or an actual event.

Vagueness and Ambiguity

Your plan can be simple, and it should be tailored to you and your specific circumstances. But your plan should NOT be too vague or ambiguous. Clarity will assist in decision making and action in times of high stress. Vagueness and ambiguity may add to the chaos and confusion and prevent you from acting quickly and decisively.

An actual event will rarely be exactly like we planned or how we trained. But the more specific our planning, and more thorough our training, the better prepared we will be to deal with the unexpected of actual emergencies. The question words who, what, when, where, and how, will assist you with your planning. Asking these of your plan will help clarify actions and eliminate vagueness and ambiguity.

Active Shooter/Active Threat Preparedness Assessment

50 Questions to Help Your Self-Assessment

These questions are designed to assist both individuals and organizations assess their preparedness for active threats (active shooters, knife wielding attackers, etc.). Use the relevant questions to assess your or your organization's level of preparedness. Not all questions will apply to every person or organization. They should be used to stimulate thought for your assessment. Once assessed, use this information to help create your plan.

Responsibility

- Do you falsely believe the police are responsible and will be able to protect you from all active threats?
- Have you accepted personal responsibility for your own safety?
- Has your organization accepted responsibility to help keep employees safe?

Knowledge of Problem

- Do you know how an active threat is defined?
- Are you aware of the history of active threat events and why this is important?
- Are you aware of the increase in active threat events?
- Are you familiar with the weapons active threats are using?
- Do you know where active threat events are occurring?

What Can Be Done Before an Active Threat Event

- Does your organization have a threat assessment team?
- Do you know behavioral indicators that could indicate a threat?
- Do you have an individual plan for an active threat event?
- Does your institution have a plan for an active threat event?
- Do you understand there is more to training than watching the "Run – Hide – Fight" video?
- Do you know there are better models than "Run – Hide – Fight?"
- Have you attended Active Shooter or Active Threat response training?
- Have you provided Active Shooter or Active Threat training to your employees?
- Do you know what kind of windows or laminate your building has?
- Are you familiar with the lock down process and are your locks easily applied?
- Do you have an efficient communication system to communicate active threats to your employees?
- Do you know how to communicate your plan, age appropriate, to your family to involve them?
- Do you know how to "harden the target" at your location?
- Have you ever conducted a workplace violence exercise?

To Survive an Active Threat

- Do you know the levels of awareness?
- Are you in the level of awareness you should be?
- Do you know physical indicators of a possible threat?
- Do you know behavioral indicators of a possible threat?
- Do you understand how people respond in a crisis?
- Do you know how to get past denial and make decisions faster when seconds count?
- Do you know the effects of fear and stress of an active threat incident?

- Do you know how to lessen the effects of fear and stress?
- Do you have a survivor's mindset?
- Do you know when, where, and how to escape an active threat event?
- Do you know the difference between cover and concealment and why this is important?
- Do you know how to deny the killer access to you?
- Do you know how to attack back when you can't escape or deny access?
- Do you have knowledge of improvised weapons and how to use them?
- Do you know the best place to ambush and attack an active killer to stop him?
- Do you know strategies to survive a knife attack?
- Do you know an excellent improvised weapon that is found in every school and public building?

After and/or During the Active Threat Incident

- Are you familiar with trauma care?
- Do you have a tourniquet in your personal first aid kit?
- Are there tourniquets in your institution's first aid kits?
- Do your or your institution's first aid kit contain pressure bandages?
- Do you know how to stop bleeding?
- Do you know what to do with a sucking chest wound?
- Do you know how to treat for shock?
- Do you know law enforcement priorities when they arrive?
- Do you know what law enforcement needs from you?

Ask Yourself This:

- Are you and your organization as prepared as you should be?
- Would the *Survive a Shooting* course help your level of preparedness?

A Training Drill for the Mall

I believe your survival plan should have on-going training which includes thinking and visualization. During an interview I did with Jeff Anderson for his *Modern Combat & Survival* on-line magazine and membership site, we discussed a drill he likes to do to stay better prepared for an active shooter or active threat situation. He likes to do this drill at his local mall, or when out-and-about at other locations. I also like to do thinking and training at malls periodically. (***Something to think about***: In 1994, Tom Clancy wrote about using a large aircraft as a terrorist weapon in *Debt of Honor*. Spoiler: The pilot crashed it into the Capitol, killing the President and many others. In 2003, Clancy wrote *The Teeth of the Tiger*, that featured simultaneous terrorist coordinated mass shooting attacks in multiple malls across America.)

Jeff performs his drill like this. He sets an alarm to vibrate sometime during his time at the mall. You can use your phone or a watch with an alarm. When the alarm goes off, he immediately kneels to tie his shoe. While doing this, he scans the area for relevant information. He notices cover, concealment, exits, potential weapons, etc. To any observers, Jeff is just tying his shoe. Heck, most people probably don't even notice because they have their heads in their apps, and you know how I feel about that. But in reality, this quick drill is valuable training.

He is conditioning himself to respond to a stimulus. Remember, movement saves lives. Immediately upon the stimulus of the alarm, he is moving and doing something. He is also recognizing all the elements in his surroundings that can aid in his survival. Performing a drill such as this over time will make you more aware of these things at times, not just when an alarm goes off or when actual bullets start flying. And that knowledge may just save your life if the unthinkable happens.

Visualize Your Plan

Visualization, also called mental imagery or mental practice, is a powerful psychological skill for enhancing performance. It's been studied extensively in high-level athletic training. Almost all the athletes and coaches at the United States Olympic Training Center, when surveyed, agree that imagery enhances performances.

In his book, *Warnings Unheeded: Twin Tragedies at Fairchild Air Force Base*, author Andy Brown writes about finding a copy of *The Tactical Edge: Surviving High-Risk Patrol* by Charles Remsberg. This is what Brown writes about this important find:

"The most important thing I learned from the book was the technique of mental rehearsal. In the same way an athlete trains by visualizing their performance, I began visualizing scenarios I might encounter and mentally practiced the actions necessary to survive them. Every night before I went to sleep, I'd mentally rehearse an incident, be it a traffic stop, a building search, an armed robbery, or a domestic dispute. I'd vividly imagine encountering a deadly threat and visualize myself successfully countering it. I also began critiquing my real-world tactics. After a traffic stop or any other interaction with the public, I'd return to my patrol car and ask myself: Did I leave myself vulnerable? What could I have done better? If I saw room for improvement, I'd work to correct it on the next encounter."

That mental rehearsal helped Brown feel better prepared to meet the challenges of his job. Visualization and mental rehearsal will also better prepare you to meet the challenges of an active threat incident. Don't dismiss this as some woo-woo mystical nonsense. The positive effects are documented and proven, and this is an important component to not only lessen your anxiety, but to increase your survivability during an active threat.

Some military and law enforcement have started using Tactical Performance Imagery, which is the use of imagination to improve specific military and police skills. It's like a mental rehearsal of skills needed for missions. The same thing can improve your performance of the skills needed to survive a shooting.

In *Warrior Mindset: Mental Toughness Skills for a Nation's Peacekeepers* (Asken, Grossman, and Christensen), the following uses for Tactical Performance Imagery to enhance military and police performance are discussed:

- Skill Improvement
- Error Analysis and Correction
- Situation Simulation and Response Preparation
- Skill Maintenance
- Confidence Enhancement

While a detailed explanation of visualization and mental imagery is beyond the scope of this book, I encourage you to further research this area for your own personal development in different skills. I do want to share also from *Warrior Mindset*, a few ways to make Tactical Performance Imagery maximally effective:

- Image in All of Your Senses
- Strive To Make Your Imagery Vivid
- Use the Best Perspective
- Image Correct Responses
- Image in Real Time
- Practice and Image Problems and Success
- Move and Use Kinesthetic Imagery

Practice Your Plan

Read all the books about swimming you can find, and detail the plans you'll take to make it to the Olympics, but you'll never be the next Michael Phelps without getting in the pool. And it's not just getting in, but getting in and putting in the grueling practice day after day, month after month, and year after year to become an Olympian. Fortunately, it doesn't take that much practice to survive a shooting or active threat.

It almost goes without saying that the more you practice, the better prepared you will be in an actual event. The question then becomes, how much practice is needed? This depends, and is a topic hotly debated in some circles. There are those that don't believe in any training or practice, and others that think we should all be training like elite military operators. The truth is somewhere in between. I do believe you should develop a plan and practice it. But I don't think you have to train and practice like those in the military or law enforcement. Just like your plan must work for you, so must your training and practice.

If you do a personal threat assessment and determine that you are at a higher risk to be involved in an active threat because of your occupation, location, and other variables, then you should probably practice your plan more and maybe look for supplemental training. If there is a very low likelihood of you experiencing an active threat event, you can adjust your training and practice accordingly so that you feel comfortable. Different people will have different comfort levels. The goal is to develop a plan, and practice that plan, so you not only will survive an active shooter or active threat event, but also so you live comfortably without fear of such an occurrence.

I've met people who live with fear and anxiety over what they see on the nightly news. That's no way to live. I want people to enjoy all life has to offer, and to go out and experience good things in this world. Yes, the frequency of these terrible events has increased, but the odds of being in an active threat situation on any given day are still quite low. Developing and practicing your plan should enable you to enjoy more of life without fear and anxiety. Practice your plan to the level you can enjoy life safely.

Training to Respond to an Active Threat

Planning and training go hand in hand. Here are some guidelines to training from author and instructor Rob Pincus:

- The goal of your training should be to establish Stimulus-Response Patterns. You don't want to be thinking about several options or making complex decisions under the emotional stress of a Spree Attack.
- The five steps of training are:
    1. Think
    2. Discuss
    3. Visualize
    4. Drill
    5. Scenario
- By thinking about the information, you can start to formulate a plan and, most importantly, make the decision to plan.
- Discussing your plan with others in your area, co-workers, classmates, students, and supervisors is the next step in the process. By talking about the plan with others, you can better work as a team in a worst-case scenario. Discussion also may bring things to your attention that you hadn't considered.
- Visualizing an actual event and your actual responses is the first practical application step in your training process. By visualizing your actions in your plan, you start to get some idea of their plausibility and the timing of events.
- After you have an idea what you will want to do, you need to actually rehearse it. If you had planned to push a desk in front of a door, you need to be sure you can actually push the desk... or know ahead of time that you need to unplug certain cords or recruit help.
- By drilling your plan, you will find flaws that may not have occurred to you until you actually performed the actions.
- Running a full scenario, if possible, is the final step of training. A Scenario is really an opportunity to run your drills in context... with some chaos and, whenever possible, a role-player who acts as a bad guy.
- Scenarios are best done in conjunction with professional trainers and special equipment. If you are part of a hospital or school, it is probably best to contact your local law enforcement agency in regard to running Spree Attacker Response Scenarios.
- After going through these five steps, you will be much more likely to efficiently execute a practical plan in the event of a spree attack.

(Source: *Spree Attacker Response* with Rob Pincus)

Discuss Your Plan with Loved Ones and Get Them on Board

It is very important that you discuss your plan with those you spend time with. Your personal plans should be discussed with family and your work plans with co-workers. I remember a gentleman from a school that procrastinated taking the course we teach in Missoula. He didn't really want to take the course, but after his co-workers told him that they didn't feel comfortable with him not having the same training and being on board with the same plan, he came to the class. At the end of the day, he told us that he understood why his co-workers wanted him to have the training and he was glad he attended.

Ideally, you work on your plans together. If your significant other isn't "into" it for whatever reason, communicate and explain why it is important and devise a plan that fits both of your needs. At work, the best case scenario is when an organization provides training for the entire staff and they can then develop their plans accordingly and together after such a training.

Talking to Kids

It's very important to discuss these things with your children at a level that is appropriate for their age and maturity. Kids understand more than we think they do at times, and even very young understand there are good guys and bad guys. It will be reassuring to them to know their parents have a plan to keep everyone safe in case of a bad guy.

As your children become older, you can explain more of your plan and include them. Obviously, your plan will change as your children grow. When I'm teaching classes to teachers, the elementary school teachers will have a different plan for the classroom than the high school teachers. A classroom full of senior football players presents a much different scenario than a classroom full of first graders.

The key is to explain to children at a level they can understand and accept without scaring them. The plan and communication are meant to help when practicing the plan, and for if an actual situation occurs. It shouldn't be an exercise that frightens or creates fear and anxiety.

Conclusion

I hope in this short chapter I've convinced you of the importance of creating plans for the different situations you find yourself in, both at work and in your private life. I want you to start working on your plans that are not too vague or ambiguous right now; and complete them. Then I want you to use visualization and practice to hone your plans into something that works for you and those included in the plan to keep everyone safe and alive. Ensure that others, including children, are included in these plans and practice at age appropriate levels.

Please understand and recognize that no plan is 100% foolproof. The information, strategies, and tactics in this book can be used to help make your plans and help increase your odds of survival. The tactics and strategies can be used individually or in combination with one another to help you escape, deny, or attack back to stop the threat. However, there is no one strategy, tactic, or technique that will work every single time. Every situation will be different, and no scenario will be exactly like another. This is why your plan must be flexible enough to adapt to the situation you find yourself in. When I was in basic training, Drill Sgt. Hernandez used to say, "I can roll left, I can roll right, or I can low crawl up the middle." This was his way of saying stay flexible and adapt. While you will have general plans, you must be able to decide in the moment which strategy, tactic, or technique will, under the circumstances, give you the best chance for survival.

Periodically review and revise your plans as things change in your life, but don't become obsessed. Use the plans and practice to free yourself from fear and anxiety and live life to the fullest. And while I hope and pray you never experience an active threat of any kind, having a plan that you have practiced will dramatically increase your odds of surviving a shooting. That's what I want. I want you to enjoy life safely, and I want you to be a survivor.

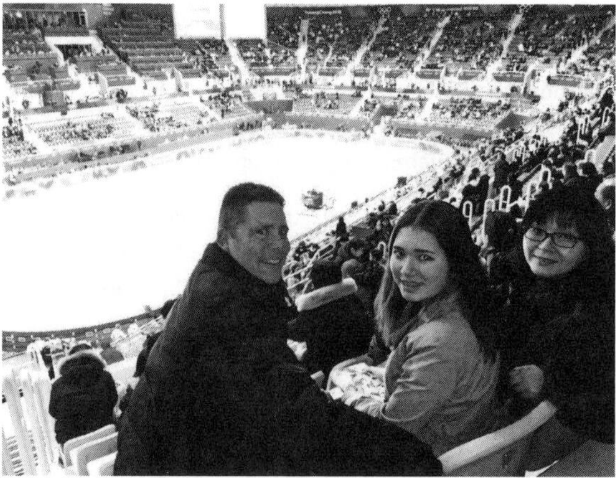

The author and his family enjoying life safely at the 2018 Winter Olympics in South Korea

A Final Message

www.SurviveaShooting.com

> ***Learn to enjoy every minute of your life. Be happy now. Don't wait for something outside of yourself to make you happy in the future. Think how really precious is the time you have to spend, whether it's at work or with your family. Every minute should be enjoyed and savored.***

Earl Nightingale

If you ever find yourself in an active shooter incident or terrorist attack, it will be the most horrific event in your life. Unless you've been in combat, nothing will even come close to the horror of seeing innocent people being shot and killed around you. Being in the middle of it will be terrifying and will forever change your life. To survive, you need to have a plan, and you must be willing to do whatever it takes to save yourself and others.

This book provides the framework to develop your own plan for both work and personal life, as well as the best actions to take in the time of an active shooter emergency to increase your chances of survival. No one can guarantee who will survive and who won't. But following the information presented in this book will definitely increase the chances of you and yours surviving such a horrific event. I'm repeating this because it is true. It's proven that having a plan and the right mindset makes a difference. I can't stress the importance of this enough. That's why I'm saying it again one final time here at the end.

I told you at the beginning that this was the most important book I hope you'll never need. I mean it when I say I sincerely hope you never face the horrors this book is about. But I do want you to form a plan, and be prepared in case you ever do. My preference would be for you to get additional training, either through my courses or others, because the more tools you have available and the more you've trained, the more likely a positive outcome. The more you learn about what to do in a life-threatening situation, and the more you train, the better prepared you will be to save your life and perhaps the lives of others. But even if you don't seek out further information or training, the information in this book can and will make a difference if you act on it. So, make a plan for survival. Do it for yourself, and do it for those you care about and love. Do it now.

And once you have your plan, and additional training if you choose to, don't obsess over it. Know that you are prepared if something does happen, but don't live in fear. Be aware to recognize the good things in life as well as the potential bad. Practice safe habits, but don't be fearful or obsessive.

Enjoy life safely!

And if something does happen: *Be a Survivor!*

Appendix A

www.SurviveaShooting.com

In an active shooter emergency, the business has one overriding goal – preserving life. There is no higher calling, no higher mission – nothing more important. This goal is not murky or elusive; it should be indelibly etched on each business license. After an emergency, what will a visitor or an employee remember about how the business faced adversity and the leadership displayed to protect life? A business must always look to the safety and security of its guests, employees, and contractors in every threat situation, as must every city, community and state. ”

Kevin T. Doss and C. David Shepherd
Active Shooter: Preparing for and Responding to a Growing Threat

Business Plan Considerations

This Appendix is a very condensed version of the information presented in several chapters of the excellent book *Active Shooter: Preparing For And Responding To A Growing Threat* by Kevin T. Doss and C. David Shepherd. It's presented here to help you understand the kinds of things to prepare for and to incorporate into your Business Active Shooter Response Plan. I encourage anyone developing such a plan for a business to add Doss and Shepherd's book to your resources and use it in your plan development. It will be invaluable for your planning.

Here are some key considerations regarding employee actions, business actions, and internal and external communications that should be thought about and addressed when planning.

Employee Actions

What can an employee do when a shooter is active? When devising an emergency plan for an active shooter incident, you want to consider the strengths and weaknesses of your work force.

Consider the following for each employee during and active shooting emergency:

- Employees know the building and shortcuts out of the area.
- Employees can guide and direct away from danger areas those who are willing to go.
- Employees can pull down gates and lock doors.
- Employees can communicate to coworkers, guests, contractors, and visitors the nature of the threat and location.
- Employees know what is behind exits and know the nearest areas of safety.
- Employees have access cards, codes, and passkeys.
- Employees know established security measures.
- Employees can facilitate an orderly exit.
- Employees can prevent guests and employees from entering the shooting area.
- Employees can communicate to employees and guests in multiple languages.
- Employees can help disabled guests away from shooting area or help them hide if they need mobility assistance.
- Employees can prevent additional vehicles from entering the business.
- Employees know the active shooter contingency plan and the location of the evacuation assembly area.
- Employees can communicate to guests to tell them whether the shooter is getting closer or moving away.
- Guests believe that all contractors, volunteers, and tenants know what to do (because they are working on property), so such persons should receive the same active shooter contingency plan or a suitably modified version.
- Contractors and tenants should understand what to do during an emergency.
- Contractors and tenants should receive active shooter training, just like they would for emergency evaluation fire procedures.
- Contractors and tenants should receive and be trained in and understand emergency communications.

- Contractors and tenants should know the procedures pertaining to their tenant space or contractor location.
- In contract and working agreements, require contractors to know the active shooter contingency plan and emergency procedures.
- Employees, contractors, and tenants can hide in and barricade rooms.

Business Actions

During an active shooter emergency, the business has a larger role than calling 911. Each business has a responsibility to alert all individuals on the property to dangers that exist. For example, when cleaning floors, signs are strategically placed around the work area to warn people of the potential danger. For many scenarios, businesses have outlined duties, roles, and assignments for staff to guide, direct, and protect employees, guests, and contractors. It should be the same with an active shooting emergency.

Consider the following areas to incorporate into the active shooter plan:

- Assign someone to meet first responders and direct them to the closest entrance to the threat.
- Describe the weapons and the number of shots fired.
- Describe the shooter's sex, race, hair color, facial hair, height, and weight.
- Describe the shooter's clothing color, clothing style, and headgear.
- Describe how many shooters are known or suspected to be present.
- Describe the number of victims and their location.
- Provide open vehicle access for first responders.
- Find out whether anyone knows the shooter's name.
- Indicate the shooter's last known location.
- List of the exits, stairwells, and elevators nearest the shooting that first responders can use or by which the shooter can escape.
- Describe the area of the shooting.
- Provide information about surveillance cameras in the area and about whether the shooting is under video surveillance.
- Allow first responders to enter the surveillance control room.
- Provide a picture of the shooter to first responders.
- Describe backpacks or other items the shooter is carrying.
- Did the shooter say anything to anyone?
- How many people are in the area?
- Prevent people from entering the shooting area.
- Provide "Go Bags" for first responders and strategically place medical kits throughout the site or facility. (This "Go Bag," as opposed to a personal "Go Bag" for evacuations, contains things to help first responders bypass security

measures such as passkeys, access cards, elevator keys, doorstops, hard keys, flashlights, property maps, and passcodes.)

- Make anyone who was in the area available for interviews by law enforcement.
- Provide information about construction issues and obstacles to a response.
- Describe any dangerous chemicals in the area of the shooting.
- Provide clear access route to the area of shooting and indicate any blockages caused by people jamming stairs and elevators.
- Let first responders know whether the business has armed security, as well as what such guards are wearing.
- If possible, contain and seal off areas so the shooter cannot expand the scope of the rampage.
- List areas that may provide a visual of the shooter.
- Relay information communicated from anyone hiding in the shooting area.
- Convey first responders to secondary entry and exit points.
- Give the location of any vehicle the shooter drove.
- Provide any equipment that first responders previously requested for this emergency.
- Monitor threats.
- Train select employees in trauma medical care.

Internal and External Communications

Communication during an active shooting emergency is critical. The better communication, the more lives that can be saved. The systems and platforms a business uses to communicate must be considered when developing an active shooter response plan.

The following methods of communications may be available at a business:

- Fire alarms: Pulled or initiated whenever a fire emergency occurs or when a full evacuation is required. Fire alarm also provides both audible sound and visual notification.
- Public address (PA) announcement: Specific directions or information can be issued to all individuals on the property. Each situation will require specific directions and can consist of its own unique pre-scripted message.
- Emergency text alert: A short message service (SMS) text message used when specific directions or information must be issued to only registered recipients. Because individuals must subscribe to this system, only subscribers will receive the alerts and messages. It may be used in conjunction with an alarm or PA announcement.
- Mass notification systems: Mass notification across multiple platforms and in multiple languages.
- Cell phones.

- Tablets and laptop computers.
- Social media (e.g., Twitter, Facebook, etc.).
- Online conferencing programs, such as Skype.
- Two-way cell phones and text messaging.
- Walkie-talkies or business handheld radios.
- Private warning subscription providers.
- PBX phone tree patterned and call-down system.
- National or local news coverage.
- Visual images and information monitors to use text for the hearing-impaired.
- GPS for alert and notification.
- Teleprompter or closed caption on monitors.
- Hardline telephones.
- Television: Hotel/resort home channel or property television network.

Messages During an Active Shooting

Besides knowing how you will communicate, you must also consider what message you will communicate over the chosen communication platform. Look at the differences in these possible messages:

- "Code silver!"
- "This is an emergency. Go to lockdown. This is not a drill."
- "Shelter in place. We have an active shooter."
- "We have an active shooter on property. Hide out now."
- "Attention! Attention! This is not a drill. There is a man with a gun, wearing a red shirt, shooting at people on the first floor in the main lobby. Take appropriate actions to protect yourself."

Things to think about when determining what message will be sent: Does everyone in the building know what a particular "code" means? Active threats have been known to use more than guns, including knives, axes, scalpels, hammers, clubs, explosives, etc. Does the term "active shooter" describe the threat? Some legal departments have debated both sides of this argument: What if a business tells a customer or employee to hide when he or she has a clear chance of safely evacuating? If the person obeys and decides to hide, then becomes a casualty, is the company responsible for that person's death?

The best practice would be for a business to use an advisory committee, including the legal department, to develop the most appropriate message to be delivered. Having a planned message available and known to employees is much better than leaving it in the hands of the person sitting in front of the communications platform at the time of the emergency.

These areas deserve consideration when formulating what messages will be communicated to different people at different times during the active shooter emergency.

- Content of warning messages. – Be specific, clear, concise, accurate, consistent, and timely.
- Should you send a second message out to individuals inside the business?
- What update message will the business send to employees and guests hiding out from the shooter?
- What is your message to the entire building when the shooter has been neutralized?
- Who prepares all the messages, and who communicates them?
- What message should be communicated to tenants?
- What message should be communicated to employees reporting to work?
- Should a message be provided to your PBX Department for when people call?
- Communication considerations for persons who have a disability.
- Signage.
- International guests.
- Communication Gaps.
- Communications after the emergency.

Recovery

Recovery is the last phase in a disaster or crisis cycle. It is no different for active shooter incidents. Businesses must have a plan for recovery. This will be different and unique to each business. Doss and Shepherd provide over 700 questions to help those making a business active shooter plan with the recovery phase. Preparing a plan and checklists to assist in times of emergency, and after, is only prudent for businesses in today's environment. I encourage all business leaders to not neglect this important area of consideration.

As you can see, there are many considerations when putting together a response plan to an active shooting emergency for a business. This Appendix should at least get you thinking about how to prepare your organization for an active threat. If you are in a position where developing a plan for your business falls under your responsibilities, again, I highly encourage you to check out *Active Shooter:*

Preparing For And Responding To A Growing Threat by Kevin T. Doss and C. David Shepherd to assist you with your planning and preparations.

Appendix B

www.SurviveaShooting.com

The cost-benefit aspect of any security counter-measure should be part of the consideration before deciding which measures should be chosen. The cost-benefit ratio is the process of determining whether a company should invest into a measure that provides a return on its investment. The 'return' does not necessarily mean only cash savings; often it is safety – or liability-focused, offering a psychological benefit to the organization. This is where the security professional can justify their security programs and initiatives using an operational business-based model to illustrate the value of security to the company leadership.

Kevin T. Doss and C. David Shepherd

Active Shooter: Preparing for and Responding to a Growing Threat

Lawsuits Over Active Shooter Events

Recent active shooter court rulings throughout the country have allowed negligence suits filed by victims of Active Shooters to proceed against employers for failing to provide defensive training to their employees. In other words, companies can no longer avoid their corporate responsibility to provide training on both how to spot potential active shooters and on how react if so confronted.

One of the allegations in the lawsuit against the town of Newtown and the Newtown Board of Education was lack of training. The lawsuit also alleges the town and school board were negligent in not having a more secure entrance to the school because it did not have bulletproof glass on the front windows, and for having classroom doors that couldn't be locked from the inside (all things covered in this book and in the *Survive a Shooting* course).

The 66-page lawsuit filed after the terrible Sandy Hook shooting lists a variety of reasons why the plaintiffs consider the school system to have been negligent, resulting in the many deaths that occurred on that fateful day.

According to the lawsuit, school officials failed to provide the school with classroom doors that could be locked from the inside, thereby making the "lockdown" aspect of that school's safety procedures virtually impossible to follow.

The lawsuit also alleges that school officials failed to sufficiently train and supervise the staff on the proper way to implement lockdown and evacuation plans. Classrooms in the school could only be locked from the outside with a key, in violation of state law, it alleges.

According to an article by James Cameron, CPP, recent active shooter court rulings relative to liability lawsuits have shown active shooter scenarios are now considered a "recognizable hazard" to employees.

One of the regulations under the Occupational Safety & Health Administration Section (OSHA) of the United States Department of Labor General Duty Clause, Section 5 (a)(1) states, "Each employer shall furnish to each of his/her employees, employment and a place of employment which are free from recognized hazards that are causing or are likely to cause death or serious physical harm to his/her employees."

Example from Cameron of recent active shooter court rulings:

In a July 2, 2013, court decision from Hennepin County, Minneapolis, MN, the court found fault with the employer for negligence and failing to train their employees. District Court Judge Denise Reilly allowed two negligence counts to proceed against the company, Accent Signage. The civil case was brought before the courts by the victims' family members in response to an active shooter incident at a place of business.

This incident occurred as the gunman, Andrew Engeldinger, walked into his place of employment on September 27, 2012, with a pistol. Once inside, Engeldinger shot and killed numerous individuals before taking his own life. Court rulings like the one above places the liability on the employer to train their employees to recognize the indicators of the potential active shooter and how to respond when they are faced with an actual active shooter incident.

The charges basically follow the OSHA guidelines set forth under the "General Duty Clause" that the employer needed to make training available, and reasonable safeguards to be put in place. One of the victim's (Beneke's) family sued the Accent Signage and Engeldinger's estate in February. Releasing the shooters estate from liability and holding the company responsible is a new shift in thoughts regarding pre-planning and prevention. Engeldinger shot and killed Beneke, and four other employees and co-workers along with a UPS deliveryman before committing suicide on September 27, 2012.

This case has now settled for an undisclosed amount of money by Accent Signage to the Beneke family.

Las Vegas Shooting Law Suit:

While it is still too early to determine what will happen with this lawsuit, on Monday, October 9, 2017, 21-year-old Paige Gasper filed a lawsuit against the Mandalay Bay and MGM Resorts International, Mandalay Bay's parent company. The complaint alleges that the hotel was "negligent or grossly negligent" in failing to notice or take precautions against the shooter stockpiling guns, and that the employees were not adequately trained to notice and report suspicious activity.

The complaint reads, "At all relevant times, Defendants MGM, and/or Mandalay Corp...knew or should have known that it was reasonably foreseeable that a breach of their duties to keep their premises reasonably safe in the aforementioned manner might result in catastrophic injury perpetrated by a gun-toting guest with an extreme intention to harm others."

The first report I read said Gasper is seeking in excess of $15,000 in damages, but that seems low for this type of case. I then saw another stating she demanded $135,000. Her case is the first reported lawsuit against MGM and the Mandalay Bay, but it is extremely likely that more victims of the shooting will try to hold the Mandalay Bay accountable by bringing lawsuits against the company. We will have to wait and see if these lawsuits will have merit and how courts will rule. This could possibly break legal ground in terms of assigning liability for mass shootings. Different experts believe that as mass shootings become more and more common, premises may be seen as legally liable to take preventative measures.

Since writing about Paige Gasper's filing, there have been numerous articles and it appears that hundreds of the victims of the October 1, 2017, mass shooting in Law Vegas have filed lawsuits against the operators of the hotel from which the gunman fired, the organizers of the country music festival he targeted, and the killer's estate. It appears that Gasper voluntarily dismissed the Nevada lawsuit she filed and is among those now filed in California.

While it is uncertain how this area of law will continue to develop, it appears that the most logical course of action based on these recent active shooter court rulings, and OSHA recommendations, is for employers to implement training and notification programs/systems to educate employees on the known risks for workplace violence and the steps that can be taken by employees to minimize the potential for workplace violence. This includes being trained on how to effectively respond to workplace emergencies to include active shooter situations.

This is not only the responsible thing to do in order to keep people safe and preserve life, but now, because of the legal liability, the most prudent course of action financially as well. I would hope keeping people alive, and providing them the training and skills to help keep them safe even when away from the workplace, would be more important than dollars, but now it appears you can argue both as reasons to prepare, plan, and train.

Some organizations believe in wishful thinking and don't want to address the possibility of violent crime and a shooting at the workplace. Pretending the problem will go away if you don't think about it isn't a very successful strategy. Statistics show that shooting violence is growing, and businesses and organizations have a responsibility to provide a safe environment for anyone on the property, as well as for staff while in the performance of company activities, whether on site or not. This doesn't necessarily mean the company has a duty to protect the employee off site, but it is the company's responsibility to prepare and educate employees if they could be exposed to acts of violence. Regardless if motivated by a sense of morality to keep employees and others safe, or the threat of increasing lawsuits, it seems clear that businesses and organizations are going to have to incorporate serious active shooter and workplace violence plans and training into their planning and budgeting.

> "There is much America can do to prevent such attacks, but the reality is that, sooner or later, an attempt will be made here in America. There are a great many things that can be done to *prepare our response* to that attack when it comes. But to accomplish this, America must be ready to endure the two things it dislikes most: A change in our lifestyles, and the spending of significant sums of money. Whether we will wait until after there has been a large body count of children to make these changes is all that remains to be seen."
>
> *John Giduck*
> *Terror at Beslan: A Russian Tragedy with Lessons for America's Schools*

Appendix C

www.SurviveaShooting.com

Nobody wants to fail in a crisis, but some of us prepare to do so inadvertently. There are those of us who take steps to prepare, and then there are those who fail to prepare, and thus are preparing to fail.

Michael Dorn, Dr. Sonayia Shepherd, Stephen Satterly, Chris Dorn
Staying Alive: How to Act Fast and Survive Deadly Encounters

Active Shooter Response Training

Active shooter training has become an important topic of discussion for many workplaces, schools, college campuses, and places of worship. However, what constitutes training varies considerably from organization to organization. The range goes from sending out the Homeland Security *Run – Hide – Fight* video link with encouragement to watch it, to 8-hour courses or more. Some businesses think once is enough, while others provide continued training for employees to reinforce and practice the concepts learned.

In response to the 2014 FBI study that examined active shooter incidents from 2000 to 2013, Special Agent Katherine Schweit, who headed the Active Shooter Initiative for the bureau, said she hoped the study would highlight, "the need not only for enhanced preparation on the part of law enforcement and other first responders, but also for civilians to be engaged in discussions and training on decisions they'd have to make in an active shooter situation."

Unfortunately, many businesses are not prepared for workplace violence or active shooter emergencies, even though there are a number of training options available, including the *Survive a Shooting* course. An article by Royal Range pointed out that Peter Martin, the CEO of a Miami-based security consulting company (AFIMAC Global) stated that, "A lot of employers, especially small and medium-sized businesses, believe even in the wake of all the things you read about: 'it can't happen here, not in my company, not with the people I know.'"

On a positive note, more businesses, schools, and places of worship throughout the country are putting emergency response and active shooter policies in place along with active shooter response training for their employees. As you read in *Appendix B: Lawsuits Over Active Shooter Events*, this is not only morally responsible for looking out for the safety and lives of employees, but fiscally responsible due to the increasing trend of lawsuits in response to active shooter incidents.

There is another important aspect of these trainings that I have seen first-hand in the thousands of people we have trained in our community, as well as those I've taught in other states. These courses empower individuals with the knowledge that they don't have to be victims, and that there are things they can do to increase their own safety and survive these critical incidents. This can be powerful for a workforce.

While there are a number of training organizations offering various active shooter response training, and more popping up all the time, I'm only going to discuss the two that I have first-hand knowledge with and have been teaching for a number of years. This does not mean I don't recommend the other trainings out there. I encourage you to research and seek out the training that fits your organization and budget, and possibly do different trainings on different years to gain a wider breadth of knowledge on the topic. (I do encourage organizations to provide semi-annual, or minimally annual, active shooter response training to best retain the strategies, tactics, and techniques to use in the accompanying drills the organization will stage.) The two different trainings I teach are the Safariland *Emergency Response to an Armed* Intruder course and my *Survive a Shooting* class. I'll describe both to provide you guidance when looking for training for your business or organization.

Safariland *Emergency Response to an Armed Intruder* Course

This is an excellent course, and I feel privileged to be part of the team that has taught this 8-hour course to over 4,000 of our community members. When I hear of companies that think sharing the link to the *Run – Hide – Fight* video on YouTube constitutes training, I sigh and shake my head. How can you compare a 6-minute video to an 8-hour course? (Or to a 4-hour course for that matter?)

The training we've provided to employees of school, university, hospital, business, and government office employees consists of a PowerPoint lecture; hands-on modules covering movement and ad-hoc barricading, weapon familiarization and disarms, basic self-defense, and rescue and trauma aid; stress-inducing scenario training with gunfire and padded suit attackers; and live practice using fire extinguishers as improvised weapons.

Without a doubt, the adrenal stress training scenarios are the best thing about this course. This training reinforces everything taught through the lecture and modules, and provides the participants a positive experience to a scary stressful situation in a safe environment. Unfortunately, it is also the most expensive aspect of putting on the course and the most logistically difficult.

To run the scenarios, we have one or two instructors wearing the Monadnock Practice Suit (These run $1600-2000 depending where you order), an instructor with a .38 revolver with blanks with each suited instructor, additional instructors serving as safety officers and for debriefing groups after each scenario. This is why you must have a team of instructors to run these scenarios safely. We usually have 4 to 8 instructors depending on the size of the class and availability of instructors. We also secure the building so no one not involved with the training, that has been cleared to be safe, is allowed inside the training area, which is often the entire building.

Each scenario is designed by the instructors to fit the training environment and to reinforce the course objectives of the "Run – Lock – Fight" model. Participants run and escape, lock and deny, or attack back and fight depending on the scenario. It's a culmination of all the strategies, tactics, and skills taught earlier in the day. It's undeniably the capstone of active shooter response training for civilians.

As I mentioned, this training is logistically more difficult and expensive. The training of so many community members over the last four years is pretty unique and involved the cooperation of multiple organizations. Safariland told the Missoula team that they don't know of any other communities that have done as much as we have here. We have trainers representing Missoula Police Department, Missoula County Sheriff's Office, University of Montana Police Department, The University of Montana, St. Patrick Hospital, Missoula County Public Schools, and more. All of these organizations sent trainers to be certified by Safariland to teach the course, and they provide the trainers on training days for the good of the community. These organizations have also purchased gear, such as the Monadnock suits, to be used for the classes. Additionally, the administrations of Missoula County Public Schools, The University of Montana, St. Patrick Hospital, and the Life Long Learning Center have supported the classes with locations and lunches for the instructors, as well as support for employees attending the classes. It truly is a community collaboration for the safety and preparation of all involved, and it really is unique.

If you have the opportunity to attend a course like this with adrenal stress training scenarios, it will be invaluable to learning and retaining the concepts of run, lock fight, or escape, deny, attack back. However, it must be taught by instructors who know how to teach scenarios. While you want to induce stress and the adrenal response, you don't want to scare people or leave them with a sense of helplessness. This is why participants never die and always survive in the scenarios. They should teach and empower people when done right. If a participant ever has a bad experience in a scenario, and it does happen sometimes, we go over what happened and redo the scenario so the person can achieve a successful and empowering outcome. Again, if you have the opportunity to go through such a course, taught like this, do so. The Safariland Group may be able to direct you to trainers they have certified in your area.

Do Short Training Courses Make a Difference?

The short answer to this question is: *Yes, they do*. The question needs to be answered because there are people out there that claim 2-hour, 4-hour, 8-hour, 16-hour, etc. courses in self-defense are not sufficient enough to do anything other than provide a false sense of security to participants. Many of these same people insist that a person will have to train consistently for years to be able to adequately defend themselves. Fortunately, there is evidence to the contrary.

I agree that it takes considerable time, practice, and commitment to learn and advance in a martial art to black belt, and even more to continue and advance to higher black belt levels. Learning a martial art and learning to defend yourself are not the same. Individuals can learn the correct mindset and simple defensive and offensive tactics in a relatively short amount of time. Sure, more training will increase a person's skill sets. But the fact is, many people have successfully defended themselves after minimal instruction and training. A little bit really can go a long way. This story from Tim Larkin exemplifies the reality of the fact:

In his book, *When Violence Is The Answer: Learning How To Do What It Takes When Your Life Is At Stake*, Tim Larkin tells the story of Sara, a young woman who reluctantly attended one of his self-defense presentations aboard a cruise ship. She attended because her father told her she was going to whether she liked it or not, because she was about to go off to college.

Three years after the seminar, Larkin met Sara again. This time she came to one of his seminars willingly, with her three younger sisters in tow. She told Larkin that shortly after the seminar on the cruise ship, she was in her college dorm room sleeping when a man snuck into her room through a window. She woke with him on top of her. She credits the training she received on the cruise ship as the determining factor of her knowing she must do something, and do something to hurt him, to stop his attack. She attacked back and the attacker was actually killed during the confrontation. (She didn't intend to kill him, but she knew she had to fight with all she had to stop him from raping her. He was killed when both of them landed on the floor with her forearm on his throat.) Later, the campus police discovered he was a serial rapist that had been terrorizing the campus for nearly six years.

Larkin's story is one of many. Numerous individuals, men, women, and children, have successfully used the mindset and skills learned in short self-defense classes to successfully defend themselves. These short classes can and do make a difference.

Survive a Shooting Course

As I shared in the introduction, I wanted to empower people and show them that people don't have to be helpless victims, like we'd been doing in Missoula with the 8-hour course I just described. But because it takes a team to teach that course, along with the expense and logistical challenges, it just wasn't feasible to take that course on the road, or more accurately, on a plane, to teach around the country.

So, I took my years of experience teaching the *Emergency Response to an Armed Intruder* course and other topics, combined with the research for this book, and created the 4-hour *Survive a Shooting* course. The benefits of this course include:

- It can be taught by one person rather than a team
- It doesn't require the large Monadnock suit
- It doesn't require firing blanks inside the building
- It doesn't require a secure location
- It can be taught in any area with space for participants and PowerPoint capability
- It provides an empowering learning experience for all attendees

The primary objective of the *Survive a Shooting* course is to provide live hands-on training of the strategies, tactics, and techniques presented in this book. The primary learning objectives cover:

- History and Overview
- The Problem Defined
- What You Can Do Before an Incident
- Disaster Response Psychology and Survival Mindset
- What You Can Do During An Incident
    - Escape
    - Deny
    - Attack Back
- Stop the Bleeding
- When Law Enforcement Arrives

The course includes detailed classroom knowledge and hands-on training in topics like:

- gun-disarms
- barricading techniques
- dealing with knife attacks
- ambush techniques
- working as a team
- stop the bleeding
- understanding the difference between cover and concealment
- disaster response psychology
- combat breathing
- how to develop a survivor's mindset

The course is designed for the average person. There are no special physical requirements, nor do you need any preliminary training before attending. The course, like this book, is designed to save lives. And that means everyone's!

I currently travel and teach this course to any business or organization that brings me in to teach to their employees or members. I can travel just about anywhere, and will work with each group to maximize the learning experience for each employee or participant. While I do support my family through writing and teaching, I sincerely have a mission to empower people and help them enjoy life safely. I want to make a difference and save lives. And because I can't be everywhere, I'm working on a train the trainer course so others will be able to take my material to their respective organizations to train and empower more people than I can reach by myself. Be sure to watch the *Survive a Shooting* website for details on this program. Together, we will make a difference.

The Next Step

Reading this book has provided you with more knowledge than most, and more than most resources provide. Following the advice in this book will make you a harder target and increase your chances of surviving an active shooter event. You definitely know more about what to do to stay safe and increase your survivability rate during an active threat than you did when you started reading. But now I want you to take the next step.

Implement and practice what you have learned in these pages. It's not enough to just read it. I want you to take action and actually make and practice your active shooter response plan. And then take it one step further by seeking out training opportunities to reinforce what you've learned here, to learn additional strategies and skills to keep you safe, and to empower yourself with the knowledge and training to be a survivor.

You, your loved ones, your friends, and your employees and coworkers are worth it!

Appendix D

www.SurviveaShooting.com

Don't feel silly about reporting your suspicions.

Kelly McCann
(as Jim Grover)
Street Smarts, Firearms and Personal Security

Suicide Bomber Threats and Improvised Explosive Devices (IEDs)

The threat of a suicide bomber is a unique threat, that unfortunately besides staying aware to recognize early warning signs, there is little most people can do to prevent or stop it. This is true for most security at large events as well. The suicide bomber is a different threat than a bomb threat and has different procedures. While this book primarily focused on shooting threats, I wanted to include a brief section on suicide bombers due to the ever-increasing situations we are seeing around the world.

The first step to stopping a suicide bomber is to harden the target in the first place. We know from history that terrorist organizations place a high value on the use of suicide bombers. We also know the standard security precautions that have been used for years to deter crime will not necessarily deter a suicide bomber from selecting a site.

Suicide bombings are not intended to be part of a normal and expected armed confrontation between two parties. The people who carry out these attacks, and all terrorist bombs, for that matter, are designed to (1) cause death; (2) inflict pain;

(3) demonstrate that the authority is powerless to prevent the attacks; and (4) generate support and finances for the terrorist group's cause.

Terrorist groups have said they use suicide bombing for three reasons: (1) This method does not require an army be outfitted with advance weapons and smart bombs; (2) it is a final method for them to get their views heard; and (3) according to al-Qaida leader Ayman al-Zawahiri, "is the most successful way of inflicting damage against the opponent and the least costly to the mujahidin in terms of casualties."

Locations with Minimal Visible Security Often Chosen

Terrorists will select a site for different reasons. Sometimes it's to make a statement and promote their cause. They may also select a location because they believe it to be a soft target due to there being little visible or detectable security in place to deter or stop the attack.

Facilities Should Be Aware of Terrorist 'Dry Runs'

There are three main operational factors to a suicide bomb attack: secrecy, reconnaissance, and rehearsals. Understanding these factors can help you protect your facility.

Secrecy: Secrecy is essential to plan and conduct a suicide mission. Because the bomber wants to keep the plan covert, it may appear to neighbors and coworkers that he/she is anti-social. The bomber may not associate with others except a few "like" individuals. After the fact, you may hear neighbors and coworkers say, "He/she was quiet, never bothered anyone."

Surveillance: Terrorists must conduct thorough reconnaissance and surveillance when choosing a target and identifying its weaknesses. This is one of the key times when staff may have the opportunity to intervene and deter a suicide bomb event. Making a facility appear to be well protected starts with each staff person and security officer taking an active role in the facility security plan.

Rehearsals: Extensive rehearsals and "dry runs" are necessary to ensure stealth and speed during the attack. The surveillance and dry-run period is another critical time for security officers and staff to detect the presence of suspicious activity. They should be alert to even some normal activity such as someone taking pictures, a small group standing outside the facility writing or making diagrams, and questions about the busiest time of the day and day of the week.

What You Can Do to Protect Your Facility

So how do you know if your location can be a target of a suicide bomber or other type of terrorist attack? If you have thought about it, most authorities will tell you that the terrorist has as well. To what degree they consider your industry a target is the unknown factor that you should evaluate along with other threats. Use of current weapons of mass destruction (WMD) or other types of threat assessment tools will help you.

Crime Prevention Through Environmental Design (CPTED) is the first step to hardening your facility. Making even minor changes to facility design such as the use of blast-resistant glass or film on exterior windows, aesthetically pleasing crash barriers and stops, and placing drop-off points away from main entrances are just a few ways to harden your facility and make it less desirable to terrorists.

Target hardening is an ongoing process. It is not something you do once and forget about. As your facility's structure, workforce, product market or plan, or significance to national security initiatives changes, you will need to reassess your threats. A threat assessment should at least contain a probability ranking, potential impact to operations, and mitigating factors such as facility hardening measures.

What Else Can You Do?

Here are some additional considerations and things you can be aware of or do regarding suicide bomber threats:

Signs to Look For

The smart suicide bomber will probably explode before anyone knows what is going on. However, not all terrorists are smart. Here are some things to look for:

- Clothing that is bulky or excessive for the weather (to hide the bomb)
- Hands hidden (possibly holding the switch to detonate the bomb)
- A strange chemical odor or excessive cologne to cover up that smell

- The bomber focused, but unresponsive. Suicide bombers often have the "1000-yard stare" and are usually unresponsive to questions or commands
- Heavy luggage or backpacks that don't fit the situation. The average weight of a bomb used by a suicide bomber is around 20 lbs. The Madrid train bombers all had very heavy backpacks. The Moscow bomber placed his bomb in a rolling suitcase. Not all the bombers wear their bombs.
- Nervousness, excessive sweating, or repeated mumbling of a prayer or mantra
- Exposed wires anywhere on a person's body
- Repeated attempts to avoid security checkpoints and/or police officers

Beware of Any Suspicious Packages

The bomber might not be a suicide bomber. He or she might just plant the bomb and walk or drive away. If the bomb is not worn by a terrorist, it is most likely to be hidden in a car, discarded backpack or duffel bag, or placed in a trash can.

Improvised Explosive Devices (IEDs) can be made from commercially available materials that are easily purchased over the counter in many places. Information on how to construct IEDs is readily available from military or survival bookstores, the Internet, and former military personnel. Sizes vary from very small to rather large. IEDs can also be disguised which gives the bomber an advantage. IEDs are an extremely dangerous threat.

Here is the toughest thing: Time, distance, and shielding are the only defense to an explosion. There is a high probability that when confronted by authority, the suicide bomber will detonate. Even if you engage with a firearm and instantly incapacitate the bomber with a brain stem shot, the bomb may still detonate. You don't know how the bomb is set to go off. It could be on a timer, it could be detonated by another person watching discreetly from afar, or it could have a dead man switch. (A dead man's switch is a switch that is automatically operated if the human operator becomes incapacitated, such as through death, loss of consciousness, or being bodily removed from control.)

Research also shows that a 20-pound suicide bomb vest loaded with shrapnel is dangerous within 400 meters. It has also been determined that 15 meters (about 50 feet) is the distance that means the difference between life and death in most suicide bombing incidents. If you are within 15 meters of the bomber when he detonates, you will likely die. If you are beyond 15 meters, you will likely live, but may be seriously injured. Whether you live or die depends on the terrain, type of bomb and shrapnel, distance away from bomb, and anything between you and the bomb. Distance combined with some type of cover that will stop shrapnel and projectiles is best.

Unfortunately, this means a suicide bomber is really a no-win situation. If someone is truly committed to blowing themselves up and taking people with him, it is going to be a terrible event and people will be killed.

Stay away from glass or heavy objects that could topple over in a blast, and while evacuating, again, try to steer clear of heavy objects that could fall over and glass that could shatter. If you are not in close proximity to the bomb, your greatest dangers in a building explosion come from flying glass and falling objects. At the sound of an explosion, dive for cover or hit the floor to avoid the shrapnel-like effects of the blast. Be careful of heavy objects that could fall over on you. Once over, evacuate the building being wary of secondary explosives and explosions. Cover your mouth and nose with a handkerchief or cloth, wetting it down if possible, to reduce the inhalation of dust, smoke, and debris.

Surviving a Grenade Attack

If you are alert enough to see the grenade before it explodes, these are tips often provided by military units to increase chances of survival.
Grenades have timers and will usually go off in two to four seconds. It is impossible to tell exactly when they will go off.

- If you can get behind cover, do so.
- If you run, you may be struck with fragments.
- If no cover is available, dive away from the grenade and get to the ground.
- Fragments radiate outward and there will be less fragments traveling parallel to the ground.
- Assume this body posture: Feet toward the grenade with feet squeezed tight together, or alternatively legs crossed (feet still together), Stomach and face down, elbows in tight to your sides, hands over ears and mouth open. The soles of your shoes, your feet, and legs will act as a shield to absorb any fragments before they penetrate vital organs. The high-pressure shock way expands from the center of the blast and can rupture eardrums and lungs. Holding your hands over the ears reduces outside pressure and minimizes tissue damage. Closing your eyes and opening your mouth helps equalize the outside and inside pressure.

If you are not wearing any protective gear, hitting the ground in this position provides you the most protection from the blast and may increase your chances of surviving and minimize your injuries.

Beware of Secondary Devices

Oftentimes bombers will use more than one bomb. The original bomb is just designed to create havoc and bring in first responders. A second bomb placed in an evacuation zone, obvious command post staging area, or near the body, is designed to injure more people, specifically fire and police officers. If an explosive device is found or goes off, you must always consider that there may be a second or third device somewhere in the area.

After one bomb goes off, look for items that seem out of place...discarded baggage or backpacks, strange pieces of trash, or recently disturbed ground. If you see any of these things, get away from them!

If a bomb goes off, don't evacuate into a parking lot. Cars are the easiest place to hide large amounts of explosives for a secondary device. One very common tactic is to place a small bomb in or near a building or public area. The terrorist knows that the small bomb will trigger an evacuation. He will then place a bigger bomb at the evacuation site to blow up all of the evacuees. Again: NEVER EVACUATE TO A PARKING LOT! It's too easy to hide a (big) bomb in a car. Get far away from anything that may conceal a secondary device!

Medical Care

Medical care will be essential to saving lives. If you are working in a position of responsibility, or decide to get involved helping others as a citizen, your goal will be to help injured people and attempt to prevent others from being injured in the aftermath of such a horrendous event.

If a bomb does go off, there will most likely be many deaths and serious injuries. If you watch videos of terrorist blasts, you see people staggering around dazed and unsure of what to do.

Expect to see serious bleeding, hearing loss, confusion, head injuries, and internal injuries. Victims may not be able to walk or hear you.

In the event of a secondary device, it can be more important to move injured people to a safe place than laying down to prevent spinal injury. C-spine stabilization won't really matter if the injured person is subject to another bomb blast. Get people to a safe place, including injured people, so no one will be subject to another blast.

The information in Chapter 9, *Stop the Bleeding*, applies to helping victims of a bombing as well as to victims of gunfire.

Antiterrorism Tips

- Beware of unattended packages.
- Beware of any suspicious vehicle activity.
- Beware of anyone asking untoward questions regarding schedules, conveyance methods, social gatherings, travel plans, police visibility, security information, or anything that doesn't appear to be normal.
- In an election year, be wary of attending political events.
- Be wary of individuals whose movements and actions are not logically motivated.
- If you attend church, make sure your church administrators are aware of the increased threat to non-Muslim denominations.
- If you work at any institution, school, hospital, government building, or corporate headquarters, make sure your administration is taking the appropriate security steps.
- Consider any travel very carefully. Make sure you check your destination for Department of State advisories, and read about its background in reference books such as the *CIA World Factbook* and Fielding's *The World's Most Dangerous Places*.
- Don't feel silly about reporting your suspicions.
- Increase your general awareness.

Source: *Street Smarts, Firearms, & Personal Security* by Kelly McCann (as Jim Grover)

Appendix E

www.SurviveaShooting.com

As a pedestrian, you must remember that prevention is far, far better than cure. Treat the threat of car attack as you would a bomber or shooter looking for a concentration of potential victims by avoiding crowds at roadsides. That also means giving up on those charming curbside cafes, be they on Melrose Avenue or the Champs Elysee. The advent of al-Qaeda means you can no longer take safety for granted with such proximity to traffic.

Itay Gil and Dan Baron
The Citizens Guide to Stopping Suicide Attackers: Secrets of an Israeli Counterterrorist

Surviving Terrorist Vehicle Attacks

Terrorist vehicle attacks are not new, but they do seem to be increasing, and have made the news frequently in the last number of years. Because I'm often asked by people in my classes what they can do when terrorists and murderers turn their automobiles into weapons of mass destruction, I wanted to provide a little information to help people deal with these kinds of attacks. Sadly, as I write this, it is only days after a 29-year-old man drove a rental truck into a pedestrian and bike path along the Hudson River in Lower Manhattan in New Your City, killing eight people and injuring 11 in the deadliest terror attack on the city since 9/11. It's a trend that I, and many experts, expect will continue and increase. Terrorist groups have specifically called for the use of vehicles and knives as weapons against the Western world as they are easy to acquire.

More places are installing vehicle-proof crash barriers where there is potential to run down groups of people. Unfortunately, there is no way to protect all areas where vehicles and pedestrians coexist in close proximity. Your first defense will always be your situational awareness. This is one more reason I insist that people get their heads out of their apps and pay attention to what's going on around them. As a pedestrian, one of the things you should be paying attention to are vehicles and traffic patterns. Being aware can provide that second needed to leap out of the way versus being run over. But I also understand that in reality, you are not always going to be aware of EVERYTHING around you. Here are some other suggestions and tips to keep you safe from vehicle attacks:

Warning

> “Dozens of times each year, confused, unfortunate souls manage to mistakenly shift into reverse instead of drive. Just as often, they might get startled and hit the gas when they intend to step on the brakes. Before they know what is happening, they have driven up onto the sidewalk or backed into the wall of the local fast-food eatery. Do not harm these poor folk; help them. They are our parents, grandparents, and grandchildren, not terrorists. You will be able to tell by their appearance, demeanor, and reaction to the accident.”
>
> Howard Linett
> Living with Terrorism: Survival Lessons from the Streets of Jerusalem

- **Be Aware!** Situational awareness is still the most important ingredient to our personal safety. Identify both risks and resources. Risks are things that may hurt us, and resources are people, places, and things that may help us. Identify both, especially at large gatherings of people, and have a plan if something happens, including a vehicle attack if in an area that is susceptible to such an attack.
- **Listen for the acceleration of a vehicle's engine.** This is another reason for not wearing earbuds and headphones when walking around in public. If you hear the sudden roar of an engine or the screeching of tires, look to identify the source and be prepared to get out of the way.

- **Walk facing traffic.** If you are walking facing oncoming traffic, you may have a better chance of seeing a vehicle hopping up on a curb and barreling toward you. This may provide an opportunity to get out of the way.
- **Stand apart from crowds on the street.** When waiting to cross the street or for public transportation, stand apart from the larger group which would be the most attractive target for a would-be-terrorist.
- **If you can, keep solid objects between yourself and traffic.** Walk along streets with blockades or cars parked at the curb. This isn't always possible, but if the street has blockades to prevent cars from driving onto the sidewalks, or if the street is lined with parked vehicles, the sidewalk would be harder for a terrorist to reach with a car and safer to walk on than others. Heavy-duty mailboxes may also provide protection. Even if they don't totally stop a careening car, they might slow it down enough for you to get out of the way. Newspaper dispensers and garbage cans are less reliable for this as they are rarely securely fastened to the ground. Trees may or may not provide protection depending on their size and how deep their roots go.
- **Pay attention to danger signs.** Speeding vehicles, sounds of collisions, revving engines, and sudden unusual vehicle movements, such as erratic driving or diverging from normal traffic patterns, can all be danger signs. Don't ignore them. Pay attention and determine if you are in danger. Seconds can mean the difference between life and death.
- **Get off the street and then out of the area.** Moving inside a building can protect you from the vehicle, but don't just stop there. Some of these terrorists, after the initial vehicle assault, continue with alternative weapons. Go through the building and out the back and continue to an area of safety. The only times you wouldn't do this are if you are with someone unable, or if you are helping the wounded. If you are with someone unable to completely escape the area, do the best you can to find a safe location. If you are helping the wounded, be aware of further attacks and don't place yourself in danger. Make sure it is safe before you assist others.
- **Be warry of secondary attacks and booby traps.** Terrorists may put explosives in the vehicle set to go off at a time after the initial attack or when the vehicle is investigated. Distance yourself from the terrorist's vehicle.
- **Don't loiter on sidewalks and open areas that are open for vehicle attacks.** If you are stopping on a busy street to talk, text, tie your shoe, take a photo, stand around, etc., you will be safer if you choose a location that isn't open for a terrorist to drive a vehicle. Blockades and cars parked on the street both provide protection from cars hopping the curb.

- **Leap out of the way.** If you find yourself in the path of an oncoming vehicle, leap aside as quickly as possible. You are more likely to survive the shock of a car's sideswipe than a full-frontal impact. Diving to the side may get your head and vital organs out of the impact zone. While it will hurt to have your legs hit, it's not as immediately deadly as an impact to your head.

Vehicular terrorist attacks date back to the early 1970s, but many experts believe this poor man's weapon of mass destruction will be used more and these attacks will continue to rise. This sort of attack is difficult to detect or deter, and the skill level necessary to execute a successful vehicle attack is low compared to using firearms and explosives. Accessing vehicles is much easier and doesn't raise the same red flags as acquiring illegal firearms and bomb-building materials. Unfortunately, the same dynamics that make large public events fun and exciting also make them attractive targets for terrorists. This means, sadly, it is one more thing we need to be aware of and have a plan to survive.

Appendix F

www.SurviveaShooting.com

 ***In an event of crisis, people need to do something.*** 

From the movie *"The 15:17 to Paris"*

Active Shooter Lessons from "The 15:17 To Paris"

I went to the new Clint Eastwood produced and directed movie ***The 15:17 to Paris***, and wanted to point out a couple of lessons we can all learn from the movie. Eastwood took a risk by having the three childhood friends turned heroes play themselves in the film. But it's a risk I'm glad he took. Those heroes-turned-actors are Spencer Stone, a former U.S. Air Force Airman, Alek Skarlatos, a former Oregon National Guardsman, and Anthony Sadler, a senior at California State University at the time of the incident. On August 21, 2015, the trio was riding on a Thalys train headed towards the French capital when a man armed with an assault rifle and pistol opened fire, shooting one passenger. Stone and Skarlatos instinctively decided to charge at the assailant, and Sadler was not far behind. Despite several injuries, including a slashed neck and thumb for Stone, the three friends managed to overpower the gunman with the assistance of a British passenger. The four were hailed as international heroes and received various honors for their valor. The movie was adapted from the three men's co-authored memoir of the same name.

It is obvious that Stone, Skarlatos, and Sadler are not actors. It is a risk Eastwood took and the film is taking some criticism for it. Personally, I didn't mind that the acting and dialogue wasn't as smooth as it would have been with A-list actors playing the three. I thought it was pretty cool that they were the actual heroes playing themselves, and I enjoyed the movie and am glad I went to see it. There are two lessons related to my work in teaching Active Shooter Response that I want to share.

There is a scene in the film when Stone is in a class at a military base when an Active Shooter alert is sounded. The instructor in the class tells people to lock the door and then get under the desks. I wanted to scream in the theater. NO, NO, NO, NO, NO!!! Hiding under desks is not a strategy to survive. Little spoiler here. Stone gets up and prepares himself at the door with a pen held in a hammer fist. If the shooter came through the door, he was going to take him out with the pen. YES, YES, YES, YES!!! I still wanted to scream at the instructor and everyone hiding under desks, but having Stone do the right thing eased my blood pressure. (Even though the instructor in the movie criticized him for it.) You lock doors and barricade to keep the shooter out, but you then prepare to ambush him at the door with whatever you have in case the locks and barricade fail. This is what I and others teach, and I was glad that at least one person in that class room figured it out on their own. It is the best strategy in a bad situation. When the instructor who told everyone to get under the desks asked Stone why he did what he did, Airman Stone replied, "I don't know, ma'am. I just didn't want my family finding out that I died hiding under a table."

The other lesson from this movie is that people, even unarmed people, can and have stopped killers. I get tired of so many people saying the only way to stop a killer with a gun is with a gun yourself. These four men, the three Americans and one British passenger, prove that quote wrong. And there have been many others in similar incidents.

As I said earlier in this book, yes, if I had to face an active shooter, I would prefer to have a firearm myself. But I refuse to say that people without a firearm must resign to being victims. I sure won't, and I don't want anyone I teach to be a victim either. I teach people to be survivors. If all they have is a ball point pen like Stone in the movie, use it. If there is a fire extinguisher handy, use it. If you are naked with absolutely nothing, use your hands, feet, elbows, knees, teeth, and anything else to attack back and stop the attacker.

I like that this movie shows regular people deciding to act, and their actions saved many lives. Not only did they stop the killer, they kept the wounded man alive until professional medical personnel could take over. That's a reason stopping bleeding is part of my book and courses. People can and do save lives. This movie was a great example of what people can do, and I applaud the men who acted on that train, and I applaud Clint Eastwood for bringing the story to us in this film.

Resources

www.SurviveaShooting.com

Everything listed here contributed to my knowledge and to the information presented in this book. I encourage everyone to seek out these resources for further study:

Books

Applegate, Rex. *Kill Or Get Killed (New Revised And Enlarged Edition)*. Paladin Press, 1976.

Arvanitis, Jim. *Battlefield Pankration The Book: Lethal Personal Combat For The Street*. Paladin Press, 2011.

Asken, Michael J. Ph.D.; Grossman, Dave Lt. Col.; Christensen, Loren W. *Warrior Mindset: Mental Toughness Skills for a Nation's Peacekeepers*. Human Factor Research Group, 2010.

Aviv, Juval. *The Complete Terrorism Survival Guide: How to Travel, Work and Live In Safety*. Juris Publishing, Inc., 2003.

Ayoob, Massad. *Gun Safety in The Home*. F+W Media, Inc., 2014.

Bird, Chris. *Surviving a Mass Killer Rampage: When Seconds Count, Police Are Still Minutes Away*. Privateer Publications, 2016.

Blair, J. Pete; Nichols, Terry; Burns, David; and Curnutt, John R. *Active Shooter: Events and Response.* CRC Press, 2013.

Branca, Andrew. *The Law of Self Defense: The Indispensable Guide for the Armed Citizen* (Second Edition). Law of Self Defense, 2013.

Brown, Andy. *Warnings Unheeded: Twin Tragedies at Fairchild Air Force Base*. WU Press, 2016.

Burrese, Alain. *How to Protect Yourself By Developing A Fighter's Mindset*. TGW Books, 2012.

Casner, Steve. *Careful: A User's Guide to Our Injury-Prone Minds*. Riverhead Books, 2017.

Cessna, Kit. *Equal or Greater Force: A Delta Force Veteran Teaches You How to Survive Crime, Terrorism, Natural Disasters, and Other Calamities*. Paladin Press, 2006.

Christensen, Loren W. *Defensive Tactics: Modern Arrest & Control Techniques for Today's Police Warrior*. Turtle Press, 2008.

Christensen, Loren W. *Surviving A School Shooting: A Plan of Action for Parents, Teachers, and Students*. Paladin Press, 2008.

Christensen, Loren, W. *Surviving Workplace Violence: What to Do Before a Violent Incident, What to Do When the Violence Explodes*. Paladin Press, 2005.

Cohen, Arthur. *Surviving A Massacre, Rampage, Or Spree Killing*. Paladin Press, 2010.

Cooper, Jeff. *Principles of Personal Defense*. Paladin Press, 2006.

Courtley, Cade. *SEAL Survival Guide: A Navy SEAL's Secrets to Surviving Any Disaster.* Gallery Books, 2012.

Divine, Mark. *The Way of the SEAL: Think Like an Elite Warrior to Lead and Succeed*. Reader's Digest, 2013.

Dorn, Michael; Shepherd, Sonayia; Satterly, Stephen; and Dorn, Chris. *Staying Alive: How to Act Fast and Survive Deadly Encounters*. Safe Havens International, 2014.

Doss, Kevin T. and Shepherd C. David. *Active Shooter: Preparing for And Responding to A Growing Threat*. Butterworth-Heinemann, imprint of Elsevier, 2015.

Dougherty, Martin J. *Special Forces Unarmed Combat Guide: Hand-To-Hand Fighting Skills from The World's Most Elite Military Units*. Metro Books, 2010.

Editors of Black Belt. *The Ultimate Guide to Reality-Based Self-Defense*. Black Belt Books, 2010.

Farnam, John S. *The Farnam Method of Defensive Handgunning*. DTI Publications, Inc., 2000.

Fowler, David. *Survive an Active Shooter: Awareness, Preparedness and Response for Extreme Violence*. Personal Safety Training, Inc., 2016.

Geddes, John and Rees, Alun. *Be A Hero: The Essential Survival Guide to Active-Shooter Events*. Skyhorse Publishing, 2017.

Giduck, John. *Terror at Beslan: A Russian Tragedy with Lessons for America's Schools*. Archangel Group Ltd., 2005, 2012.

Giduck, John, with Bail, Joseph M. Jr. *Shooter Down! The Dramatic, Untold Story of the Police Response to the Virginia Tech Massacre*. Archangel Group Ltd., 2011.

Gil, Itay and Baron, Dan. *The Citizen's Guide to Stopping Suicide Attackers*. Paladin Press, 2004.

Grossman, Dave. *On Killing: The Psychological Cost of Learning to Kill in War and Society*. Back Bay Books, 1996.

Hanson, Jason. *Spy Secrets That Can Save Your Life: A Former CIA Officer Reveals Safety and Survival Techniques to Keep You and Your Family Protected*. Perigee, 2015.

Hattingh, Garth. *The Outdoor Survival Handbook: Life-Saving Skills for the Lost, Stranded, or Injured*. The Lyons Press, 2001.

Jones, James C. *The Live Free Book of Total Survival: Principles for Organizing Your Life, Home, Vehicle, And Family for Natural Disasters, Civil Unrest, Financial Meltdowns, Medical Epidemics, And Political Upheaval.* Paladin Press, 2016.

Kahn, David. *Krav Maga Weapon Defenses*. YMAA Publication Center, 2012.

Kane, Lawrence A. *Surviving Armed Assaults: A Martial Artist's Guide to Weapons, Street Violence, & Countervailing Force*. YMAA Publication Center, 2006.

Kaplan, Michael I. *Edge of Freedom: Knife Defense Tactics for a Changing World*. Paladin Press, 2014.

Kendall, Laura J. MICP. *Active Shooter Response Training: Tactical Trauma Care for First Responders.* TTR Publishing, 2015.

Kendall, Laura J. MICP. *Active Shooter Response Training: Tactical Trauma Care for Laypersons.* TTR Publishing, 2015.

Kenik, David. *Armed Response: A Comprehensive Guide to Using Firearms for Self-Defense*. Merril Press, 2005.

Kipp, Bill. *Turning Fear into Power: How to Prevail in Verbal Confrontations and against Physical Assaults*. Paladin Press, 2005.

Klarevas, Louis. *Rampage Nation: Securing America From Mass Shootings*. Prometheus Books, 2016.

Larkin, Tim. *When Violence Is the Answer: Learning How to Do What It Takes When Your Life Is At Stake*. Little, Brown and Company, 2017.

Lawrence, Erik. *Tactical Pistol Shooting: Your Guide to Tactics that Work*. Gun Digest Books, 2005.

Lichtenfeld, Imi Sde-Or and Yanilov, Eyal. *Krav Maga: How to Defend Yourself Against Armed Assault*. Frog, Ltd., 2001.

Linett, Howard. *Living with Terrorism: Survival Lessons from the Streets of Jerusalem*. Paladin Press, 2005.

Lonsdale, Mark V. *CQB: A Guide to Unarmed Combat and Close Quarter Shooting*. S.T.T.U., 1997.

Machine, Garret. *Israeli Security Warrior Training*. Paladin Press, 2011.

McCann, Kelly. *Combatives For Street Survival: Hard-Core Countermeasures for High-Risk Situations*. Black Belt Books, 2009.

McCann, Kelly (as Jim Grover). *Street Smarts, Firearms, & Personal Security: Jim Grover's Guide to Staying Alive and Avoiding Crime in the Real World*. Paladin Press, 2000.

McNab, Chris. *Special Forces Survival Guide: Wilderness Survival Skills from The World's Most Elite Military Units*. Ulysses Press, 2008.

Miller, Rory. *Facing Violence: Preparing for the Unexpected*. YMAA Publication Center, 2011.

Morrison, Lee. *The Complete Book Of Urban Combatives*. Paladin Press, 2015.

Nance, Richard. *Gun Fight! An Integrated Approach to Shooting And Fighting In Close Quarters*. Looseleaf Law Publications, Inc., 2016.

Plaster, Maj. John L. USAR (RET.). *The Ultimate Sniper: An Advanced Training Manual for Military and Police Snipers (Updated and Expanded)*. Paladin Press, 1993, 2006.

Province, Charles M. *Patton's One-Minute Messages: Tactical Leadership Skills for Business Managers*. Presidio Press, 1995.

Rawls, Neal with Kovach, Sue. *Be Alert Be Aware Have A Plan: The Complete Guide to Protecting Yourself, Your Home, Your Family*. The Lyons Press, 2002.

Remy, Steven. *Indomitable Spirit: How to React and Survive in a School Shooting*. IEM Texas, 2015.

Richardson, Robert. *The Ultimate Situational Survival Guide: Self-Reliance Strategies for A Dangerous World*. Living Ready Books, 2014.

Rosen, Lester S. *The Safe Hiring Manual: The Complete Guide to Employment Screening Background Checks for Employers, Recruiters, and Jobseekers. (Revised 2nd Printing)* Facts on Demand Press, 2012.

Scali, Robert. *The Unconventional Close Protection Training Manual: Learn How to Defend Yourself and Protect Others*. (E-Book) Pineland Productions/Vector Defensive Systems, 2017.

Siddle, Bruce K. *Sharpening The Warrior's Edge: The Psychology & Science of Training*. PPCT Research Publications, 1995.

Sockut, Eugene. *Secrets of Street Survival – Israeli Style: Staying Alive in a Civilian War Zone*. Paladin Press, 1995.

Steiner, Bradley J. *The Tactical Skills of Hand-to-Hand Combat*. Paladin Press, 2008.

Styers, John. Cold Steel: Technique of Close Combat. Paladin Press, 1952.

Suarez, Gabe. *The Combative Perspective: The Thinking Man's Guide to Self-Defense*. Paladin Press, 2003.

Suarez, Gabriel. *The Tactical Advantage: A Definitive Study Of Personal Small-Arms Tactics.* Paladin Press, 1998.

Suarez, Gabriel. *The Tactical Pistol: Advanced Gunfighting Concepts and Techniques.* Paladin Press, 1996.

Sutton Chris & Graden, John. *The Cobra-Defense Active Shooter Response Plan.* ITBD, Inc., 2013.

U.S. Army. *TC 23-14 Sniper Training and Employment.* Paladin Press, 1988.

U.S. Army. *Combat Lifesaver Course: Student Self-Study* manual.

U.S. Army. *The Ultimate Guide to U.S. Army Survival Skills, Tactics, And Techniques* (edited by Jay McCullough)

Van Horne, Patrick and Riley, Jason A. *Left of Bang: How the Marine Corps' Combat Hunter Program Can Save Your Life*. Black Irish Entertainment, LLC, 2014.

Willink, Jocko. *Discipline Equals Freedom Field Manual*. St. Martin's Press, 2017.

Wilson, Orlando. *Counter Terrorist Bomb & Active Shooter Procedures* (E-Book). Risks Incorporated, 2004.

Wilson, Orlando. *International Security: Personal Protection in an Uncertain World*. Glenbridge Publishing Ltd., 2012.

DVD Programs

Benbenisty, Doron. *Active Shooter Massacre Survival Israeli Method: 12 DVD Video Program*. CRI School, 2013.

Cale, Paul "JJ" and Davies, "Taft." *Dealing with An Active Shooter*. Target Focus Training & International Combative Concepts, 2017.

Cale, Paul "JJ" and Davies, "Taft." *Extreme Close Combat Shooting DVDs 1-6*. Target Focus Training & International Combative Concepts, 2017.

Duncan, John. *Crucible All-Access Training Vol. 5 Tactical Combat Casualty Care*. Paladin Press, 2012.

Howe, Paul. *Make Ready with Paul Howe: Civilian Response To Active Shooters*. Panteao Productions, 2013.

Machine, Garret. *Combat First Aid: A Citizen's Guide to Treating Battlefield Injury*. Paladin Press, 2010.

McCann, Kelly (AKA Grover, Jim). *Jim Grover Defensive Shooting Series*. Paladin Press, 1995.

McCann, Kelly. *Inside the Crucible Volume 1: Combat Shooting Essentials.* Paladin Press, 2003.

McCann, Kelly (AKA Grover, Jim). *Living Safely in Dangerous Times: Defending Yourself and Your Family Against Terrorism.* Paladin Press, 2002.

Miller, James. *Under the Gun: Fundamentals of Handgun Disarming*. Paladin Press, 1997.

Pincus, Rob. *Active Shooter Response*. TNM Media, 2012.

Pincus, Rob. *Spree Attacker Response*. TNM Media, 2013.

Suarez, Gabriel. *Close-Range Gunfighting: Reality-Based Firearms Training for Realistic Situations*. Paladin Press, 2005.

Stivi, Alon. *Active Shooter Survival*. Directmeasures, 2012.

Tudjan, Branimir. *Street Krav Maga II Vol. 1: Gun Threat Survival Tactics*. Paladin Press, 2012.

Magazine Articles

Alton, Joe, M.D. "Deadly Impact: Dealing with Gunshot Wounds During An Active Shooter Scenario." *American Survival Guide*, May/June 2016. Vol. 5, Issue 5.

Amweg, Rick and Denton, Paul S. "What Does Terrorism Look Like on a College Campus?" *Campus Safety*, January/February 2017. Vol. 25, No. 1.

Campbell, Bob. "Death in Seconds: To Survive an Active Shooter Incident, You Need A Plan and Quick Execution." *American Survival Guide Doomsday*, 2015.

Davis, Kevin R. "Stop The Killing: Preparing armed school personnel to take down an active shooter." *Personal & Home Defense: Gun Buyer's Annual #174*, 2016.

Dorn, Michael. "20 Active Shooter and Active Killer Prevention Strategies." *Campus Safety*, September 2016. Vol. 24, No. 6.

Harris, Steve and Capt. Silk, Dan, PhD. "How the University of Georgia Embraces 'Stop the Bleed.'" *Campus Safety*, November/December 2016. Vol. 24, No. 8.

Junod, Tom. "A Radical New Look at Mass Shooters." *Esquire*, October, 2014. http://www.esquire.com/news-politics/a30024/mass-shooters-1014/

Kenik, David. "What It Takes to Survive." *Gun Buyer's Annual #196 Presents Personal & Home Defense*, 2017. Athlon Publications.

Mastison, Fred. "Survive A School Shooting: Lifesaving crisis plans for grade schools and college classrooms." *Survivor's Edge*, Winter 2016. Vol. 2, Issue 3.

Schwartz, Larry. "Cover and Concealment." *American Survival Guide*. April, 2017. Vol. 6, Issue 4.

Topper, Martin D. "Out of the Crosshairs: Prepare yourself to escape an active shooter anywhere, anytime." Survivor's Edge, Summer 2016. Vol. 3, Issue 1.

Weinstein, John M. Lt. "Active Incident Training: Preparing for the Future Threat." *Campus Safety*, March 2017. Vol. 25, No. 2.

Whaley, Bob. "A Different Look at 'Run, Hide, Fight' How to Respond to The Active Killer." *Stay Alive*, Fall/Winter 2016.

Winn, Zach. "10 Years Later, Colleges Still Feel the Impact of the Virginia Tech Mass Shooting." *Campus Safety*, April/May 2017. Vol. 25, No. 3.

On-Line Articles

Berg, Arthur Z. MD. *Violence and Survival: Denial and the Ultimate Threat*

http://www.psychiatrictimes.com/articles/violence-and-survival-denial-and-ultimate-threat

Black, Alan. *How to Survive a Stampede: What to do if you're caught in a crowd crush or surge*

http://www.safebee.com/health/how-survive-stampede

Burch, Cecil. *The Counting Game*

http://www.iacombatives.com/2017/07/26/the-counting-game/

Cameron, James, CPP, *Legal aspect regarding Work Place Violence and Active Shooter Preparedness*

https://www.linkedin.com/pulse/legal-aspect-regarding-work-place-violence-active-shooter-cameron/

Carlson, Tucker. *'God, Get Me Home to My Girls': Navy SEAL Shot 27 Times by Al Qaeda Tells His Amazing Survival Story*

http://insider.foxnews.com/2014/09/21/god-get-me-home-my-girls-navy-seal-shot-27-times-al-qaeda-tells-his-amazing-survival

Cassidy, Megan. *Las Vegas first responders leaned on training, improvised for chaos*

http://www.azcentral.com/story/news/nation/2017/10/05/las-vegas-first-responders-leaned-training-improvised-chaos/737766001/

Duckworth, Ron. *EMS trauma care: ABCs vs. MARCH*

https://www.ems1.com/trauma-assessment/articles/319159048-EMS-trauma-care-ABCs-vs-MARCH/

Ellifritz, Greg. *Armed Citizen Response to the Terrorist Bomber*.

http://www.activeresponsetraining.net/all-about-bombs

Ellifritz, Greg. *Active Shooter Response for the Armed Citizen.*

http://www.activeresponsetraining.net/active-shooter-response-for-the-armed-citizen

Ellifritz, Greg. *'Don't Run in a Straight Line' and other Bad Advice*.

http://www.activeresponsetraining.net/dont-run-in-a-straight-line-and-other-bad-advice

Ellifritz, Greg. *Playing Dead?*

http://www.activeresponsetraining.net/playing-dead

Ellifritz, Greg. *Naked and Afraid: Fighting an Active Shooter When You are Unarmed.*

http://www.activeresponsetraining.net/naked-and-afraid-fighting-an-active-shooter-when-you-are-unarmed

Ellifritz, Greg. *Are Those Really Gunshots?*

http://www.activeresponsetraining.net/are-those-really-gunshots

Ellifritz, Greg. *Recognizing the Sound of Gunfire.*

http://www.activeresponsetraining.net/recognizing-the-sound-of-gunfire

Ellifritz, Greg. *Should I Pull the Fire Alarm During a Mass Shooting?*

http://www.activeresponsetraining.net/should-i-pull-the-fire-alarm-during-a-mass-shooting

Ellifritz, Greg. *Weapon Malfunctions in an Active Shooter Event.*

http://www.activeresponsetraining.net/weapon-malfunctions-in-an-active-shooter-event

Ellifritz, Greg. *10 Tips for Surviving a Terrorist Vehicle Attack.*

http://www.activeresponsetraining.net/10-tips-for-surviving-a-terrorist-vehicle-attack

Ellifritz, Greg. *The Orlando Pulse Nightclub Shooting.*

http://www.activeresponsetraining.net/the-orlando-pulse-nightclub-shooting

Fisher, Andrew. *The MARCH Algorithm in Tactical Combat Casualty Care.*

http://havokjournal.com/fitness/medical/march-algorithm/

Forliti, Amy. *Settlement Reached in Accent Signage Shooting Suit.*

http://www.twincities.com/2014/09/21/in-minneapolis-accent-signage-shooting-suit-settlement-reached/

Gorosko, Andrew. *Settlement Offers Made in Sandy Hook School Lawsuit.*

https://newtownbee.com/settlement-offers-made-in-sandy-hook-school-lawsuit/

Haskins, Aaron. *Col. Cooper's Color Code – You're Doing It Wrong.*

http://www.breachbangclear.com/rethinking-coopers-colors/

Hatmaker, Mark. *Do You Choose Situational Blindness?*

http://paladin-pressblog.com/2017/07/06/do-you-choose-situational-blindness/

Hsoi. *Finally Found A Solution for Carrying A Tourniquet!*

https://blog.hsoi.com/2017/05/06/finally-found-a-solution-for-carrying-a-tourniquet/

Jannetti, Aaron. *The Myth of Perfect Situational Awareness.*

http://mailchi.mp/07f2914463ff/asr-newsletter-june14

Jones, Jerry. *The Movie Theater Active Shooter Equation*

http://modernserviceweapons.com/?p=14853

Jorgustin, Ken. *How to Survive A Stampede.*

http://modernsurvivalblog.com/security/how-to-survive-a-stampede/

Lah, Kyung and Mungin, Lateef. *Train riders too consumed with phones to see gun before shooting.*

http://www.cnn.com/2013/10/10/tech/san-francisco-shooter-phone/

McKay, Brett and Kate. *What to Do in an Active Shooter Situation.*

http://www.artofmanliness.com/2015/11/30/what-to-do-in-an-active-shooter-situation/

Pincus, Rob. *3 Tips for Talking to Your Kids After the Connecticut School Attack.*

https://www.personaldefensenetwork.com/article/3-tips-for-talking-to-your-kids-after-the-connecticut-school-attack/

Pincus, Rob. *Active Shooter Training Resources.*

https://www.personaldefensenetwork.com/article/active-shooter-training-resources/

Police Executive Research Forum. *Critical Issues in Policing Series: The Police Response to Active Shooter Incidents. March 2014.*

http://www.policeforum.org/assets/docs/Critical_Issues_Series/the%20police%20response%20to%20active%20shooter%20incidents%202014.pdf

Royal Range. *The importance of active shooter training.*

http://www.royalrangeusa.com/importance-active-shooter-training/

Stewart, Scott. *How to Counter Armed Assaults.*

https://worldview.stratfor.com/article/how-counter-armed-assaults

Telegraph Men. *Meet the Navy SEAL who was shot 27 times and lived to tell the story.*

http://www.telegraph.co.uk/men/thinking-man/11503612/Meet-the-Navy-SEAL-who-was-shot-27-times-and-lived-to-tell-the-story.html

Williams, John. "Suicide Bombers: Are you a target?" *Campus Safety*.

http://www.campussafetymagazine.com/article/Suicide-Bombers-Are-you-a-target

Wood, Mike. *Why 'Move! Escape or Attack' is superior to 'Run, Hide, Fight.'*

https://www.policeone.com/active-shooter/articles/196375006-Why-Move-Escape-or-Attack-is-superior-to-Run-Hide-Fight/

On-Line Videos

Active Killer presentation from Lt. Colonel Dave Grossman by In the Line of Duty. Hero99 Network. Published on Jan 10, 2016. https://youtu.be/kRZb1oskAtI

ACTIVE SHOOTER. Doctors Community Hospital. Published on Mar 3, 2015. https://youtu.be/8yWPnbuGNh4

Active Shooter Response Training for High School and Middle Schools. John First. Published on Jan 17, 2014. https://youtu.be/V5_-5O5fGzY

Active Shooter Prevention Training with OSHA Message. Chris Grollnek M.S. Published on Jun 18, 2014. https://youtu.be/nKA_l8il7nc

Active Shooter Video for Muscogee County School District in Columbus, GA. Roger Hart, published on July 14, 2015.

https://www.youtube.com/watch?v=cO5FJ0v_tuc

DeSAT SAFER Active Shooter Training Video. DeSAT. Published on Aug 24, 2016. https://youtu.be/3yoOq809SU0

How to Survive an Active Shooter. SormTX. Published on Feb 26, 2016. https://youtu.be/w9nldEZv16k

Practical Response to Active Shooter. Rock Valley College. Published on Jul 3, 2014. https://youtu.be/pplrzuYlvDk

Run, Hide, Fight: Armed Intruder Training for Schools. Wichita Public Schools - WPS-TV. Published on Jun 16, 2015. https://youtu.be/eydFlxX-1dQ

RUN. HIDE. FIGHT.® Surviving an Active Shooter Event – English. Ready Houston. Published on Jul 23, 2012. https://youtu.be/5VcSwejU2D0

Shooter on Campus: Know You Can Survive. Concordia University of Edmonton, Published on Jun 3, 2014. https://youtu.be/zQ3U9boa6Xg

Surviving an Active Shooter Event - Civilian Response to Active Shooter. ALERRT Center. Published on Feb 10, 2015. https://youtu.be/j0lt68YxLQQ

SURVIVING AN ACTIVE SHOOTER - LA County Sheriff. LA County Sheriff's Dept. Published on Mar 17, 2015. https://youtu.be/DFQ-oxhdFjE

Unarmed Response to an In-School Active Shooter Event. Indiana State Police Information Channel. Published on Jan 26, 2016.

https://www.youtube.com/watch?v=zeoZmsXpc6k

Wagner, Jim. *Jim Wagner my self-defense instructor: Playing dead during a shooting*. https://www.youtube.com/watch?v=rZOVZZ0_jxo

Web Sites

Active Response Training

http://www.activeresponsetraining.net/

Active Shooter Defense

https://www.activeshooter-defense.com/

Alice Training Institute

https://www.alicetraining.com/

Delta Situational Awareness Training

https://desat.org/

Domestic Security Alliance Council: Active Shooter Resources

https://www.dsac.gov/topics/active-shooter-resources

FBI Active Shooter Resources

https://www.fbi.gov/about/partnerships/office-of-partner-engagement/active-shooter-resources

FEMA: How to Prepare for an Active Shooter Incident

https://www.fema.gov/media-library/assets/documents/123184

FEMA: IS-907: Active Shooter: What You Can Do

https://training.fema.gov/is/courseoverview.aspx?code=IS-907

Homeland Security: Active Shooter Preparedness

https://www.dhs.gov/active-shooter-preparedness

https://www.dhs.gov/xlibrary/assets/active_shooter_booklet.pdf

Homeland Security: Active Shooter Pocket Card

https://www.dhs.gov/publication/active-shooter-pocket-card

https://www.dhs.gov/xlibrary/assets/active_shooter_pocket_card.pdf

Homeland Security: Active Shooter Event Quick Reference Guide

https://www.dhs.gov/publication/active-shooter-pamphlet

https://www.dhs.gov/sites/default/files/publications/active-shooter-pamphlet-2017-508.pdf

Homeland Security: Planning and Response to an Active Shooter

https://www.dhs.gov/sites/default/files/publications/isc-planning-response-active-shooter-guide-non-fouo-nov-2015-508.pdf

Homeland Security: Stop the Bleed

https://www.dhs.gov/stopthebleed

No Nonsense Self-Defense

https://www.nononsenseselfdefense.com/

Personal Defense Network

https://www.personaldefensenetwork.com/

PHLster Holsters

https://www.phlsterholsters.com/

The Safariland Group

https://www.safariland.com/

State of New Jersey Office Of Homeland Security and Preparedness

https://www.njhomelandsecurity.gov/

Tennessee Tech Response to an Active Shooter Situation

https://www.tntech.edu/police/dealing-with-an-active-shooter-situation/

Washington County Sheriff, Oregon

http://www.co.washington.or.us/sheriff/

Wikipedia

https://www.wikipedia.org/

Live Training

Survive a Shooting Course

This intensive in-depth course begins with approximately 2-hours of detailed classroom knowledge that includes background, strategy, and the Active Shooter Triangle model of "Escape – Deny – Attack Back." The course then transitions to 2-hours of hands on training in topics like:

- gun-disarms
- barricading techniques
- dealing with knife attacks
- ambush techniques
- working as a team
- stop the bleeding
- understanding the difference between cover and concealment
- disaster response psychology
- combat breathing
- how to develop a survivor's mindset

This course is designed to SAVE LIVES!

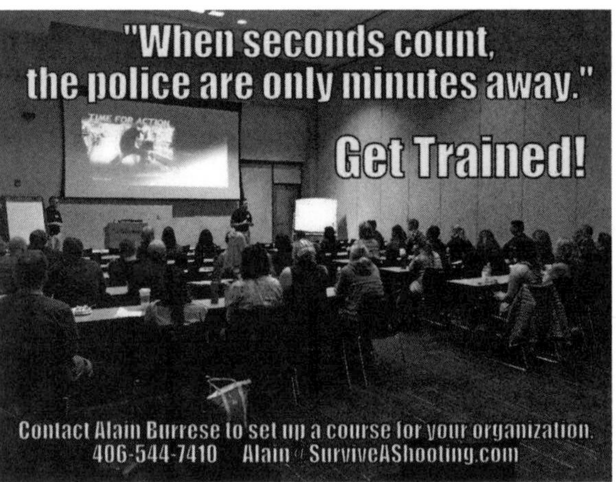

Further Resources

All of the resources listed, and the latest resources on this topic, can be found at:

www.surviveashooting.com/bookbonus

If you know of a resource that should be added, or if there is a resource listed that is no longer valid, please contact me through the contact page on the Survive a Shooting site, or e-mail me at alain@surviveashooting.com, and help me ensure this resource page is the best available on the topic of active threats.

Schools – I have resources to assist you with funding for the Survive A Shooting live course. Contact me at alain@surviveashooting.com for details.

Additional information on personal safety and self-defense can be found on the sister site:

www.SurviveandDefend.com

Acknowledgements

www.SurviveaShooting.com

This book was a lengthy project. And while there were many days and nights sitting in front of the keyboard alone, I had a lot of help along the way. There have been many that I've learned from, and others who helped with the process. I owe thanks to all of them.

Kevin Brett, besides being a voice of encouragement throughout the process, assisted tremendously with format, layout, and direction. The presentation of the material wouldn't have been nearly as good without him. I'm lucky to have such a good friend.

Tim Boehlert helped clean up the manuscript and provided valuable editorial suggestions. Much thanks! (If there are any typos, don't blame Tim, they are on me.) Dan LoGrasso also provided input to make the book better. Thank you!

I want to thank Bryan Whitney, Tavis Johansson, Jamar Galbreath, and Paul Shaffer for assisting with the photographs and bonus videos for the book; and to Carolyn Glidewell and Glidewell Investments & Insurance Group for providing a location to take photographs and film videos.

An outstanding group of subject matter experts read an advanced manuscript and provided feedback and endorsement blurbs. Thank you to Barry Eisler, Greg Ellifritz, Rory Miller, Dale Comstock, Wim Demeere, Jason Hanson, Marc MacYoung, Dave Spaulding, Lawrence Kane, and Richard Nance.

A special thank you to Loren W. Christensen for encouragement and writing a Foreword for the book between his many writing projects.

I've had the distinct honor of being part of a team of trainers certified by The Safariland Training Group to teach the Safariland *Emergency Response To An Armed Intruder* course. I learned from every one of the trainers I worked with; and I owe a tremendous thank you to each of them. They include: Sandy Wall, Brad Giffin, Rob Taylor, Dave Conway, Mark Puddy, Angie Puddy, Ben Gladwin, Bryan

McCravy, Shannon Parsons, Josh Herbold, Shawn Paul, Brandon Gale, Mike Juhola, Robert Kennedy, Steve Kendley, Hannah Singleton, Larry McElravy, Christy Meurer, Liz Roosa Millar, Luke Hoerner, John Weber, Darren Ginn, Casey Gunter, Pat Malone, Gordon Schmill, and Garrett VanHoose.

Each and every person listed in the research section contributed to my knowledge, and to the writing of this book, and I owe a thanks to all of them.

I want to thank my father, who taught me much throughout my life and was proud of the work I'm doing to help others. Unfortunately, he passed away unexpectedly as I was completing the first draft of this book and he never got to see the finished product. Thank you, and I miss you.

Last and most important, my wife, Yi-saeng, and daughter, Cosette, for their support and for providing a reason to do what I do. Thank you.

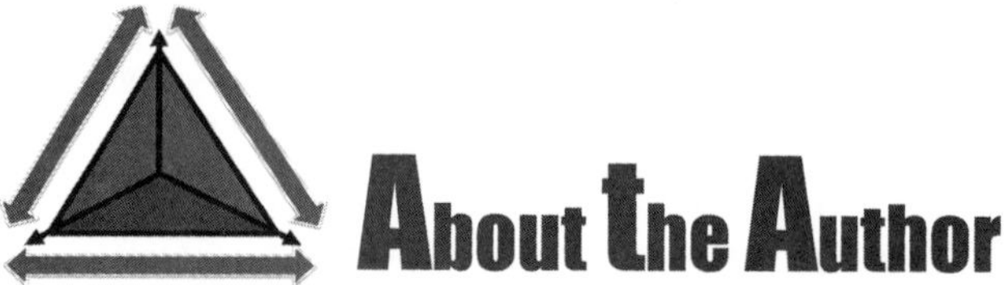

About the Author

www.SurviveaShooting.com

Alain Burrese, J.D., is a former U.S. Army Sniper, a fifth-degree black belt, and a certified Active Shooter Response instructor. He is the author of 9 books and 11 instructional DVDs and teaches a common-sense approach to staying safe and defending yourself through his *Survive a Shooting* and *Survive and Defend* programs and websites. He's combined his experience, education, and training to design programs to teach you how to survive.

- Certified Active Shooter Response Instructor (Safariland Training Group)
- Appeared in the PBS Documentary: *Active Shooter: Are Montana Colleges Ready?*
- Creator of the *Survive A Shooting* course and website
- Author and producer of numerous books and DVDs on self-defense
- Contributor to *Black Belt Magazine, American Survival Guide*, and many other publications
- Attorney
- 5th Degree Black Belt Instructor in Hapkido
- Former U.S. Army Sniper and Sniper Instructor with the 2nd Infantry Division
- Former U.S. Army Paratrooper with the 82nd Airborne Division

Alain divides his time between spending quality time with his family and friends, writing, and teaching. He practices what he preaches by enjoying life safely.